ANDERSON, Donald F. William Howard Taft; a conservative's conception of the Presidency. Cornell, 1973. 355p il bibl 73-8408. 15.00.   ISBN 0-8014-0786-0.   C.I.P.

Anderson seeks to assess Taft's Presidency in terms of the categories and questions formulated in Clinton Rossiter's *The American Presidency* (rev. ed., 1960) and Richard Neustadt's *Presidential power* (1960). Taft is historically identified as an adherent of the "constitutional" or "literal" theory of the Presidency, with its emphasis upon the limited nature of Presidential power, and in his 1915 Columbia University lectures, published as *Our Chief Magistrate and his powers* (currently available under title *The President and his powers*), he became the leading theoretical exponent of that view. But Anderson concludes that, judging on the basis of his "actual conduct of office," Taft in fact did attempt to be "a strong, energetic president." He "simply lacked the energy, imagination, and political skill to fill the role." Unlike Paolo Coletta's *The Presidency of William Howard Taft* (CHOICE, Nov. 1973), which was primarily a synthesis based upon published materials, Anderson has done thorough research in the Taft Papers. Yet his final assessment is much the same: "an upright, dedicated, and courageous public servant," but a political failure. And though his

Continued

ANSERSON

account is more balanced than Henry F. Pringle's laudatory *The life and time of William Howard Taft* (2 v., 1938), the definitive history of the Taft Administration remains to be written.

WILLIAM HOWARD TAFT

William Howard Taft, President, 1908–1912. From the Collection of
the Library of Congress.

WILLIAM HOWARD TAFT

A Conservative's Conception of the Presidency

DONALD F. ANDERSON

CORNELL UNIVERSITY PRESS
ITHACA AND LONDON

Copyright © 1968, 1973 by Cornell University Press

First published 1973 by Cornell University Press.
Published in the United Kingdom by Cornell University Press Ltd., 2-4 Brook Street, London W1Y 1AA.

International Standard Book Number 0-8014-0786-9
Library of Congress Catalog Card Number 73-8408

Printed in the United States of America by York Composition Company, Inc.

Librarians: Library of Congress cataloging information appears on the last page of the book.

To Peg, Stephen, and Rebecca

Preface

William Howard Taft has been associated historically with the "constitutional" and "literalist" theory of the presidency, which has emphasized the limited nature of presidential power. Until recently, this restricted view of the presidency has been in ill repute among most historians and political scientists, who have been mesmerized by the strong presidency and oblivious to its potentiality for evil. Although scholars have frequently attributed Taft's uninspiring administration to his limited view of office, that explanation fails in many significant respects to explain his presidency. In reappraising Taft, I have examined his personal political style as well as his views and convictions about his office. I could not escape, as he himself could not, continual comparisons with the successful style of Theodore Roosevelt, which plagued him in all that he did, or failed to do. Nor could I avoid comparing Taft's and Roosevelt's theories of the presidency, which were generated simultaneously in reaction to each other and which cannot be understood alone. The result, I believe, is a more objective and balanced picture of our twenty-seventh president.

The personal papers of William Howard Taft became available to interested scholars and the public in 1960. They reveal important aspects of his presidency that Henry F. Pringle, who did have special access to these papers, neglected in his major authorized biography. Other works on Taft or the progressive period are incomplete because they did not have the benefit of access to the Taft Papers, are too partial to Roosevelt, or do not deal with the techniques of presidential leadership. I have found that our new knowledge about this presidency sheds significant light upon the problems of leadership in a democratic system of government.

Clinton Rossiter's *The American Presidency* provided the categories of presidential roles around which I have organized my discussion (Chief Executive, Chief Legislator, Chief of Party, Voice of the People, and Chief Diplomat). Richard Neustadt in *Presidential Power* posed the specific questions about presidential sensitivity to power upon which I have focused. The postpresidential writings of Taft and Roosevelt have furnished the classic presidential apologia from which I have filtered out the rhetoric, personal animosity, rationalizations, and forgetfulness which so often plague such documents. The result is a clearer picture of Taft's basic conceptions of office.

Extensive quotations from Taft's letters and papers have been included in order to convey his difficulties in using the written and spoken word—in contrast to the effectiveness of the vivid, almost electrifying verbal style of Roosevelt—difficulties which help to explain Taft's lack of success as a popular leader.

Although this volume raises many broader questions about the nature of democratic leadership and, indeed, of democracy itself, I have not pursued them here. This is neither a definitive biography of Taft nor a chronicle of the period, but an in-depth study of one conservative's exercise of presidential power.

I wish to extend my appreciation to Andrew Hacker, Peter Amann, Donald Proctor, and those who read the manuscript for Cornell University Press for their helpful comments and suggestions; to Walter LaFeber for setting me on the trail of the Taft Papers; to the late Clinton Rossiter, whose continued encouragement made this work possible; and to my wife Peg for sustained editorial assistance beyond the call of human or wifely duty. I also wish to thank the staffs of the Manuscript Division of the Library of Congress, the Diplomatic Division of the National Archives, and the John M. Olin Library Department of Manuscripts and University Archives at Cornell University for their help in securing materials on the Taft period. However, I am fully responsible for the approach, for the interpretation, and for any errors that may appear in the work.

I acknowledge my extensive reliance upon the papers of William Howard Taft, Philander Chase Knox, Theodore Roosevelt, Elihu Root, and Walter L. Fisher in the Manuscript Division of the Library of Congress. I wish to thank Charles P. Taft for permission to use material from the Taft Papers; James Knox Tindle and Robert McGrew Tindle for permission to quote from the Knox Papers; Michael Straight for permission to quote from the papers of Willard D. Straight in the John M. Olin Library Department of Manuscripts and University Archives; the Diplomatic Branch, Civil Archives Division, of the National Archives for permission to use the diplomatic correspondence of the State Department; Harvard University Press for authorization to quote from *The Letters of Theodore Roosevelt*, edited by Elting E. Morrison and John M. Blum, Cambridge, Massachusetts, copyright 1954 by the President and Fellows of Harvard College; Charles Scribners' Sons for permission to quote from *Selections from the Correspondence of Theodore Roosevelt and Henry Cabot Lodge*; and to the Library of Congress for the use of photographs of the Taft period.

Dearborn, Michigan   DONALD F. ANDERSON

Contents

Illustrations

WILLIAM HOWARD TAFT

Introduction

William Howard Taft was an outstanding public servant, ruthlessly honest, aristocratically disdainful of political humbug, and incapable of hypocritically flattering the American public or catering to their baser whims. In a calmer, less hysterical age, Taft would have earned a respectable place among the ranks of our presidential heroes. But the times were extraordinary, and his predecessor Theodore Roosevelt was an impossible act for Taft to follow, especially since Roosevelt refused to leave the political stage.

The Taft period, 1908–1912, obscured by the spectacular presidencies of Roosevelt (1901–1908) and Woodrow Wilson (1912–1920), offers disturbing lessons for those who would attempt to understand the American presidency and, indeed, American political life. Of course it is easy with hindsight to fault a by-gone president. Failure is often easier to explain than success, and memories of conflicting forces grow dim with time, making generalizations easier. And perhaps Americans are quicker to find fault with conservative presidents, who seem destined to squirm uncomfortably in an office that belongs preeminently to the people. Nevertheless, no president who enters office with broad public support, leading a dominant national party, and who then fritters away his popularity, barely winning eight electoral votes four years later, can be considered an unmitigated political success.

Throughout his term as president, Taft remained chained to Theodore Roosevelt and the popular expectations he had created about the presidency. Roosevelt had entered the White House in September 1901, after the assassination of William McKinley, when public confidence in American political institutions had reached a low ebb. The progressive movement, already emerging in many communities throughout the land, soon found an eloquent and energetic spokesman for its ideals in the new president, who proved to be both a child and the midwife of the movement.

The progressive phenomenon was not merely a rerun of the Populist crusade of the 1890s, although that strain was certainly evident throughout the West and Midwest. It included many new recruits from the urban middle and upper classes who felt threatened by the new barbarians of corporate wealth who were fast replacing them in influence and status across the country. Not only did the progressives push for a new relationship between the national government and business in which private greed would be subordinated to the public interest, but they were responsible for a bewildering array of proposals designed to bring about a more responsive and efficient government on the state and local levels, proposals such as the commission form of government for municipalities, nonpartisan elections, the short ballot, municipal ownership of utilities, extension of the merit system, better social services, the direct primary, and the initiative, referendum, and recall. According to Russel Nye, progressivism as it manifested itself both locally and nationally "simply meant that the rule of the majority should be expressed in a stronger government, one with a broader social and economic program and one more responsive to popular control."[1]

Although Roosevelt sympathized with most of the goals of the progressives, he did not always share their enthusiasm for dismantling or radically democratizing American institu-

tions to achieve them. Roosevelt actually staved off more drastic changes in American institutions by preaching and dramatizing the need for a new relationship between government
and private enterprise. Into the growing breach between the
traditional American ideas of democracy and the shabby world
of corporate greed strode Roosevelt, determined to preserve
the best of both worlds while rooting out corruption and
privilege in the national government. By combining the Jeffersonian ideal of government by the people with the Hamiltonian concept of a strong national government, Roosevelt
harnessed burgeoning popular desires to the power of the national government and thereby prepared the way for the subsequent growth of the welfare state. Roosevelt met with some
successes as president—the passage of the Hepburn Act (1905)
strengthening the Interstate Commerce Commission, the increase in the number of antitrust suits of which the Northern
Securities Case (1904) is most famous, the reclamation of
public lands for conservation, the intervention in the anthracite coal strike of 1902, food and drug legislation—but, for
the most part, he had to remain content preaching reform to
the nation and setting the stage for the accomplishments of
the Taft and Wilson administrations which followed. Although Taft was able to continue many of the Roosevelt policies and achieve some successes of his own, he lost the confidence of the American people, who grew increasingly restive
under his uninspiring leadership and who turned to the Democratic party for leadership four years later. Although Taft
was an upright, dedicated, and courageous public servant, he
has never become a model for succeeding presidents to emu-
late.

1. The Road to the White House

Politics, when I am in it, makes me sick.
William Howard Taft,
1906[1]

The road to the White House is long and hazardous. Age, geography, religion, nationality, ideology, personality, and simple quirks of fate have conspired to eliminate presidential hopefuls all along the way.

For some men, however, the road has been shorter, straighter, and less hazardous than for others. Military heroes such as Ulysses S. Grant and Dwight D. Eisenhower have been catapulted into the presidency with a minimum of experience in the give and take of national politics. Other men such as William Howard Taft and Herbert Hoover have reached the presidency through apprenticeship in top administrative posts in Washington. All came to power deficient in the political skills of experienced elected officials. All too soon, the nation discovered that success outside of elective office was no guarantee of success in the presidency.

For William Howard Taft, the road to the White House was devoid of any major obstacles, political crises, or personal tribulations. Propelled into the presidency by his successes as a judge, administrator, and political handyman for Theodore Roosevelt, Taft soon found himself cursed with the defects of his virtues. In rising to the presidency through the appointive route, Taft acquired certain professional skills and personality traits which, though appropriate for the confined world of a judge or administrator, became liabilities in a popularly elected leader. In the former posts, Taft had been insulated from the press and the public, and had never found it necessary to develop the political skills or antennae of the other-directed politician. Primary responsibility for these constituencies lay with elected officials, not their appointees.

Taft's effectiveness as President was deeply influenced by his social background and previous political experiences. An understanding of certain aspects of his personality which were evident in his judicial and administrative career is crucial to an understandng of his presidency.

I

If high birth can help boost a man into the presidency, Taft was blessed with an auspicious beginning as a member of the politically prestigious family of Alphonso Taft of Cincinnati, Ohio. Although Alphonso Taft rose to national prominence as secretary of war and attorney general in the Grant administrations, his life-long ambition, never realized, was to become a justice of the United States Supreme Court. He bequeathed this ambition to his son "Will."[2]

The story of Taft's early career has been told before.[3] What should be emphasized here is that Taft rose to national prominence through cooptation and appointment, with a minimum of personal effort in electoral politics. After graduating, second in his class, from Yale University in 1878 and from the Cincinnati Law School in 1880, Taft immediately became involved in Republican politics at the urging of his father. In 1880, he was appointed assistant prosecutor of Hamilton County, encompassing Cincinnati. In January 1885, he was appointed assistant county solicitor for Hamilton County. In March 1887, Governor Joseph B. Foraker appointed him to the Superior Court of Ohio. In April 1888, Taft won election to the Superior Court post for a five-year term—the only elected position he was to fill until his election as president twenty years later. In February 1890, he was appointed solicitor general of the United States and served until March 1892, when he was appointed to the Federal Circuit Court of the Sixth Judicial Circuit (including Ohio). There Taft served with distinction until February 1900, when William McKinley appointed him to the recently created Philippine Commission to oversee the new island possessions of the United States. Taft's steady climb to national prominence can be attributed to his father's reputation and influence in the Ohio Republican party, and also to his own strong party loyalty, congenial disposition, ability, and political opportunism.[4]

Taft's decision to go to the Philippines marked a critical point in his public career. The Spanish-American War had brought the United States far-flung possessions and new responsibilities in the Philippines, Puerto Rico, Cuba, Guam, and Hawaii. The spirit of expansion was abroad in the world, and the United States was not immune from its heady effects. President McKinley's offer of a position on the Philippine Commission came as a complete surprise to Taft. The relations between the two men had been formal and distant, but apparently McKinley desired a fellow Ohioan with integrity and legal experience for the job. At first Taft hesitated to accept the offer because of his antiimperialist sentiments. McKinley argued, however, that imperialism or antiimperialism was not the real question: the United States was stuck with the islands, and he now wanted Taft "to go out there and establish a civil government."[5] Secretary of War Elihu Root also appealed to Taft's sense of duty by indicating his obligations to the Republican party and the nation.

You have always had your platter up. You have caught the offices that have fallen; you have had an easy time; you have done good work enough but now you have an opportunity to serve your country. You are at the parting of the ways and the question is whether you are going to take the easy or the heavy task.[6]

It was a difficult decision for Taft, for he really desired to pursue a judicial rather than an administrative career. "In my early married life," he once confessed, "I told my wife that I was so fond of judicial work that if I could be made a Common Pleas Judge in Hamilton County, in Cincinnati, I would be content to remain there all my life."[7] But by 1900 Taft had set his sights on a Supreme Court seat. Only after he was assured by McKinley that his judicial ambitions would not suffer from the appointment did he reluctantly agree to accept, and then on condition that he would become chairman of the commission.[8]

As chairman of the Philippine Commission and, by July 4, 1901, the first governor-general of the Philippines, Taft exercised broad, almost dictatorial powers over the islands. McKinley, Roosevelt, and Secretary of War Root, however, were the ultimate policy-makers. Root had set the course of civil administration in the islands by drafting, with the approval of McKinley, the civil constitution of the Philippines. Taft believed that his initial success in the islands was due primarily to Root's modification of the military government there and his transformation of the commission into the legislative arm of the government.[9] Taft himself made valuable contributions to the government of the islands. He tackled issues involving health, education, economic development, and pacification, and he tried to mediate the thorny and emotionally explosive church-state issue among the islanders. Given the slow means of communication between Washington and the Philippines, the governor-general was necessarily left with extensive powers and discretion to deal with these problems.

On September 6, 1901, William McKinley was assassinated,

and, within a few days, was succeeded by Theodore Roosevelt. The new president was an old and respected friend of Taft and wisely continued to give him a free hand in the islands. Taft's conscientious work fed his growing reputation in Washington as an able executive and a dedicated public servant. According to Roosevelt, one of the major reasons for this growth was Taft's primary concern with doing his job well and his secondary concern with his own political interests or image back home.[10] This trait—the desire to do the job properly regardless of its effect on his own interests—contributed greatly to Taft's success in the Roosevelt administration and, indeed, as we shall see, to his subsequent problems as president.

Roosevelt saw that Taft's accomplishments did not go unnoticed, partly because the President genuinely admired Taft, but also for domestic political reasons. The Republican acquisition of the Philippines and the bloody insurrection which followed had generated strong dissent against the new American imperialism in the Pacific. Taft's success in bringing about political stability in the islands helped neutralize that dissent and strengthened the dominant position of Roosevelt and the Republican party in Washington.

Later, when Taft ran for the presidency in 1908, his experience as governor-general was used as an argument on behalf of his candidacy. As often happens in presidential campaigns, a candidate's partisans create an image of the man which eventually turns out to be quite false or inappropriate for the office. Taft's presidential boosters believed that his Philippine experience had provided him with valuable political training for the presidency. This was hardly the case. True, Roosevelt had once acknowledged that the ideal qualities for the first governor-general of the Philippines "ought to combine the qualities which would make a first-class President of the United States with the qualities which would make a first-class Chief Justice of the United States" and that Taft was "the only man he knew who possessed all these qualities."[11] But Taft's experience in the Philippines did not really prepare him for the White House. As Taft's biographer Henry Pringle pointed out, Taft's position was more akin to that of a dictator than that of an American chief executive.[12] When Taft was a colonial governor, his words were tantamount to law, just as they had been during his tenure as a federal circuit court judge; he never really had to contend with such independent political figures as congressmen, governors, and other prominent party leaders. Being lawgiver to a subject nation was quite different from traveling, hat in hand, to the American Congress or a party boss to seek cooperation and support. Moreover, Taft could afford to ignore his public image back home, for he had a skilled news manager and promoter in Roosevelt. Taft's executive experience was invaluable, but it was no substitute for the training most conducive to developing the manipulative and bargaining skills necessary in a democratic leader, skills rarely developed outside of elective office itself.

II

The friendship between Taft and Roosevelt, begun in the early 1890s in Washington, was marked by a steady growth of mutual trust and admiration. In 1900, for example, Roosevelt had described Taft as "the whitest man I have ever met in politics."[13] Always the flatterer, Roosevelt had written Taft while still vice-president that "if I had the naming either of President or Chief Justice, I should feel in honor bound to name you." When apprised of Taft's selection to the Philippine Commission, Roosevelt had warmly congratulated Taft as "one of the very few men instead of being fit for only one job is able to do well almost any job which needs to be done."[14] The Vice-President's admiration, however, was tinged with envy over Taft's good fortune in heading the Philippine government. Recognizing the political potentialities of Taft's new office and the traditional liabilities of the vice-presidency, Roosevelt confided to a friend, "The one position that I should like to have had was that of Governor General of the Philippines with the proper powers."[15]

After his succession to the presidency in September 1901, Roosevelt repeatedly offered Taft a Supreme Court appointment. Roosevelt undoubtedly was concerned about the Republican presidential nomination in 1904. A Taft appointment to the Supreme Court would help smooth Roosevelt's own path to renomination by eliminating a potential competitor. Although Taft himself would have preferred a judicial career, his wife and brothers were eager to see him in the presidency and were anxious to avoid sidetracking his potential presidential candidacy. The subtle but persistent pressures of his family kept Taft off the Supreme Court as long as the presidency loomed on the horizon and remained a constant factor in his career decisions. In October 1902, Roosevelt offered Taft a seat on the Court vacated by the retiring Justice George Shiras: "You can at this juncture do far better service on [the] Supreme Court than any other man. I feel that your duty is on the Court unless you have decided not to adopt [a] judicial career."[16] Because of the "gravity of the situation" in the Philippines, Taft declined the offer, "even if it is certain that it can never be repeated." To avoid any misunderstanding of his motives, Taft explained to Secretary Root that his desertion of the Philippines would represent a "violation of duty" unless it was "absolutely compulsory" for political reasons.[17]

But Roosevelt was not to be sidetracked so easily. One month later, he renewed his insistence upon Taft's appointment to the Court. When rumors of Taft's possible departure from his post led to genuine popular protests from the Philippine leaders and people, Roosevelt reluctantly agreed to leave Taft in the islands.[18] Realizing that his second refusal might be misinterpreted as a possible threat to Roosevelt's nomination in 1904 or as a bid for the vice-presidency, Taft disavowed any ambition in a letter to Root: "Nothing is further from the truth. Neither office has the slightest attraction for me and the horrors of a campaign are like a nightmare. As compared with a judicial life, it seems to me as if they were not to be considered in the same class."[19] Taft's sense of obligation to the Philippine people, not presidential ambitions, lay behind his refusals to accept a Supreme Court appointment. Despite Mrs. Taft's yearning to return to the United States and her presidential ambitions for her husband, Taft felt he could not leave the islands with the task of reconstruction unfinished.[20] He had become committed to the development of the Philippine Islands.

Taft also suspected other motives behind Roosevelt's offers. For months after his refusal of a Supreme Court appointment, Taft thought he had become a political liability to the administration for having offended American Catholics in negotiating a settlement between the Roman Catholic and nationalist-catholic churches in the islands. When word reached Roosevelt of Taft's attitude, the President immediately reassured him of continuing support: "[I]t simply never occurred to me that you could dream I wanted to change you, except for the reason that I wanted to put you in what I regarded as an even bigger post, near me."[21]

A "bigger post" became available in the fall of 1903, when Secretary of War Elihu Root expressed his intention to resign. Roosevelt needed a replacement of comparable stature and loyalty; Taft fit the bill perfectly. The President must also have recognized that if Taft became a member of his cabinet, it would be virtually impossible for him to oppose Roosevelt's renomination in 1904. Recognizing Taft's commitment to the

Philippines, Roosevelt offered him Root's position in most appealing terms, arguing that "from the standpoint of the interest of the islands alone you could well afford to take the place, which involves the general regulation, supervision, and control of the Philippine government."[22] Control of the Philippines from Washington represented only part of Roosevelt's bait; there was also the prospect of greater power and prestige for Taft as the President's personal confidant. The offer was too tempting for Taft to decline; it might lead to a seat on the Supreme Court—perhaps the chief justiceship itself—and it would allow him to pursue what by now had become an important mission in his life, the development of the Philippine Islands. Although he felt unqualified to fill Root's shoes and confessed "no knowledge of army matters and no taste for or experience in politics," he agreed to leave Manila for a more comfortable and politically advantageous position in Washington.[23] Another appointment had brought him one step closer to the White House.

Roosevelt was relieved by Taft's acceptance, for he liked, trusted, and needed Taft. "If only there were three of you!" Roosevelt lamented. "Then I would have put one of you on the Supreme Court . . . one of you in Root's place as Secretary of War . . . one of you permanently as Governor General of the Philippines."[24] Roosevelt was more perceptive than his flattery at first glance might indicate, for he realized that Taft's administrative abilities, party loyalty, and subordination of self were just the qualities the President needed in his lieutenants.

Roosevelt, of course, expected the new secretary of war to fulfill political as well as administrative tasks. His secretary would be expected not only to supervise the small American army, but also to lobby for the Philippines in Congress, advise Roosevelt on domestic policy, and, like most of his cabinet members, deliver an occasional speech on behalf of the administration. Aware of Roosevelt's expectations, Taft raised no objections. His complete adherence to the Roosevelt policies for the next four years can be fully appreciated only in the light of his virtues, the conditions under which he was appointed, and his ambitions for the chief justiceship or the presidency.

III

Taft's new position as secretary of war entailed more than just the routine supervision of the armed forces. In 1904 the War Department was engaged in administering the new territories which the United States had acquired, directly or indirectly, as a result of the Spanish-American War. The Philippines, Puerto Rico, Guam, Panama, and even Hawaii and Cuba at times came under the province of the War Department. The secretary of war was a de facto colonial secretary.

Roosevelt was quickly impressed by his new secretary. "He is . . . the greatest imaginable comfort to me here," he wrote to General Leonard Wood, "and I think the only man in the country who could have taken Root's place."[25] In his first year in office, however, Taft became so involved in Philippine legislation before Congress, supervision of the construction of the Panama Canal, and electioneering for the President that insiders faulted him for neglecting the routine administrative tasks of his office at which Root had excelled. As Roosevelt's first lieutenant and "troubleshooter," Taft was never able to absorb himself in the purely military aspects of his office. He left "most of the details to his subordinates" and, according to White House military aide and former newspaperman Major Archie Butt, thereby "permitted the department to accumulate a dozen different heads and factions."[26] Roosevelt, however, was willing to pay the price as long as such major concerns as the Panama Canal and the Philippines were carefully supervised: "I realized the War

Department suffered through Taft's activity in politics, but one such big-brained man is necessary for each administration, for he can say and make explanations which the President cannot do."[27] Taft could not juggle the diverse roles thrust upon him by the President. His inability to curb administrative factionalism and to coordinate the activities of his subordinates was becoming evident. These deficiencies in his executive ability would become more obvious during his own administration.

In the fall of 1904, Taft plunged into Roosevelt's reelection campaign and defended the entire record of the administration at every opportunity. The kind of loyalty which he showed toward Roosevelt and the Republican party was a quality which he was sternly to expect from others when he became president. The only personal disagreement between Taft and Roosevelt during that fall campaign resulted from Taft's proposal to lower the American tariff on the principal Philippine products of sugar and tobacco. The tobacco interests complained bitterly and refused to contribute to the Republican party coffers if Taft continued what the president of the Cigar Manufacturers' Association termed his "fanatical hobby" of trying to "smash" Philippine tariff barriers.[28] Piqued by the criticism of his tariff views and Roosevelt's obvious annoyance, Taft offered to resign from the cabinet but was quickly reproved by Roosevelt as suffering from "nerves or something!"[29]

After Roosevelt's election in 1904, Taft's role shifted from that of partisan spokesman for the administration to de facto assistant president. Roosevelt's increasing confidence in Taft, combined with the failing health of Secretary of State John Hay, earned Taft the temporary job of acting secretary of state in 1905. Roosevelt informed Hay of his intention to leave "the burdens of state on Taft's broad shoulders" during a one-month vacation in the wilds of Colorado in April 1905.[30]

Although Roosevelt retained ultimate decision-making powers during his five-week western sojourn, he left Taft to grap-
ple with such problems as the termination of the Russo-Japanese War, the United States mediation in the Moroccan
dispute, racial friction in Hawaii, and disturbances in Vene-
zuela and the Dominican Republic. In particular, Roosevelt
left Taft with "large discretion" in sounding out British intentions regarding Morocco so that Roosevelt could better
assess the possibilities of mediation between France and Germany. Taft was also given a role in seeking to obtain United
States mediation in the Russo-Japanese War. Roosevelt was
quite satisfied with Taft's performance as assistant president
and congratulated him, "I think you are keeping the lid on
in great shape!" The President's confidence in Taft's ability
to handle such diplomatic matters was not difficult to understand. As he intimated to his lieutenant, "Fortunately you and
I play the diplomatic game alike."[31]

The death of John Hay that summer forced Roosevelt to
find a new secretary of state. Taft, of course, was an obvious
possibility, but Senator Henry Cabot Lodge urged Roosevelt
to offer the post to Elihu Root and allow Taft to finish his
work in Panama and the Philippines. At first Roosevelt hesitated to bypass Taft for fear of slighting him, but he eventually decided upon Root. For Roosevelt, it was not a choice of
one or the other, but "a choice of having both instead of one."
Root's appointment as secretary of state naturally placed him
high among the ranks of possible successors to Roosevelt, but
Taft was unconcerned. In fact, Roosevelt admitted to Lodge
that Taft himself had "urged me to bring Root into the Cabinet."[32]

The President interpreted Taft's indifference toward the
Root appointment as an indication of his secretary's continuing desire for a Supreme Court appointment rather than for
the presidency. In March 1906, despite Taft's increasing

"availability" for the presidency, Roosevelt offered Taft another chance for the Supreme Court. Taft declined. The President had erred once again about Taft's feelings: "You say that it is your decided personal preference to continue your present work. This I had not understood. On the contrary, I gathered that what you really wanted to do was to go on the bench, and that my urging was in the line of your inclination, but in a matter in which you were in doubt as to your duty." To prevent any misunderstanding, Roosevelt proceeded to praise Taft as the "most likely" Republican candidate for 1908, the "best man" to receive the nomination, and the one "under whom we would have most chance to succeed."[33] One can only speculate about the motives of a president who at one moment was willing to appoint Taft to the Supreme Court and, at the next, to acknowledge his increasing availability as the Republican nominee of 1908.

Taft found it necessary to offer Roosevelt an explanation for his third refusal of a Court appointment. He admitted that he had "almost" made up his mind to accept the appointment when he was imposed upon by Philippine leaders to continue his efforts on behalf of the Philippine tariff reductions. As he confessed to the President, "I looked into my motives and saw that what I was about to do was the result of a desire to avoid controversies that were mine to fight and that it was my duty to my Filipino friends . . . to stay and fight them." Taft was quite aware of the political consequences of his third refusal of a Court appointment:

I know that few, if any, even among my friends will credit me with anything but a desire, unconscious perhaps, to run for the Presidency and that I must face and bear this misconstruction of what I do. But I am confident that you credit my reasons as I give them to you and will believe me when I say I would much prefer to go on the Supreme Bench for life than to run for the Presidency and that in twenty years of judicial service I could make myself more useful to the country than as President even if the impossible event of my election should come about.[34]

It is conceivable that Taft, like his wife and family, had been bitten by the presidential "bug," but his commitment to work for the development of the Philippines cannot be completely overlooked. Perhaps it was simply easier for Taft to fulfill his duty to the islands while the presidency loomed on the horizon. What does seem certain, however, is that Taft's sense of duty to the Philippines would not have precluded him from accepting an appointment to the Court as chief justice.[35] At this point in his public career Taft preferred the chief justiceship, would have settled for the presidency, but was determined to finish his work on behalf of the Philippines before accepting a mere associate justiceship on the Supreme Court.

IV

Taft's duties in the War Department kept public attention focused upon him for the remainder of the Roosevelt administration, partly because Roosevelt supported Taft for the Republican nomination in 1908, and partly because of the rather exotic nature of Taft's work and his accomplishments. In Roosevelt's view, the most important task that he had entrusted to his secretary of war was the construction of the Panama Canal—"the biggest thing" of his administration.[36] After Senate approval of the Hay-Bunau-Varilla Treaty granting the United States the right to build a canal through Panama, Congress, on April 28, 1904, directed the President to take possession of the Canal Zone and to build the canal by means of a newly created Isthmian Canal Commission. On May 9, 1904, by executive order, Roosevelt placed the work of the commission, including the construction of the canal and the exercise of governmental powers in the Canal Zone, under the control of his newly appointed secretary of war.

Taft was not particularly pleased with this arrangement. When he was apprised of Root's appointment as secretary of state, he suggested to Roosevelt that the canal work be transferred to the State Department because of Root's "more constructive" executive ability.[37] Roosevelt brushed the suggestion aside as unfeasible and pushed on with his plans to have the Army Corps of Engineers build the canal.

The canal occupied much of Taft's time and energy. He traveled to Panama for onsite inspections and consultations numerous times, pressed by Roosevelt's desire to "dig that canal as quickly and as effectively as possible" and by a host of delicate problems which plagued the project.[38] The most significant problems involved treaty adjustments with Panama regarding the American presence in the Canal Zone, internal Panamanian politics, the selection of competent engineers, the choice of the proper type of canal, labor disputes, and the necessity of explaining and defending canal decisions before Congress. Taft's knowledge of the canal enterprise became very extensive. The Secretary's supervision of the canal construction continued from May 1904, until his retirement from the presidency in March 1913.[39] Roosevelt would later brag that "I took the canal zone."[40] "But I built the Canal," Taft could have answered.

Occasionally Taft was called upon to act as the President's special envoy to solve a serious political crisis. In September 1906, for example, he was sent to Cuba to quell an incipient revolt against the fragile regime of President Estrada Palma. Secretary of State Root was away from Washington at the time on an extended goodwill tour of Latin America.

Roosevelt was reluctant to intervene in the face of impending congressional elections and Root's Latin American trip, but eventually he dispatched Taft to negotiate an end to the Cuban political crisis. Faced with the distasteful prospect of military intervention, Roosevelt decided to handle the crisis without consulting Congress and to establish a strong precedent for future presidents:

> If it becomes necessary to intervene I intend to establish a precedent for good by refusing to wait for a long wrangle in Congress. You know as well as I do that it is for the enormous interest of this Government to strengthen and give independence to the Executive in dealing with foreign powers, for a legislative body, because of its very good qualities in domestic matters, is not well fitted for shaping foreign policy on occasions when instant action is demanded. Therefore, the important thing to do is for a President who is willing to accept responsibility to establish precedents which successors may follow even if they are unwilling to take the initiative themselves.[41]

Taft then was no stranger to Roosevelt's conscious expansion of executive power. He participated in Roosevelt's scheme without a murmur of dissent.

Taft's legalistic approach to a political settlement in Cuba produced a minor disagreement between himself and the President. Confronted with a situation bordering on anarchy, Taft decided to help Palma retain his presidency because no "suitable" alternative existed among the feuding factions and also because Taft himself desired to preserve the "constitutional continuity" of the regime.[42] Roosevelt was rather piqued by Taft's fastidious concern with constitutional technicalities and urged him to be more realistic:

> Upon my word, I do not see that with Cuba in the position it is we need bother our heads much about the exact way in which the Cubans observe or do not observe so much of their own constitution as does not concern us. . . . Neither do I understand why the fact that [the] government is not within the constitution as you state would alter your control of the situation for pacification.

Since Taft was only the President's lieutenant, he had to subordinate his concern for constitutional appearances to Roosevelt's demand for a quick solution. Violent feuding between the Cubans ultimately forced Taft to request limited military intervention to restore order and install a new provisional government. Despite the minor differences, Roosevelt was "especially pleased" with the arrangements negotiated by Taft.⁴³ Elihu Root, on the other hand, sorely embarrassed during his Latin American trip by American military intervention, did not share the President's glowing opinion of Taft's work. Root felt that a more skillful approach to the Cuban crisis could have avoided military intervention; Taft felt that he had done his best, given the troubled situation he inherited from Root.⁴⁴ Cuba remained a sensitive issue between the two men for the remainder of their careers.

Roosevelt's extraordinary use of an executive agreement to bypass the Senate and its treaty-making powers produced a second disagreement between Taft and Roosevelt on constitutional principles. Although Taft's biographer admittedly searched "in vain for a major issue on which Taft took a stand, even in private, against Roosevelt,"⁴⁵ Roosevelt's signing of an executive agreement with the Dominican Republic in 1905 met with Taft's private disapproval. Fearing the possible involvement of European powers in the chaotic political and financial affairs of the Dominican Republic, Roosevelt negotiated a treaty with the island on January 21, 1905, in which the United States agreed to appoint Americans to control the customs houses of the island in order to restore its financial stability. The theory behind the scheme was simple: if the customs houses were eliminated as potential booty for revolutionaries, revolutionaries would cease to exist, peace and prosperity would reign, creditors would be paid off, and the threat of foreign intervention and a possible American-European power clash would be avoided. When the Senate stalled on the treaty, Roosevelt then negotiated an identical executive agreement with President Carlos Morales of the Dominican Republic for American control of the customs houses.[46] Root was horrified by the President's action, and even Taft was heard to raise his voice against the President's policy. Roosevelt confided to Secretary of State John Hay:

> There has been rather a comic development in the Santo-Domingo case. Morales asked us to take over the customs houses pending action by the Senate. I decided to do so, but first of all consulted [Senators] Spooner, Foraker, Lodge, and Knox. All heartily agreed that it was necessary for me to take this action. Rather to my horror Taft genially chaffed them about going back on their principles as to the "usurpation of the executive." But they evidently took the view that it was not a time to be over-particular about trifles.[47]

Roosevelt, moreover, neglected to consult Taft on the use of the executive agreement "for fear of meeting opposition."[48] Although Taft was good-natured about the matter, in retrospect, he must have been alarmed about Roosevelt's "usurpation" of the treaty-making power, for he refused to use Roosevelt's precedent in similar situations during his own administration.[49]

With the exception of these relatively minor incidents over Cuba and the Dominican Republic, Taft never openly challenged a major policy of the Roosevelt administration. As a staunch Republican disciple of party government, he found little difficulty in subordinating his personal views to those of the President. Since party regularity had paved his way to political success, Taft would have been foolhardy suddenly to desert the path that could lead him to the chief justiceship or the White House.

v

As governor-general of the Philippines and de facto colonial secretary for the United States, Taft had acquired more firsthand knowledge of the Far East than any previous presidential candidate. Not only did he continue to oversee affairs in the Philippines as secretary of war, he also found time to carry out diplomatic duties assigned him by Roosevelt in the Far East. In the summer of 1905, Taft accompanied a large group of American congressmen on a fact-finding tour of the Philippines and the Far East. The official party traveled to Hawaii, Japan, the Philippines, and China before returning home. Besides lobbying on behalf of the islands, Taft performed a number of important tasks for Roosevelt. In Hawaii, he stopped briefly to assess labor unrest. In Japan, he tried to reassure officials about American attitudes toward the planned Portsmouth Conference and American policy in the Far East. The Japanese believed that Taft, who earlier in the year had been acting secretary of state, had come empowered to do some hard bargaining over the ultimate terms of the Russo-Japanese peace, the Philippines, China, and immigration problems. Taft was given an extremely warm reception and drawn into diplomatic conversations in which he tried to explain American policy. The conversations resulted in the Taft-Katsura Memorandum, an "unofficial alliance" between the United States and Japan guaranteeing Japanese influence in Korea in return for American suzerainty in the Philippines.[50] Taft, however, had not come to Japan to conduct serious negotiations. He cabled Roosevelt:

> I sent Mr. Root from Tokio a long cable concerning a conversation which I had with Count Katsura. They were anxious that it should be sent and I did not know but it might help you in your conferences with Komura. They [the Japanese] sought the interview. I did not because I did not wish to butt into the affairs of the State Department, but they probably thought it important because I had had some relation with State Department business.

Roosevelt cabled back that Taft's conversations with Katsura had been "absolutely correct in every respect" and asked Taft to assure Katsura that he, Roosevelt, had confirmed "every word" of his secretary of war.[51]

Taft returned to the Philippines and then journeyed on to China under instructions from Roosevelt to meet with the viceroy to discuss American-Chinese relations, particularly the Chinese boycott of American goods and anti-Chinese sentiment on the West Coast of the United States. After an exchange of views, Taft reported that the anti-American agitation and boycotts were receding in strength even though anti-American demonstrations occurred during his visit.[52] With his Chinese talks over, Taft returned to the United States. On the whole, it had been a very successful trip.

In the fall of 1907, Taft again journeyed to the Far East ostensibly to open the first Philippine Assembly, but also to soothe the ruffled feelings of the Japanese over anti-Japanese sentiment on the West Coast and to discuss the question of Japanese immigration into the United States. The Japanese, evidently concerned about war talk in the United States, received him even more impressively than in 1905. Discussion ranged from such topics as the rumored American sale of the Philippines to the thorny problem of immigration. Taft reported back to Roosevelt that the "Japanese government is most anxious to avoid war" and "in no financial condition to undertake it."[53]

From Japan, Taft traveled on to China. At Shanghai he delivered a rousing and significant speech to the American business community. As heir apparent to the President, he pledged full American support for the growth of American commerce and influence in China.[54] After stopping off in the Philippines to open the Philippine Assembly, he proceeded to Siberia. There he met the indefatigable Willard D. Straight, American consul at Mukden, China, who presented his case for American commercial expansion in Manchuria and China before the prospective Republican nominee. Straight notably found the secretary of war "unusually well informed about the entire Eastern situation" and "was surprised at the amount of information he possessed."[55] Seven years of experience overseeing various aspects of American colonial interests had given Taft a degree of expertise in foreign relations unparalleled by any other presidential hopeful.

VI

Taft's apprenticeship under Roosevelt had given him valuable experience in administration and foreign affairs. His public reputation as an administrator earned in the Philippines and Panama was high, but as his neglect of the War Department indicated, it was not his greatest asset as a prospective president. Foreign affairs was Taft's forte. He had learned through firsthand experience how Roosevelt conducted diplomacy and had won recognition from the President for the similarity of their diplomatic styles. Taft was known in China, admired in the Philippines, feared in Cuba, and respected in Japan and Panama. The flattering compliment of Japanese Premier Count Taro Katsura that Taft was "more familiar than any other foreigner" with the Far East, although uttered while Taft was president, was not without substantial foundation.[56] Taft represented a new breed of American statesmen who had become acutely conscious of America's expanding power in the world. His knowledge of foreign countries had been perhaps his biggest asset as a potential presidential candidate. He noted later during his presidency:

I have been twice to the Philippines and back. I have been twice around the world, in going to and from the Philippines. And in those four trips I visited Japan four times, Siberia and Russia once, China three times, Rome once, the Isthmus of Panama seven times, Cuba twice, and Porto Rico once. . . . Such an experience has enabled me to breathe in the atmosphere and environment of many countries and many nationalities, and I hope given me a less provincial view of many international questions than one is likely to have who learns of foreign countries by books and whose Americanism is so narrow and intense that he be indisposed to learn anything either of government or society from the experiences of other peoples.[57]

Not even Theodore Roosevelt could boast of such broad foreign experiences upon becoming president.

In addition to his foreign policy expertise, Taft possessed a number of traits which Roosevelt found appealing and complementary to himself. The secretary of war's indifference to the presidency (and no other term quite describes his attitude!) assured Roosevelt that his own power would not be undermined by an overly ambitious subordinate. Taft's dedication to duty, moreover, impressed Roosevelt greatly for it meant that the President could always depend upon Taft to carry out the tasks assigned to him. In addition, Taft's judicial temperament provided a useful check upon the more impulsive, result-oriented approach of the President, and Roosevelt knew it. The President also admired his lieutenant's integrity, perhaps because he could not always afford the luxury of it himself. "I know of no man in public life," he once wrote Taft, "who would be prompter than you to follow his own conscience without regard to the fact whether it hurt his future or not."[58] Roosevelt was absolutely correct. All of these qualities—indifference toward the presidency, dedication to duty, judicial temperament and integrity—made Taft an ideal political lieutenant and assistant president, but they did not necessarily guarantee success in the White House.

Pringle has aptly characterized Taft as a valuable "conciliator" for the Roosevelt administration.[59] His reputation appears to have been earned primarily while he was secretary of war. His visits to the Philippines, Panama, Cuba, China, and Japan were made to iron out American problems with those countries, and obviously Roosevelt trusted his lieutenant to do the job properly. But Taft's most significant successes occurred in situations in which he negotiated with political inferiors whose bargaining power was unequal to that of the personal representative of the president. In the Philippines, Cuba, and Panama, where he scored his greatest successes as a mediator and administrator, Taft was able to wield the greatest amount of discretion and power. In the Philippines, he had been a benevolent dictator who could invoke the ultimate sanction of superior force to win his way if necessary. In Panama, he inherited a situation where a fragile new republic had granted the United States canal-building rights and where the expressed desire of the President to finish the canal as quickly as possible placed enormous power and responsibility in his hands. In Cuba he could claim success in placing the Cuban regime back upon its feet because of the military power of the United States which he represented, and which he ultimately invoked. In all these cases, Taft was not dealing with the political equals he would have to confront as president. His judicial and administrative experience did not equip him for bargaining with domestic political barons like Speaker of the House Joe Cannon, Republican Senate leader Nelson W. Aldrich, or party bosses and governors across the country. Taft had not learned enough about the domestic political process or the public with whom he would have to contend as president. He eventually recognized the inadequacy of his preparation after he became president. In an interview for the *Outlook* in December 1911, he ruefully admitted, "Though I had had some executive experience in the Philippines and as Secretary of War, it was no adequate preparation for the multifarious duties of the Presidency."[60] His congenial nature and notoriously infectious chuckle, though valuable for any conciliator, were no substitute for a sophisticated understanding of the nature of power in a democratic system.

By working in the shadow of one of the most popular leaders in America who served as his mentor, press agent, and champion, Taft was never forced to develop the knowledge and skills of the professional politician concerned with winning and maintaining public support. He was neither a stirring orator, flatterer of the people, nor a sensitive barometer of the passing whims and fancies of the populace. He had risen to power, not by his ability to win votes, but by his knack of impressing those who had already done so. He did not enjoy campaigning or party politics and performed his partisan duties for Roosevelt out of loyalty to the administration and ambition for higher office. Surprisingly, he could admit to his wife in the midst of the 1906 congressional campaign, "Politics, when I am in it, makes me sick."[61]

2. "A Forced Succession to the Presidency"

I believe with all my soul Taft, far more than any other public man of prominence, represents the principles for which I stand . . . and I should hold myself false to my duty if I sat supine and let the men who have taken such joy in my refusal to run again select some candidate whose success would mean the undoing of what I have sought to achieve.

Theodore Roosevelt,
January 27, 1908[1]

Political analysts have often praised national party conventions as institutions designed to select candidates who possess the qualities required for the presidency, qualities such as drive and determination, the ability to bargain and compromise, organizational skill, sensitivity to public opinion, and genuine popular appeal. But such qualities can triumph only in a nominating convention which is competitive. In 1908, Theodore Roosevelt was such a popular and commanding figure in the Republican party that he was virtually able to appoint William Howard Taft as his successor. In imposing Taft upon the Republican party, Roosevelt succeeded in frustrating the inherent logic of the nominating process and helped nominate and elect a man who did not possess a number of qualities necessary for effective party and popular leadership.

I

There were not many things Theodore Roosevelt was inclined to regret in his long and active public life, but two stand out distinctly: his public pledge, taken the evening of his presidential victory over Alton B. Parker in November 1904, that "under no circumstances will I be a candidate for or accept another nomination,"[2] and his selection of William Howard Taft as his successor. The self-denying pledge returned to haunt him during the last two years of his term and led to his abdication in favor of Taft. Although he must have agonized over keeping his pledge, he finally decided to do so for three major reasons; understanding these is necessary for an understanding of Roosevelt's effectiveness as president and of his subsequent falling out with Taft. First, he found it proper to follow the two-term precedent, for he believed it was "a very unhealthy thing that any man should be considered necessary to the people as a whole, save in the way of meeting some given crisis."[3] Second and most significant, a violation of his pledge would have tarnished his public reputation as the defender of morality in politics and as a disinterested public servant. He explained to Whitelaw Reid, ambassador to Great Britain:

My value as an asset to the American people consists chiefly in a belief in my disinterestedness and trustworthiness, in the belief that I mean what I say, and that my concern is for the good of the country; and if they should now nominate me, even under circumstances that would force me to take the nomination, I could only take it as the least of two evils, and with the bitter knowledge that many good people would have their faith in me shaken, and that therefore my influence for good would be measurably, and perhaps greatly, diminished.[4]

As a successful democratic leader, Roosevelt had learned the necessity for preserving a spotless public image, even if the substance beneath was somewhat tarnished. Finally, he might have reconsidered his pledge if no able successor could have been found, but this was not the case, as he related to George Trevelyan, the British historian:

In Taft there was ready to hand a man whose theory of public and private duty is my own, and whose practice of this theory is what I hope mine is; and if we can elect him President we achieve all that could be achieved by continuing me in the office, and yet we avoid all the objections, all the risk of creating a bad precedent.[5]

For these reasons, Roosevelt decided to retire from office at the zenith of his political career and at the relatively young age of fifty-one.

Taft, of course, was not the only possible successor to Roosevelt. Among the men Roosevelt considered as presidential material at one time or another were Elihu Root, secretary of state and former secretary of war; Charles Evans Hughes, progressive governor of New York; Philander Chase Knox, senator from Pennsylvania and former attorney general; and "Uncle Joe" Cannon, Speaker of the House of Representatives. Of all these potential candidates, including Taft, Roosevelt would have preferred Root as his successor. He once admitted to Oscar King Davis of the *New York Times*, "I would rather see Elihu Root in the White House than any other man now possible" and "would walk on my hands and knees from the White House to the Capitol to see Root made President."[6] Although Roosevelt recognized the political liability of Root's background as a corporation lawyer, he felt that Root as president would work as energetically on behalf of the people as he had for his Wall Street clients. Roosevelt, moreover, did not consider Taft equal to Root in ability. He had once epitomized the differences between the two while explaining why he thought Root was the greatest secretary of state: "The trouble with Taft was that he had once been a Judge, and if he came up against the law in a policy which he wanted to pursue, he had such a respect for the law that he gave in, while Secretary Root was such a great lawyer that he always could find a way to get around it."[7] Taft himself admired Root's abilities and suggested to Roosevelt that Root run for the governorship of New York in 1906 as a step toward the Republican nomination in 1908. "A test of this sort," he wrote to Roosevelt, "and a successful one, would do much toward dissolving the feeling of doubt as to his running powers."[8] Root, however, had little taste for campaigning for either the governorship or the presidency. Roosevelt reluctantly concluded that "wild horses couldn't drag him into making a public campaign."[9] By October 1906, Roosevelt had been forced to rule out Root as a potential successor and had tentatively committed himself to work for Taft's nomination.

Charles Evans Hughes, winner of the New York governorship which Root had shunned, presented Taft and Roosevelt with the most formidable threat to the nomination in 1908. Hughes was a proven vote-getter and quickly began to establish a progressive record for himself as governor. As early as November 1906, Roosevelt had warned Mrs. Taft that if her husband did not provide more personal impetus to his own presidential ambitions, then he, Roosevelt, might be forced to support a candidate like Hughes with stronger grass-roots sentiment behind him. Roosevelt recognized Hughes's ability and came to fear his ambition. "He has the kind of quality which is apt to win out in conventions as against a man of bold generous type like Taft, who looks out too little for his own interests," he wrote to his son Kermit in 1908.[10] Earlier he had written that "one man's chief concern is himself, and the other man's chief concern is to do well the job at which he is working."[11] Because the governor was so "inordinately conceited," Roosevelt feared that Hughes, as president, "would not carry out the so-called Roosevelt policy because it was known as Roosevelt."[12] Taft presumably was above such pettiness: "Taft's great ambition in office is to do the job in the best way it can possibly be done, and he simply never thinks as to whether he is under obligations to anyone or whether anyone is under obligations to him."[13] Roosevelt also found Hughes woefully deficient in his knowledge of foreign affairs, naval policy, and the administration of American territories, all matters of prime importance to the President. Finally, Roosevelt feared that Hughes might become a rallying point for the vested interests he had antagonized while president— "the anti-imperialists . . . Wall Street, the *Sun*, the *Evening Post*, the mugwumps, the big corporations, all will be for him."[14] This ragtag assortment of interests preferred Hughes because "they would hope that his unfamiliarity with the needs of the country as a whole, and his lawyer-like conservatism, would make him a President like Cleveland instead of a President like me." Roosevelt preferred a successor with a wide knowledge of foreign affairs, long experience in government, and an impartial attitude toward capital and labor—a man who would carry out his basic policies unchanged. He had convinced himself that although Hughes might make a "good" president, he could "not begin to compare with Taft, either morally, intellectually, or in knowledge of public problems."[15]

Philander Chase Knox presented another potential threat to Taft's nomination. Although Knox had been identified publicly as less progressive than Taft on domestic issues, Roosevelt viewed his candidacy more favorably than Hughes's. As Roosevelt's attorney general, Knox had distinguished himself by securing the complicated title to the Panama Canal and by vigorously enforcing the antitrust laws, particularly in the Northern Securities Antitrust Case. Neither his lack of experience in foreign affairs nor his reputation as a corporation lawyer was a bar to his nomination in Roosevelt's eyes, for Knox, Roosevelt wrote in 1907, "has the extremely lawyer-like mind which would make him as President treat the country as his client, with as a result . . . some very unpleas-

ant surprizes to the wealthy men who now think he could be
trusted to be their ally in the White House." Because Knox
was also more familiar with Republican foreign policies than
Hughes, he would have been an acceptable replacement for
Roosevelt.[16]

"Uncle Joe" Cannon, Speaker of the House, was another
possible Republican choice for president. A powerful leader
of men and experienced in public life, Cannon would have
made a "good" president, according to Roosevelt in 1907, "except on one or two lines."[17] Those "one or two lines" were
tariff reform and Roosevelt's naval policy. During his eight
years in office, Roosevelt continually broached the question of
tariff reform to the Speaker, only to have him throw cold
water on the idea. Cannon was also known as a foe of large-
scale naval expansion, a policy dear to the President's heart
and central to his foreign policies.[18] By June of 1908, however, Cannon had alienated Roosevelt by bottling up his
legislative program in the House. The Speaker's increasing
"standpattism" in the face of rising progressive sentiment, his
authoritarian methods of running the House, and his barnyard
language had eliminated him as a serious contender for the
nomination. By 1908, Roosevelt would have sought a third
term rather than see Cannon nominated.

Taft had been a logical choice to succeed Roosevelt ever
since the President's self-denying pledge of 1904. With no
suspicious ties to Wall Street or the trusts, a sterling reputation for integrity, and a solid political base in the strategically
important Midwest, Taft appeared to be the most "available"
candidate. Although his friendship with Roosevelt was a factor in his nomination, Taft's commitment to Roosevelt's policies was the real basis of his strength with the President. "I
believe with all my soul Taft, far more than any other public
man of prominence, represents the principles for which I
stand," he wrote his son Kermit, "and I should hold myself

false to my duty if I sat supine and let the men who have taken such joy in my refusal to run again select some candidate whose success would mean the undoing of what I have sought to achieve."[19] Roosevelt undoubtedly hoped to harness Taft's selfless loyalty to his own policies and thereby guarantee their perpetuation in the next administration. Furthermore, with Taft so indifferent toward the presidency and so interested in becoming chief justice, Roosevelt could leave the door ajar for a political comeback eight or perhaps four years later.

Experience in public affairs was another plus for Taft. As Roosevelt explained to Nicholas Murray Butler, a popular vote-getter without experience in government would never do as his successor:

The business of the nation is complicated. There is no excuse whatever, when we have such an abundance of really big men, strong men of high character, who do know all about this business, for failing to take advantage of this knowledge. Nobody can learn about the navy, and Panama Canal, and the Philippines, and our foreign policy, and what it is possible to do in federal regulation of trusts, save by experience; that is by being predominantly identified with office-holding. To put a good man with a good character who has not been "prominently identified with office-holding" into the Presidency, is just the kind of inanity of which you speak. He has got to learn all of these things during his first months or years of the Presidency, instead of knowing them already. A man like Root or Taft does not have to learn any of them and can do his best work from the beginning.[20]

Roosevelt's expressed concern about foreign affairs was genuine. His criteria for a "good" president included experience in public office (though unfortunately not elective office!) and foreign affairs. Roosevelt could consequently assure Arthur Hamilton Lee: "Of course if Taft succeeds me our foreign policy will go on absolutely unchanged. Indeed, I think this will be the case with almost any Republican."²¹ But Taft's participation in the making and execution of Roosevelt's foreign policies had made his personal stake in defending those policies greater than that of any other potential candidate except Root. That is why Roosevelt preferred Taft above all the other Republican hopefuls.

II

The Republican presidential nomination in 1908 was a prize eminently worth seeking. The Republican party had dominated national life since the Civil War and, with William Mc-Kinley's victory over William Jennings Bryan in 1896, had repulsed a Democratic challenge to its control over national life. Although McKinley had polled only 51 per cent of the popular vote in 1896 and 1900, Roosevelt had increased the Republican presidential margin to a whopping 57 per cent and was leaving office with his party in an almost impregnable position. Although Roosevelt had expressed misgivings after the 1906 elections that the pendulum of public opinion might have begun to swing back toward the Democratic party, that pendulum had a long way to go before the Republican hold on the nation would be broken. In grappling with the dominant issue of government regulation of economic life, Roosevelt had inspired great popular confidence in himself and in the ability of American political institutions to curb the growing excesses of corporate power. He had become the symbol and champion of the rising hopes of progressives throughout the country. His support for any Republican candidate would probably have guaranteed that candidate's nomination and election to the presidency. As Roosevelt's choice, Taft was handed what most men could only dream of—the presidency of the United States.

This is not to deny the difficulties that Roosevelt faced in naming a successor. By the fall of 1906, he had decided to support Taft, barring, of course, any cataclysmic changes in the political climate. The President's major obstacle was Taft's own indifference to the "politics" necessary for winning the nomination, for Taft remained a reluctant candidate who continued to long for the chief justiceship rather than the presidency. What he lacked in ambition for the office, however, was more than offset by the zeal of his wife and family for his candidacy.[22]

Roosevelt was well aware of his lieutenant's reluctance. In October 1906, Mrs. Taft had come away from an interview with Roosevelt with the distinct impression that the President was somewhat "discouraged over my husband as a candidate because he had avoided co-operation with certain political organizations in the West, and, further thought he might have to join with other Republicans in supporting Governor Hughes, because Mr. Taft was such a poor politician."[23] Taft attributed his behavior to a desire to remain free of embarrassing commitments and did not appear unduly alarmed at the prospect of Roosevelt's supporting another candidate:

If you do you may be sure that you will awaken no feeling of disappointment on my part. While I very much appreciate your anxiety that I shall be nominated, and regard is [sic] as the highest compliment possible to me and a most gratifying evidence of your good will, you know what my feeling has been in respect to the Presidency, and can understand that it will not leave the slightest trace of disappointment, should your views change and you think it wise to make a start in any other direction.[24]

Part of Taft's attitude toward the presidency stemmed from his recognition of his inability to strike a responsive chord among the party leaders and people of the country. His stumping for the Republican party in the 1906 elections had left him acutely aware of his deficiencies as a campaigner, politician, and successor. He explained his misgivings to Roosevelt:

The truth is that I find on this trip, and find it everywhere, that the strong feeling is not for me but it is for your renomination, and then in case of desperation if you will not accept, they flatter me by saying that I must come next, but the second choice is so far from the first choice that I only warn you that the ground swell for your renomination is beginning, not among the politicians, but among the people, and you are going to have bad quarters of an hour during the next eighteen months on account. The people are delighted with your course. They are anxious to have you given an opportunity to continue for four years longer, and they are not content with any substitute.[25]

Had Taft craved public adulation, empathized with the crowds, or enjoyed power more than he did, perhaps he would have become a more enthusiastic candidate for the presidency, but as Roosevelt's successor, he realized that he could never escape comparison with his mentor. Little wonder that Mrs. Taft could write of him during this period that "never did he cease to regard a Supreme Court appointment as vastly more desirable than the Presidency."[26]

Despite his intense desire to remain president, Roosevelt labored hard for Taft's nomination. Always the skillful politician, the President refused to renew publicly his election-eve pledge. Roosevelt believed that a public reaffirmation of the pledge would create trouble in the South, where delegates could easily be purchased by the big financial interests. For western Republicans, however, he privately was "positive" in his refusal to run again; for eastern Republicans not inclined to support Taft, he remained "delphic" about his plans.[27] Following this dual strategy, the President was able to prevent candidates like Hughes and Knox from tying up delegates in the eastern states who were inclined toward the President, while Taft's lieutenants—Charles P. Taft, Arthur I. Vorys, Myron T. Herrick, Nicholas Longworth, and former Assistant Postmaster General Frank Hitchcock—busily gathered commitments from delegates in the West and South. As a result of this strategy, Taft's opponents were skillfully maneuvered into anti-Roosevelt positions, thus easing the way for Taft's nomination as the pro-Roosevelt candidate.

By the time the Republican National Convention opened in Chicago on June 16, 1908, the only doubt about the convention was whether it might offer a third term to Roosevelt, a prospect the President had considered, secretly longed for, but had resolutely planned against. When permanent chairman Henry Cabot Lodge referred to Roosevelt by name in a keynote address as "the most abused and most popular man in the United States today," the convention exploded with a spontaneous demonstration of support for him, interspersed with chants of "Four, Four, Four Years More." The demonstration lasted forty-seven minutes and surpassed the tumult over Bryan's Cross of Gold Speech at the Democratic Convention of 1896. Lodge, however, deflated the movement by reminding the delegates that Roosevelt was determined to retire and that "anyone who attempts to use his name as a candidate for the presidency impugns both his sincerity and his good faith."[28] The convention then proceeded with its business, finally nominating Taft overwhelmingly on the first ballot with 702 votes out of a possible 980. His nearest competitors, Hughes and Knox, could muster only 67 and 68 votes respectively.[29]

Despite the emotional demonstration on his behalf, Roosevelt felt that the convention machinery was controlled by a "rather ultraconservative set of delegates" who were willing to vote for Taft to dump the President.[30] Roosevelt and Taft, for example, encountered difficulties in dictating the platform to the convention and had to compromise on the labor injunction and tariff revision planks. Both men, moreover, were outmaneuvered in their choice of a vice-presidential candidate. Roosevelt had deferred to Taft's wish to wait until after the presidential nomination before supporting a candidate. By postponing the question, the two found it impossible to find a progressive partner at the last minute who was both "available" and willing to take second place. Senators Jonathan P. Dolliver and Albert J. Beveridge both flatly refused the proffered nomination and left a political vacuum into which a united conservative bloc thrust "Sunny" Jim Sherman of New York, a senator closely identified with "standpattism" within the party. Thus, the conservative backlash of the delegates against Roosevelt left the Taft forces with the presidential nomination, a "safe, sane, and conservative platform," and little else.[31]

Charges that Roosevelt had forced Taft's nomination upon the Republican party were, for the most part, true. Although Roosevelt had tried to avoid the appearance of dictating anybody's nomination, he acknowledged his right to protect his own policies and to voice an opinion on his successor. "I am quite sincere when I say that I am not trying to dictate the choice of anyone," he wrote to William Allen White, "and I stand for the kind of man rather than any particular man."[32] It just happened that Taft was the right kind of man. Despite the grumbling of some Republicans about the President's favoritism toward his lieutenant, Roosevelt consistently denied the use of coercion to secure Taft's nomination. Although the President had forbidden federal officeholders from pushing his own nomination in his letter of November 19, 1907, to all department heads, he certainly did not use his patronage powers to favor any other candidate.[33] As he ingeniously tried to explain, "I appointed no man *for the purpose* of creating Taft sentiment; but I have appointed men *in recognition* of the Taft sentiment already in existence."[34]

The voices of criticism, however, could not be stilled. The Democratic party adopted a plank in its platform which condemned Roosevelt's support for Taft as "a forced succession to the Presidency."³⁵ Neither Taft nor Roosevelt, however, thought of the nomination in that fashion. Roosevelt pointed out to his critics that Taft had won more votes in the northern states than in the South, which gave "twice as many" votes to Taft's opponents as did the North. The President maintained that the federal officeholders had actually followed "the drift of their several communities" in supporting the various candidates. "The only way in which I dictated to the officeholders," he explained, "was to dictate to them that they should not support me for a renomination."³⁶ Taft, moreover, later indicated in a letter of gratitude to Roosevelt the limitation the President had encountered in trying to name a successor:

The first letter I wish to write is to you, because you have always been the chief agent in working out the present status of affairs, and my selection and election are chiefly your work. You and my brother Charley made that possible which in all probability would not have occurred otherwise. I don't wish to be falsely modest in this. I know, as you have said to me when we have talked the matter over, that neither you nor he could probably have done the same thing with any other candidate, under the circumstances as they were, but that doesn't affect the fact as I have stated it, or my reason for feeling the deep gratitude which I do.³⁷

Although the letter upset Roosevelt because he felt that he alone was responsible for Taft's nomination, it did indicate the candidate's belief that he was the most "available" person in the Republican party at the time. Taft had been such a nationally prominent figure in the cabinet that the President had found it easy to enhance his secretary's reputation. After the convention, the *New York Times* appropriately described Taft as "a Republican who has more elements of strength with the people than could be asserted on behalf of any other of the prominent aspirants for the honor."³⁸ Had Roosevelt decided to boost Hughes or Knox, he would have had to begin improving their image one or two years before the convention. By June 1908, the President had narrowed his choices. He could have secured his own renomination or vetoed the nomination of any other candidate. However, after encouraging and supporting Taft for years, he was no longer free to abandon his lieutenant at will. Roosevelt was no longer the complete master of the Republican party.

III

When the Democratic party renominated its old standard-bearer William Jennings Bryan, a Republican victory seemed assured. Twice defeated by McKinley in 1896 and 1900, the silver-tongued orator had emerged from a divided Democratic party to challenge the Grand Old Party again. The battle between Taft and Bryan was soon joined, but it was not half as interesting as the emerging differences in political style between Taft and Roosevelt which the campaign began to reveal, differences which foreshadowed the party split of 1912. As early as November 1906, Roosevelt had criticized Taft for being too "aloof" from the early campaign for the nomination. A master at self-dramatization himself, Roosevelt thought Taft should get out in public more and "give everybody a fair show at you."[39] Once Taft's nomination was secured, Roosevelt felt that his role as Taft's promoter had come to an end. "Of course everything I can do for Taft's success will be done," he explained to Senator Lodge, "but after all, most of what I can thus do has already been done, and I do not wish to become officious or a busybody."[40] Taft's lackluster political style, however, soon forced Roosevelt to throw himself into the campaign "with greater energy" than ever.[41]

The event which compelled Roosevelt to reenter the campaign on an active note and which revealed a significant difference in style between the two men occurred when Ohio

Senator Joseph B. Foraker proffered Taft his support for the presidency. In 1907, Foraker had approached Taft and offered to support him for the nomination in return for Taft's assistance in the senator's bid for reelection. Because of Foraker's unsavory reputation as a spokesman for the trusts, Taft declined, maintaining, "I do not care for the Presidency if it has to come by compromise with anyone on a matter of principle."[42] After the Republican Convention, while both men shared a campaign platform in Ohio, Foraker publicly extended his support to Taft, thereby creating the false impression among the audience that the two men had settled their political differences. Oblivious to the effects of Foraker's support upon his public image, Taft, to the chagrin of Roosevelt, let the episode pass unchallenged. Shortly thereafter journalist William Randolph Hearst sensationally exposed Foraker's financial subservience to the Standard Oil Company and utterly destroyed his chances for reelection. Roosevelt could no longer restrain himself and urged Taft to disassociate himself immediately from Foraker lest the people believe that "all Republicans are tarred with the same brush." The President saw nothing to be gained by "temporizing":

I would like to see you in the strongest and most emphatic way do what I should do in your place—make a fight openly on the ground that you stood in the Republican party and before the people for the triumph over the forces which were typified by the purchase of a United States Senator to do the will of the Standard Oil Company, and that you had been opposed by him because of this fundamental antagonism and that for the American people to beat you was to serve notice that they were willing to see a man punished because he declined to yield on such an issue.[43]

But Taft was not Roosevelt. He had no stomach for denouncing a man whom Hearst had just demolished, the very man who had given his early judicial career a boost by appointing him to the Superior Court of Ohio. The President was understandably angered by his lieutenant's impotence. He confided his misgivings about the campaign to Lyman Abbott of the *Outlook:*

> Oh Lord, I do get angry now and then over the campaign. Of course I suppose everyone always feels that he would manage things a little differently if he had the doing of them; but certainly I would like to put more snap into the business. In this Foraker affair I made up my mind that I would hit from the shoulder inasmuch as Taft did not. Taft is quite right in saying that he does not wish to hit a man when he is down; but this is not a case of that kind. This is a case of a fight to the finish.[44]

Taft was not oblivious to the opportunity for dramatizing the issue of corporate corruption of high officials, but he could not bring himself to the unsportsmanlike course of kicking a man who was already down. He knew he could have increased his popularity by attacking Foraker, but he felt his own integrity would have suffered in the process. Unlike Roosevelt, Taft had no political instinct for the jugular.

The fall campaign revealed other important aspects of Taft's character and political style. For example, Taft adopted a rather novel and daring attitude toward campaign financing. Since political contributions were not regulated by federal law, Taft decided to set an example for his party and nation by voluntarily publicizing campaign contributions to the Republican National Committee after the election. Although his attitude delighted progressives across the country, his selection of George R. Sheldon, a prominent Wall Street lawyer, as treasurer of the Republican National Committee disappointed many. In 1906, Sheldon had earned a reputation for integrity as treasurer of the New York State Republican Committee by publicizing campaign expenditures required by New York law. Taft hoped that Sheldon's integrity would neutralize objections to his background as a corporation lawyer and, as Taft wrote to Roosevelt, "enable us to eliminate from the campaign any substantial argument against us, on the ground that we favor corruption funds or the undue use of money in campaigns." The President agreed that Sheldon was the "best selection that could be made."[45]

Complaints about Taft's campaign contribution policy soon began to filter into campaign headquarters. George W. Perkins of the banking firm of J. P. Morgan, for example, protested against Sheldon's appointment and announced his unwillingness to contribute to the Republican campaign for fear of subsequent publicity. Taft, however, stood firm on Sheldon and his contribution policy. He explained to Roosevelt:

I am, as you are, in favor of the publicity of contributions and the receipts and expenditures. I think it is necessary to prevent the great use of money for corrupt or quasi-corrupt purposes, and I am willing to have it begin with this campaign, although it may work to our comparative disadvantage. Following the publicity law in New York in reference to national expenditures will doubtless decrease the amount of money which we can raise, but much as I would like to have an ample fund to spread the light of Republicanism, I am willing to undergo the disadvantage in order to make certain that in the future we shall reduce the power of money in politics for unworthy purposes.[46]

Taft's good intentions were soon tested when William Nelson Cromwell, a friend and prominent Wall Street lawyer, offered Taft $50,000 for his campaign. Embarrassed by the amount and the prospect of having to publicize the contribution later, Taft declined the offer. "The size of the subscription will be misunderstood and the inferences drawn from it will not be just to you or to me,"[47] he wrote to Cromwell. Surprisingly, Roosevelt thought that Taft was "altogether over sensitive."[48] For the remainder of the campaign, Taft kept a sharp eye on party finances. At one point he even found it necessary to warn Sheldon to refrain from soliciting contributions from the Standard Oil Company or any other company that had violated the antitrust laws. Although Taft's attitude stands in marked contrast to his generally cavalier concern for his public image, it can be explained, for the most part, by his almost ruthless integrity and overriding desire to reduce the power of money in politics.

Problems with the Republican National Committee continued to plague Taft throughout the campaign. Taft had appointed Frank Hitchock, former assistant postmaster general and his own convention manager, as chairman of the Republican National Committee. Taft explained to the President that Hitchcock was "far and away the ablest organizer that we can get. He is able to step into the business at once and lose no time about it, and he is one of the hardest and most efficient workers I know." Despite protests from Ohio and from progressives suspicious of Hitchcock's conservatism, Roosevelt approved of Taft's choice as "wise."[49]

Taft soon found himself unable to control Hitchcock. Allegedly misunderstanding Taft's desires, Hitchcock had appointed Thomas C. duPont, Charles F. Brooker, and Frank O. Lowden to the executive committee of the Republican National Committee without consulting Taft. DuPont was closely connected with the so-called "Powder Trust," Brooker was vice-president of the New York, New Haven and Hartford Railroad, which was being prosecuted by the federal government for violation of the antitrust laws, and Lowden was the son-in-law of George Pullman of the infamous Pullman strike of 1894—all men associated with the worst abuses of corporate wealth! Taft complained to Roosevelt of the arbitrary manner in which the party chairman had gone about his work "without consulting with me at all." Roosevelt's solution to the problem was characteristic of his political style. He suggested that Taft quickly discipline Hitchcock "without the slightest hesitation and with all needful severity. He is a man who needs to have a strong hand kept on him."⁵⁰ Although Taft then complained to Hitchcock of duPont's appointment and of the lack of consultation, he did not reprimand the party chairman or ask for duPont's resignation. It was not surprising, then, that progressives began to cast suspicious glances toward's Taft's campaign organization, which was heavily stocked with men identified with the business community.

Hitchcock remained undaunted by Taft's mild complaints. In early August, he decided to appoint William Nelson Cromwell chairman of a newly created advisory committee to aid in formulating campaign strategy. Taft was forced to intervene and asked Cromwell not to accept "to avoid the inference, however unfounded, as it certainly is, that I am under the control in any way of the interests against whom the movement in the West is a protest."⁵¹

Although Cromwell declined to serve, Taft's troubles with his campaign manager persisted. Taft continued to complain to Roosevelt about Hitchcock; he still found it "very difficult to get him to do things which I wish him to do in the matter of smoothing down people." Roosevelt in turn urged Taft to "keep your hand on Hitchcock a little" and to light some fires under the National Committee to counteract "a pretty widespread feeling that things are not quite as lively as they should be at headquarters."⁵² The President had little sympathy with Hitchock's strategy of waiting until late in the campaign for a whirlwind finish. Toward the end of September, Roosevelt again expressed misgivings to Taft about the way in which the campaign was being conducted and encouraged Taft to "dominate more than you have yet done the National Committee" and to "take the most aggressive kind of attitude toward Bryan." Roosevelt also suggested that Hitchcock be ordered to replace duPont because of his identification in the public mind with the trusts. The public clamor against du-Pont soon reached such a pitch that Taft was forced to urge Hitchcock to reverse what Roosevelt now described as a "grave blunder."[53] DuPont finally resigned under pressure.

Taft's difficulties with Hitchcock highlighted his propensity as an administrator (already evident from his handling of the War Department) to delegate extensive powers to his subordinates without providing the necessary control and coordination from the top. By failing to keep a tight reign on Hitchcock, Taft permitted a number of important political decisions to be made which damaged his image among progressives across the country. To associate himself and his party with men like duPont, Lowden, Cromwell, Sheldon, and Pullman was to tar and feather the party as a special interest group before the campaign had even begun. To have delegated extensive powers to Hitchcock may have been an admirable technique of administration, but to have allowed him to determine the character of the campaign organization was clearly poor politics on Taft's part.

As the campaign developed, differences between Taft and Roosevelt became more evident. Whereas Roosevelt enjoyed combat, Taft found it a continuous trial to be endured stoically. Taft naturally encountered difficulties, for it was his first major campaign for elective office. He was admittedly "a bit nervous" over being a presidential candidate since he was "unused to occupying a personal position in a campaign."[54] Although he had originally planned to run only a "front-porch" campaign, distress calls from the West led him to recognize that "the necessity for stirring up interest in the campaign is so imperative that I am willing to run the risk of breaking a precedent or following the course that Blaine took."[55] The prospect of electioneering, however, was distasteful to him. "I hate to go out on the stump because it is hard work," he confessed to Senator Lodge, "and yet I don't know that it is any harder work than sitting at home doing nothing but being opposed by Bryan."[56]

Exasperated by the campaigning deficiencies of his successor, Roosevelt began to offer more advice to Taft. Shortly after the Republican convention the President urged Taft to take the offensive against Bryan. "My own voice is always for aggressive warfare," he wrote to Taft, "and in your position I should go hard at Bryan and the Bryanites." The President also returned Taft's Speech of Acceptance of the nomination with general approval but criticized various sections as "weak," "apologetic and hesitating," and as indicating too much "self-depreciation or undue subordination" to the President. In late August, Roosevelt again attempted to light a fire under Taft. "I earnestly want your personality put into this campaign," he urged Taft, "and I want us to choose our ground and make the fight aggressively." When it appeared that Taft would take to the stump, Roosevelt again prodded him on to do battle: "Do not *answer* Bryan; attack him! Don't let *him* make the issues."[57] But Taft did not possess the combative personality of a Roosevelt. Even Elihu Root, who hated campaigning as much as Taft, began to express his doubts about the campaign. "For reasons which I am absolutely unable to fathom," he wrote to Roosevelt, "Taft does not arouse the enthusiasm which his record and personality warrant us in believing he ought to arouse."[58] If Roosevelt had already discerned the reasons, as is likely, he was loathe to express them. After all, it was he who had foisted Taft on the party.

But Taft could not change his personality and essentially judicial temperament overnight. When one irate Republican complained about the lackluster speeches he had been giving, Taft replied:

I am sorry, but I cannot be more aggressive than my nature makes me. That is the advantage and disadvantage of having been on the Bench. I can't call names and I can't use adjectives when I don't think the case calls for them, so you will have to get along with that kind of a candidate. I realize what you say of the strength that the President has by reason of those qualities which are the antithesis of the judicial, but so it is with me, and if the people don't like that kind of a man then they have got to take another.[59]

Republicans were left with a take-it-or-leave-it proposition. The campaign had highlighted the differences between the basically aggressive, self-righteous nature of Roosevelt and the more passive, judicial nature of Taft. Taft's lack of political aggressiveness and his insensitivity to opportunities for creating a more favorable public image were plainly evident to those near him. He had failed to learn one of the first lessons of elective politics and one of the oldest known to political man, which Sir Francis Bacon so aptly expressed in his essay "Of Boldness":

Question was asked of Demosthenes, *what was the chief part of an orator?* he answered, *action;* what next? *action.* what next? *action.* He said it that knew it best, and had by nature himself no advantage in that he commended. A strange thing, that that part of an orator which is but superficial, and rather the virtue of a player, should be placed so high, above those other noble parts of invention, elocution, and the rest; nay almost alone, as if it were all in all. But the reason is plain. There is in human nature generally more of the fool than of the wise; and therefore those faculties by which the foolish part of men's minds is taken are most potent. Wonderful like is the case of Boldness, in civil business; what first? Boldness: what second and third? Boldness. And yet boldness is a child of ignorance and baseness, far inferior to other parts. But nevertheless it doth fascinate and bind hand and foot those that are either shallow in judgment or weak in courage, which are the greatest part; yea and prevaileth with wise men at weak times. Therefore we see it hath done wonders in popular states.[60]

IV

Although the presidential campaign had disclosed differences in political style and temperament between Roosevelt and Taft, it failed to reveal any significant discrepancies in their views on public policy. In numerous appearances throughout 1908, Taft strongly defended the Republican foreign policy of "expansion" and all its corollaries. He vigorously denounced the traditional political isolationism of the United States as irrelevant in the modern world; he pledged to continue the American presence in the Philippines until those islands were thoroughly prepared for self-government; he emphasized his desire to lend greater support to American trade expansion throughout the world and, in particular, to maintain the Open Door Policy in the Far East. He recognized the need to complete the Panama Canal as soon as possible; and, finally, he energetically supported the continued strengthening of the American navy, promising Roosevelt to back the construction of two battleships per year.[61] On all the great foreign policy issues of the day, Taft echoed Roosevelt's views—indeed, he had been the architect of some of them—and occasionally, as with foreign trade, championed them even more vigorously than had the President himself. Both men realized that the old rhetoric of isolationism and nonentanglement was inappropriate for America's emerging role as a great power.

For the American public, however, domestic issues were of prime concern, particularly the question of government regulation of growing corporate power. Although Taft tended to be more legalistic and rigid in his views on the extent of federal power to regulate the trusts, he basically agreed with Roosevelt's antitrust policies. As he explained in 1907, "*Mr.*

Theodore Roosevelt with Taft, 1909. Photograph by Harris & Ewing.

Robert M. La Follette and Taft, 1908.

Henry Cabot Lodge and Taft, 1909. Photograph by Underwood & Underwood.

Taft and Major Archibald Butt, 1911.

The first family: Taft with his wife, Helen, and their children Helen, Charles, and Robert, 1909. Photograph by W. Fawcett.

The President and his cabinet: (*clockwise*) Franklin MacVeagh, George W. Wickersham, George von L. Meyer, James Wilson, Charles Nagel, Richard A. Ballinger, Frank H. Hitchcock, Jacob M. Dickinson, Philander C. Knox. Photograph by Clinedinst.

Taft at his desk. Photograph by H. E. French.

Taft speaking at Manassas Court House, 1911.

The President throws out the first ball, 1909. Photograph by Clinedinst.

Taft leaving the St. Antho[nio]
Hotel, San Antonio, Texas, 19[

Charles P. Taft in the gard[en]
with his brother, 1908.

Roosevelt's views were mine long before I knew Mr. Roosevelt at all."[62]

Taft expressed his support for Roosevelt's policies against concentrated wealth while he was still governor-general of the Philippines. While congratulating Roosevelt on the Republican congressional victories of 1902, Taft wrote of his apprehension at the "blindness," "greed," and "unconscious arrogance" of men of wealth which threatened to precipitate a socialist upheaval and destroy private property. Taft hoped that Roosevelt, while proceeding with the necessary task of social and economic reform, would be able to so channel popular feeling against the trusts that the public would not threaten the principles of private property and "freedom of contract." Whether men of property realized it or not, Roosevelt was saving them from a "cataclysm" of popular reaction which could bring about economic collapse in its wake. Roosevelt's subsequent attempts to bring the trusts and railroads under responsible public control met with Taft's hearty approval. Even Roosevelt's controversial message of January 31, 1908, calling for greater public control over corporations found favor with Taft, who characterized it as "a bugle call for renewed support of the policies of the Administration."[63]

The attitudes of both Taft and Roosevelt on the great issues of government regulation of the economy could be classified as "middle of the road." As public opinion had become more progressive toward the end of his administration, so had Roosevelt, at least in rhetoric. But the consummate politician of the age could likewise confess to Taft that "the great virtue of my radicalism lies in the fact that I am perfectly ready, if necessary, to be radical on the conservative side."[64] Taft had kept pace with Roosevelt and public opinion and could be classified as a moderate on the political spectrum. Roosevelt applauded Taft's position as a great asset in a president:

If elected, he has shown by his deeds that he will be President of no class, but of the people as a whole; he can be trusted to stand stoutly against the two real enemies of our democracy—against the man who to please one class would undermine the whole foundation of orderly liberty, and against the man who in the interest of another class would secure business prosperity by sacrificing every right of the working people.[65]

Taft was firmly pledged to the Roosevelt policies of enforcing the antitrust laws, regulating the railroads, and reducing the great personal aggregations of wealth, but all within the framework of the sanctity of private property and respect for law. Although not committed to destroying all combinations of wealth indiscriminately, Taft did intend to apply the laws impartially and let the chips fall where they might.

On the issue of tariff reform, which had agitated the nation for over a decade, Taft pushed more aggressively than Roosevelt for downward revision, and during his campaign he pledged to call a special session of Congress to dispose of the issue.[66] Although Roosevelt had been able to dodge the issue for seven years, Taft felt that he could no longer do so. Ethics rather than expediency guided his position.

Taft's attitude toward labor created definite problems for him during the campaign. As a federal judge, Taft had earned the reputation as "the injunction judge" for having issued numerous restraining orders against striking workers. In fact, the Knights of Labor had branded him "the father of government by injunction by star-chamber methods," so strong was labor's bitterness against him.[67] Like the more popular Roosevelt, however, Taft believed in labor's right to organize and strike, but not their right to destroy property, "unlawfully injure the business of their employers," or "institute a secondary boycott in such a dispute."[68] To appease labor, Taft and Roosevelt sought a strong antiinjunction plank in the Republican platform calling for a more precise definition of the rules of procedure in federal courts governing the issuance of injunctions in labor-management disputes. A conservatively inclined convention adopted a watered-down injunction plank which satisfied neither Taft nor labor.[69] Indeed, Samuel Gompers, president of the American Federation of Labor, walked out of the convention in protest against the plank and his unfriendly reception by the delegates. Taft's old reputation as the "injunction judge" continued to haunt his campaign and differentiate him from Roosevelt in the eyes of many laborers.

In general, the similarities between Taft and Roosevelt on domestic and foreign policies were remarkable; the differences still lay submerged beneath the president-lieutenant relationship of the two. Perhaps the point to remember is that Roosevelt found it unnecessary to leave his successor a detailed legacy of policies to follow. Taft himself was the prime legacy.

v

The real threat to the continuity of Republican policies came from the Democratic party and its standard bearer, William Jennings Bryan. Bryan had dominated the Democratic party for fourteen years and, though twice-defeated for the presidency, was renominated for the presidency for an unprecedented third time. In previous campaigns, he had frightened many middle class Americans by his support for free silver, direct democracy, and government ownership of the railroads, but by 1908 he had moderated or discarded some of his more extreme ideas. Bryan could find no single issue like "free silver" or "antiimperialism" to exploit as he had in 1896 and 1900. He addressed himself rather to numerous issues such as the control of trusts, business domination of the Republican party, a square deal for labor, "Cannonism," and the direct election of senators.[70]

Bryan and his party were too populistic for Taft's own liking. Taft had been appalled by previous Democratic campaigns which tended to place the "good name" and the "social order" of the country at stake.[71] Although the rather extreme nature of Democratic rhetoric had been tempered since 1896, Taft still viewed Bryan as a dangerous demagogue pandering to the vices of the people. "He is in favor of the punishment of the rich," Taft wrote to the President, "but opposed to a strong government, which shall punish both the poor and the rich." His policies would lead directly to "the rule of the mob."

Bryan's attitude is that of one who would weaken the sanction of all government, would reduce the army and the navy, would take away all power in the courts to enforce their own order, and would reduce the government to a mere town meeting by whom the laws should be enforced against the rich, but should be weakened as against the poor.[72]

Taft believed that a president should be an impartial judge between the conflicting demands of the various classes in society. Bryan was just too partial toward the poor for the good of the nation.

When the Democrats, in contrast to an equivocal Republican plank, advocated that all articles in competition with trust-controlled products be placed on the duty-free list, Taft rebelled at such "a fool notion" which would "mean the destruction of the business in which some of the so-called 'trusts' partake." It was "impossible to separate the innocent from the guilty in such widespread devastation."[73] He preferred instead the creation of a tariff commission that would consider the problems of each industry separately.

The issue of "Cannonism," Speaker Cannon's alleged despotic control over the House of Representatives for reactionary ends, also plagued Taft during the campaign. The Democrats condemned Cannon's authoritarian tactics, and in their platform called for the democratization of the House procedures.[74] Taft stoically bore the attacks against "Cannonism" and the lackluster record of the last Republican Congress. He was unable to condemn openly such a powerful Republican figure without destroying his chances for election. He wrote to a loyal friend, "I do not hesitate to say to you confidentially that the great weight I have to carry in this campaign is Cannonism, which is the synonym for reactionaryism."[75] The only alternative available to Taft was to inform his friends that he would not be disappointed if the next House elected a new Speaker.[76] This, however, did not prevent the Democrats from scoring heavily against the Republicans in the West.

Other issues—the amendment of the antitrust and railroad laws, currency reform, and the guarantee of bank deposits—were bandied about by both parties, but, for the most part, Roosevelt and his party had cleverly stolen much of the Democratic program of the previous decade and left their opponents without any major issue.

Taft and Roosevelt remained apprehensive over the Democratic party's antiimperialist tradition, which threatened to undo a decade of Republican foreign policy. The Democratic platform, for example, included its quadrennial attack upon the American presence in the Philippines, condemning it as an "experiment in imperialism," and called for "an immediate declaration of the nation's purpose to recognize the independence of the Philippine Islands as soon as a stable government can be established." The platform, however, hedged by calling for the American government to "retain such land as may be necessary for coaling stations and naval bases."[77] Whether or not independence could be granted in the light of such contradictory statements, Republicans feared the demoralizing effects of Democratic promises of independence upon the effective administration of the islands.

A Democratic victory would also interfere with the construction of the Panama Canal. Although the Democrats had pledged to continue the building of the canal, Roosevelt and Taft feared that a victory by patronage-hungry Democrats would produce lowered standards of performance, "scandal," and a "far-reaching disaster." Roosevelt was quite content to leave the canal in Republican hands. After the election, he wrote to Colonel George W. Goethals, chief engineer of the project, "I tell you it is a great comfort to feel that this thing is to be left in the hands of Taft. It would indeed have been a calamity if Bryan had come in."[78]

The Democrats also threatened Roosevelt's big navy policy by pledging to build only "a navy sufficient to defend the coasts of this country and protect American citizens wherever their rights may be in jeopardy."[79] This in effect meant a de-emphasis upon new naval construction and the offensive capabilities of the navy. Roosevelt's policy of two new battleships a year would have been seriously endangered by a Democratic victory.

The Democratic platform also expressed opposition to continued Asiatic immigration. Roosevelt felt this position contradicted the Democratic commitment to a defensive navy and encouraged Taft to take advantage of it. "They desire to insult Japan by excluding all Japanese immigration, and at the same time recommend cutting down the navy so that it could only be used for coast defense," he wrote to Taft. "They might as well say that they advocate provoking Japan to go to war with us, and at the same time abandoning the Philippines, Hawaii, and Alaska to her, not to speak of the Canal."[80] This contradiction was the crux of the foreign policy differences between the two parties. The Democrats were in favor of the broad goals of the McKinley-Roosevelt policies of "expansion," but not the specific means adopted. As Taft put it, "Our friends, the democrats, are in favor of the result, but they are opposed to paying the piper and maintaining the means to bring it about."[81]

Despite Republican fears of Bryan and his party, differences between the two parties had narrowed significantly since 1896. The overriding issue of the campaign was really which candidate could best continue the Roosevelt policies. On November 3, the American electorate accepted Roosevelt's choice and elected Taft.

The Republican victory contained ominous warnings for the future. Although Taft swamped Bryan in the electoral college, 321 votes to 162, he captured only 51.6 per cent of the total vote. Because of the vote for the Socialist and Prohibitionist candidates, Bryan was able to capture only 43 per cent of the vote. Taft's popular vote margin over the Democrats had declined 50 per cent from Roosevelt's showing in 1904. Taft, however, had generally run stronger than his party. He ran ahead of the successful Republican gubernatorial candidates in New York, Illinois, Ohio, Indiana, and Minnesota. Despite his sweep of Ohio, Indiana, Minnesota, North Dakota, and Montana, Democratic governors were elected in those states. Outside the South, Taft lost only Oklahoma, Nevada, Colorado, and Nebraska, all of which, with the exception of Oklahoma, had been Roosevelt states in 1904. There was no doubt that the most significant consequence of the election was the marked growth of progressive strength in the West and Midwest.[82]

Disregarding the danger signs for the moment, Republicans were generally elated by the results. Roosevelt congratulated Taft: "You have won a great personal victory as well as a great victory for the party. . . . The returns of the election make it evident to me that you are the only man whom we could have nominated that could have been elected."[83] Although Elihu Root, in a more sober mood, considered the result "a vote more against Bryan than for Taft,"[84] Roosevelt had only praise for his successor:

Taft has pitched this campaign on a higher plane than any campaign in the history of the country. He has not made one demagogic appeal. Every statement has been based on some principle he believed to be right and honest, and the other candidate has appealed to every prejudice or passion he could think of. It was a wonderfully intelligent vote.[85]

And so it seemed at the time.

In retrospect, Taft's candidacy for the Republican nomination and his dull campaign for the presidency had revealed glaring deficiencies in his atrophied political skills. Mrs. Taft herself most appropriately put the finger on her husband's faults when she reflected that "there was nothing to criticize him for except, perhaps, his unfortunate shortcoming of not knowing much and of caring less about the way the game of politics is played."[86]

3. The Rule of Law

We have a government of limited power under the Constitution, and we have got to work out our problems on the basis of law. Now, if that is reactionary, then I am a reactionary.

William Howard Taft,
June 29, 1909[1]

Taft's previous judicial and administrative careers had imbued him with a strong respect for the rule of law and a firm belief in a juridical administrative style in which power was clearly delegated to subordinates, who were then, in theory at least, held strictly accountable for their actions. To close observers, however, Taft's administrative style had already been found wanting in the internal affairs of the War Department and the management of his presidential campaign. His administrative approach contributed to his political problems as president and eventually helped undermine his standing in the Republican party and the country. Emphasis upon a formal, hierarchical structure may have added to the apparent "efficiency" of his administration, but it left Taft at the mercy of subordinates with little political sophistication or presidential perspective.

I

The first significant political task of the President-elect was the selection of a cabinet. Although still considered Roosevelt's lieutenant by the public, Taft set out to become his own president. In his speech of July 28, accepting the Republican nomination, he indicated that the function of his administration would differ from that of the old:

The chief function of the next Administration, in my judgment, is distinct from, and a progressive development of that which has been performed by President Roosevelt. The chief function of the next Administration is to complete and perfect the machinery by which these standards may be maintained, by which the law-breakers may be promptly restrained and punished, but which shall operate with sufficient accuracy and dispatch to interfere with legitimate business as little as possible.[2]

The function of the administration would be what sociologist Max Weber would have termed the "routinization of charisma."[3] Taft lacked the charisma of Roosevelt; his career had instilled in him a passionate respect for law and authority, the very antithesis of the qualities of the charismatic personality. However, he was determined to transform the ideals of Roosevelt into permanent social institutions and policies. His was a most difficult role to play. In many ways, the preaching of reform is much easier than reform itself, for compromises must be struck and interests injured by the enactment of new laws.

Despite pressures to retain as many of the old cabinet members as possible, Taft felt that a new cabinet was needed for his task. He informed the outgoing members not to expect reappointment "because of a difference of function that the new administration is to perform in carrying out the policies of the old."[4] Roosevelt had informed Taft about "a certain number of men who had been *his* [Taft's] staunch and ardent supporters,"[5] but he did not specifically ask Taft to retain any member of the cabinet. As Roosevelt explained to his military aide Major Butt:

If Mr. Taft were to ask my advice as to his cabinet I would not know what to say. I would possibly suggest to him to retain the present Cabinet and to make changes as he saw fit, but he cannot ask me and I cannot volunteer advice in the matter. If he should ask my advice he would feel compelled to take it, whereas if he asks Root's advice, he can take it or not as he chooses.[6]

The only offices Roosevelt was particularly anxious to influence were those essential to the continuity of his foreign policies.[7]

Taft had indicated to the President that he might not keep any of the Roosevelt cabinet. Although Roosevelt would have preferred no changes, he recognized that Taft was "big enough" to fashion his own administration. "Taft," he maintained, "is going about this thing just as I would do."[8] But as new cabinet members were appointed, the magnanimous Roosevelt became disturbed by the independent line Taft was taking. By the time of the inauguration, "Ike" Hoover, chief usher at the White House, noted that Taft's appointments evoked a strong trace of bitterness in Roosevelt.[9] In refashioning the cabinet. Taft had slowly begun to drift away from Roosevelt and the progressive wing of the party.

As Roosevelt's influence faded, Philander Chase Knox, senator from Pennsylvania and former attorney general under Roosevelt, emerged as one of the most influential men near the President-elect. Although Mrs. Taft and Charles P. Taft were encouraging Taft to take an independent line, they did not possess the political experience and knowledge of Knox. As secretary of state and the new "premier" of the cabinet, Knox became an important force in Taft's selection of the remainder of the cabinet. The President-elect solicited Knox's advice regarding the appointment of George von L. Meyer to Treasury, Luke Wright to the War Department, George W. Wickersham to Justice, John Hays Hammond to Navy, Charles Nagel to Interior, and Frank Kellogg to Commerce and Labor, and used Knox as a sounding board for subsequent cabinet appointments. Knox was also given the task of inves-

tigating the qualifications of George Wickersham and negotiating the appointment of Franklin MacVeagh as secretary
of the treasury.[10] Knox's advice may well have been the last
heeded by Taft before his final cabinet selections. "After I
talk with Knox on the subject of the Cabinet," Taft wrote to
Roosevelt, "I shall do something definite in the way of action
toward those who are now in office."[11] No other nonfamily
figure could boast of such a relationship with Taft during this
crucial period of cabinet selection.

Taft also consulted Republican senators Nelson W. Aldrich
of Rhode Island, Eugene Hale of Maine, and Lodge, Elihu
Root, Speaker Cannon, attorney Nelson Cromwell, and railroad magnate James J. Hill in the process of choosing his
cabinet. His subsequent assertion that "I made up my own
Cabinet and did not confer with anybody except as to the
Secretary of the Treasury and the Secretary of State"[12] belies
the record. Unfortunately, he did not seek advice from any
person, excepting the President, closely connected with the
progressive wing of the party who might have exerted greater
influence over some of his appointments. It was Taft's misfortune to have chosen Knox as a confidant, a man who was not
only a conservative and former corporation lawyer, but who,
according to Archie Butt, had "a perfect contempt for the
people when spelt with a big P."[13] Taft's preference for such
an adviser, partially the consequence of his own political inexperience, contributed to the selection of a cabinet heavily
weighted with lawyers and slightly right of center.

The final cabinet consisted of Knox as secretary of state;
George W. Wickersham, a New York corporation lawyer, as
attorney general; Charles Nagel, another professional lawyer,
as secretary of commerce and labor; Richard A. Ballinger,
attorney and former chief of the Land Office, as secretary
of the interior; Jacob Dickinson, a railroad attorney and former Democrat, as secretary of war; Franklin MacVeagh, a

Chicago banker and former Democrat, as secretary of the treasury; and Frank H. Hitchcock, former assistant postmaster general as postmaster general. The only two holdovers from the Roosevelt cabinet were James Wilson of the Department of Agriculture and George von L. Meyer, who was shifted from the Post Office to the Department of the Navy.[14]

The selection of a cabinet is one of the first important symbolic acts of an administration. From it the nation takes its first definite impression of the new president's political judgment, policies, and philosophy of government. The growing progressive wing of the party which had so strongly supported Taft's nomination and election was understandably disappointed in a cabinet staffed by five former corporation lawyers and devoid of an acknowledged spokesman for their views. The inclusion of two Democrats, Jacob Dickinson and Franklin MacVeagh, also created unnecessary resentment among western Republicans who felt slighted for their loyalty. If the function of the new administration was to draft and enforce laws, and if it is true that lawyers are best qualified for that task, then of course Taft had been wise in his selection. Although the new cabinet was endowed with men of executive ability, Taft would learn too late that it possessed little political sophistication.

Thus, while the electorate was becoming more progressive in orientation, Taft was shifting the balance of power within his cabinet to the right of center and setting the stage for his own political demise. Since the cabinet would become the primary advisory and decision-making agency, Taft was bound to be affected by the conservative-legalistic bias of the body.

While intellectually aware of the need for a diversity of opinions within his cabinet, Taft was temperamentally reluctant to appoint the kind of progressives who would bring his government ideological balance. He found it too painful to try to reconcile their conflicting views or styles with his own.

In this sense, Taft lacked the self-confidence of Roosevelt, who could work with a wide range of persons without undue threat to himself or his policies.

The President-elect had been relatively free to choose his immediate subordinates, but found himself more restricted in transforming the subcabinet level of government. He had to retain most of the old Roosevelt crowd because of their support for his nomination. Shortly after assuming office he lamented:

My chief trouble comes from the fact that I have no offices to distribute. If it were not for Roosevelt, I would in all likelihood not be President. I know some differ, but that is my opinion nevertheless. Not only did I have his support, but the support of all his friends. The whole administrative part of the government was for my nomination and election. I can no more turn out these men than Roosevelt could have done without some just cause. I suppose I have fewer offices to fill than any man who ever found himself in the White House.[15]

Although many of his supporters were hungry for jobs, the new President disappointed most of them. "You must understand," he wrote a job-seeker, "that I have come into office very much as if I were Mr. Roosevelt succeeding himself, and that the men who fill the offices to which you refer are men who are friendly to me and appointees of Mr. Roosevelt."[16] Because of his "forced succession" to the White House, Taft entered office with more political debts to the outgoing administration than any of our modern presidents.

It came as a surprise, then, when the new President peremptorialy dismissed career diplomat Henry White, ambassador to France and a good friend of Roosevelt. The sudden dismissal revealed a weakness in Taft's character and deep political insensitivity. Roosevelt had informed Taft about those diplomats who merited retention, and White, possibly the best-trained member of the American diplomatic service, was among them. Taft apparently had assured Roosevelt that White would be kept, but upon becoming president, he swiftly dismissed the ambassador and did not reappoint him to any other diplomatic post. Taft had miscalculated Roosevelt's deep concern about White. The immediate reaction among the informed circles of government was shock and disbelief. Not only was White a diplomat of recognized ability, but his dismissal had allegedly been made for personal reasons. Taft offered no reasons and consequently left observers free to believe the worst. The rumor circulated throughout Washington that Taft had been slighted twenty-five years earlier during his European honeymoon by White, then a minor diplomatic official, and that the President had remembered and fired him.[17] Although Root attempted to persuade Taft to reconsider, he found the new President's determination to fire White "inexorable" and, along with many other admirers of White, felt "very badly" about the whole affair.[18] The firing could probably be attributed to the President's propensity to hold grudges. Archie Butt once explained:

When he takes a dislike to anyone it is for some reason known to himself, and he does not easily forgive. He is persistent in his antipathies. Mr. Roosevelt once said that Mr. Taft was one of the best haters he had ever known, and I have found this to be true . . . and those whom he dislikes never suspect it until the crucial moment.[19]

Taft's decision was a serious and needless blunder, for it diminished his reputation in Washington as a man above the petty politics of personalities. Even the appointment of Robert Bacon, a close associate of Roosevelt, to succeed White at Paris could not repair the damage. Roosevelt of course was quite disturbed at the news and found it necessary to explain the inexplicable to White:

I wish you to know that everything I could do was done on your behalf, not because of my affection for you, great though that is, but because I told Taft I regard you as without exception the very best man in our diplomatic service. I told Taft that I had no personal request whatever to make of him, but there were certain men whose qualifications for the public service were of so high an order that I felt I ought to dwell on them, and that conspicuous among these was yourself. To me as well as to Cabot Lodge he said without any qualification that he intended to keep you. It was, of course, *not* a promise. But it was an expression of intention which I was at liberty to repeat.[20]

Roosevelt undoubtedly began to wonder about the man he had foisted upon the Republican party as his successor. He was sorely embarrassed. The new President, on the other hand, had apparently misunderstood Roosevelt's concern over White. "I had no idea that his heart was set on Harry White," he wrote to his brother Charles months later. "If I had known it I would not have relieved White, but I supposed I was doing exactly what he approved when I put Bacon in White's place."[21]

Henry White was not the only person relieved of his position for personal reasons. "Personal likes and dislikes seem to be governing," Lodge wrote to Roosevelt, and he could "see trouble gathering" on some of Taft's dismissals and appointments.[22] Although relatively few changes were made in the lower levels of the administration, those that were made sometimes appeared arbitrary to outsiders looking in. The President offered no reasons or excuses for his changes and, as in the White episode, left rumors free to circulate in Washington circles without comment.

Taft's appointments and dismissals actually weakened the new administration, for they provided needless ammunition to those of the old Roosevelt crowd who felt the new President could never measure up to their idol. Many of Taft's supporters were also dismayed by his poor judgment. Henry Cabot Lodge accurately reflected the attitude of Washington officialdom when he wrote to Roosevelt:

The one thing which surprises me about Taft is that he does not know more about politics. With all his great experience and all his great success in administration he does not seem to have got hold of the elements of politics which must enter into so many matters, especially appointments, and which has to be considered. He is all we believed him to be and I have great affection and respect for him, but I am surprised that he has not, in all his years of public life, learned more about politics, and you will understand that I do not mean this in any bad sense of the word, but as one of the conditions with which a man has to deal, especially a President.[23]

Taft was so insensitive to the political consequences of his appointments and dismissals that it would take two years of buffeting in office before he would begin to appreciate their significance. By then, he had wrought irrevocable political damage to himself and his party.

II

With the launching of the new administration, differences in style between Taft and his predecessor quickly emerged. Whereas Roosevelt had frequently ignored formal lines of authority and often interfered in the routine affairs of his departments, Taft adopted the strictly formal policy of "leaving departmental affairs to the head of the Department and making the head of the Department responsible to me."[24] Taft made it clear to all that he did not intend to destroy the morale of his cabinet by bypassing his secretaries or allowing their subordinates to undercut them through the White House. He was determined to transfer to the presidency what he considered to be good habits and principles of administration, which accented formal lines of authority and communication. Unfortunately, Taft's inclination to delegate authority was not matched by his ability to keep his departments responsible to himself.

Taft's administrative style is best exemplified in his relationship with Philander C. Knox and the State Department. Taft entered office with the firm intention of reorganizing the State Department from top to bottom. He considered the department completely inadequate to America's expanding role in the world. "The truth is the State Department does not cost the government as much money as the Govt. ought to spend to make it effective," he noted. "It needs reorganization. It is organized on the basis of the needs of the Government of 1800 instead of 1900."[25] The President realized that American foreign policy could only be as good as the eyes, ears, and voice of the United States abroad. Knox was appointed secretary of state to help speed the reorganization of the department.

Taft had originally offered Elihu Root the position, but Root, his health declining, preferred to become a senator from New York. Root recommended Knox for the job. Roosevelt acquiesced in Knox's appointment and even helped persuade the senator to accept.[26] Knox had previously served as Roosevelt's attorney general but, in an effort to boost his own presidential ambitions, had left the administration to become senator from Pennsylvania in 1904. He had gained experience in foreign affairs only as attorney general, when he secured the legal title to the Panama Canal from the old French Panama Canal Company, and as chairman of the Senate Interoceanic Canal Committee. Knox had impressed British Ambassador Lord James Bryce as "having cared little, known little, or thought little of foreign politics until he became a minister."[27] In Knox, however, Taft found an able lawyer in whom he could repose great trust and responsibility for the daily conduct of diplomacy.

Once Knox and the President had reached an understanding on their respective roles in the administration, Knox began to build a department personally loyal to himself. Taft had desired to appoint Beekman Winthrop, his former secretary in the Philippines, as first assistant secretary of state. Advised by his friends to secure loyal subordinates, however, Knox dropped Winthrop and appointed Huntington Wilson, former third assistant secretary of state and former chief of the Far Eastern Division. Knox's action was not surprising in view of the free hand he had been granted in staffing his department. "I want you to know that the arrangement of the State Department is to suit you, and you can take any course you see fit," the President wrote to Knox. "Whatever you do will satisfy me."[28]

Huntington Wilson had been selected first assistant secretary because his diplomatic experience, his comprehensive plans for departmental reorganization, his desire for American trade expansion, and his immediate rapport with Knox impressed the new Secretary, who hurriedly appointed Wilson before Taft's inauguration. According to Wilson, Knox appointed him with a "carte blanche" to go ahead with his reorganization plans for the department, plans he had been championing since 1906.[29]

The special relationship between Taft, Knox, and Wilson became the most important factor affecting the foreign policy-making of the new administration. Since both Taft and Knox saw eye to eye on the need to continue the policies of previous administrations and to promote American commerce abroad, the President had few qualms about entrusting the conduct of foreign relations to Knox. Despite his inexperience, Knox ran the department with a firm hand and, according to Bryce, was "inclined to be autocratic and rapid in his decisions."[30] There was no doubt in Washington who ran the department, for, according to Wilson, Knox "had it tacitly understood, that, outside of Congress, no official from the President down was to say or do anything that touched upon foreign relations without his approval in advance." Moreover, Taft "practically never interposed in any matter of foreign relations" and left his Secretary free to evolve policy within the general guidelines set down by the President.[31] Although Taft occasionally grumbled at Knox's laziness, Major Butt reported that he continued to rely heavily upon the secretary's judgment on domestic as well as foreign affairs: "There is no one whose approval he [Taft] desires more than the Secretary of State's." Knox was apparently able to capitalize upon the President's deference toward him by subtly suggesting ideas which Taft almost unconsciously incorporated into some of his speeches. "He is very adroit in this—auto-suggestion some call it," wrote Butt. "He has a great influence upon the President."[32]

In spite of Knox's rather autocratic disposition, his administrative style, like the President's, was characterized by the delegation of extraordinary responsibility and power, particularly to his ambitious assistant Wilson. Although he usually arose at 5:00 A.M. each morning, Knox rarely arrived at his office before 10:00 A.M., at which time he expected telegrams, letters, and other papers of interest from the previous day to be on his desk for perusal.[33] Rarely would he return to his office after lunch, except on Thursdays. According to Henry Lane Wilson, ambassador to Mexico, "The details of the work of the Department of State wearied him almost to the point of cynicism, and he fled from them as frequently as the executive work would permit."[34] He preferred to golf, drive his horses, or simply read during the afternoons. Knox, however, would regularly invite Wilson to lunch (usually three times a week) to discuss departmental business. During lunch, Wilson would explain the pending business, recommend a course of action, and, "almost always be told to go ahead."[35] On many occasions, Knox would be away from Washington either visiting his farm in Pennsylvania, fishing in Maine, vacationing at Cape May, New Jersey, or traveling abroad on official business. In his absence, Wilson became acting secretary, consulting Knox by letter or wire on important matters, but often dealing directly with the President. Responsibility for the department lay with Knox, but great power had slipped into the hands of his indispensable assistant. As Wilson candidly admitted, virtually the whole Department was responsible "in practice, usually to the secretary through the Assistant Secretary." Wilson aptly described himself as Knox's "alter ego."[36] Wilson exercised power out of all proportion to his position or his status with the President.

Whereas Knox found his assistant congenial and competent, Taft found him insufferable. Perhaps it was Wilson's self-confessed arrogance, his aristocratic disdain for the public, or his fetish for protocol which offended the President. Whatever the reasons, Taft felt little affection for the man who had replaced his first choice for the position. "I would like to sit on Wilson and mash him flat," Taft once admitted to Major Butt. "What Knox sees in him I do not see." Butt thought that if Knox did leave the State Department to run for governor of Pennsylvania in 1910, the President would not hesitate to replace Wilson.[37] In fact, Taft later attempted to kick Wilson upstairs by offering him an ambassadorship to Russia, but Wilson elected to remain close to his powerful patron in Washington.[38]

The President had obviously delegated too much power to Knox, who, in turn, had allowed his ambitious assistant to assume too much of it. Perhaps power would have slipped away from any inexperienced secretary of state, but the fact remains that Taft was saddled with a powerful figure in the State Department whom he disliked and who was more loyal to the secretary than to the President. A more forceful chief executive would have nudged Wilson into another position, but Taft dared not offend his own secretary of state. His administrative style had left him as much the prisoner as the master of the State Department.

III

Other facets of the President's approach to administration emerged during the celebrated dispute between Secretary of Interior Richard Ballinger and Chief of the Forest Service Gifford Pinchot. Taft had appointed Ballinger, a former lawyer and chief of the Land Office in the Interior Department, with the intention of legalizing Roosevelt's conservation policy. Former Secretary of the Interior James Garfield, under instructions from Roosevelt, had withdrawn millions of acres of public land along the national waterways for conservation purposes. Although the withdrawal of lands had allegedly been based upon a 1902 statute authorizing the withdrawal of water power sites, Taft and Ballinger believed that many of the withdrawals had been illegal. They believed some of the land should be returned to the private domain until Congress enacted legislation clarifying the rights of the national government over the lands.[39] The legalistic policy of the new administration produced immediate friction between Ballinger and Pinchot. When Ballinger began to return land to the public entry lists, thus opening them to private exploitation, an outraged Pinchot urged Taft to rescind the action. Although the President compromised temporarily and agreed to withdraw some of the land until Congress acted, progressives began to doubt the sincerity of the President's commitment to conservation.[40]

There was no doubt in the President's mind about his commitment. He desired only to preserve Roosevelt's achievements through legal means, a policy which impatient progressives found difficult to understand. In December 1908, Taft had pledged Roosevelt that he would rely on Gifford Pinchot as "a kind of conscience" to be followed on conservation policy.[41] Despite his pledge, Taft later discovered that he valued law and orderly administration more than the self-righteousness of his chief forester. When progressive congressman William Kent of California complained of Taft's "reactionary" policy, the President replied: "One of the propositions that I adhere to is that it is a very dangerous method of upholding reform to violate the law in so doing, even on the ground of high moral principle, or saving the public." "We have a government of limited power under the Constitution," Taft wrote, "and we have got to work out our problems on the basis of law. Now, if that is reactionary, then I am a reactionary."[42]

The simmering battle between Pinchot and Ballinger over conservation policy came to a boil with the public charges of Louis R. Glavis, an obscure employee of the General Land Office, that Ballinger had been party to a fraudulent attempt by the Morgan-Guggenheim syndicate to seize federal coal lands in Alaska. Pinchot seized upon the charges to launch public attacks upon Ballinger and, by implication, the President himself.[43] When Taft asked Attorney General Wickersham to investigate the sensational Glavis charges, progressive Henry L. Stimson of New York feared that the President had erred in allowing a cabinet member to pass upon the propriety of the actions of another. Stimson distrusted Wickersham's "feel" for the political issues involved and considered it unsafe to "leave the question to the danger of cabinet bias."[44] Nevertheless, the President relied heavily upon the conclusions of the attorney general and, after a cabinet discussion, exonerated Ballinger of any wrongdoing.[45] Pinchot continued to champion his cause in public and eventually forced the President to choose between Ballinger and himself.

At first, Taft viewed the dispute as merely an administrative problem of conflicting jurisdictions between the Forest Service, located in the Agriculture Department, and the Interior Department. In August 1909, he described the conflict to Congressman Nicholas Longworth as merely "a row over nothing very serious, except a kind of jealousy and friction between Departments that ought to be avoided," but by early September Taft felt that Pinchot had become a severe disciplinary problem. Roosevelt had permitted Pinchot to undercut the heads of the Interior and Agriculture departments and become "the power behind the throne" on conservation policy. The President wrote his brother Horace that he considered this "very bad governmental discipline." By October, the President had begun to lose patience with Pinchot, whose head, Taft felt, had been "swelled" by his popularity and status in the previous administration. Taft would not permit his department heads to be undermined by anyone, not even by Pinchot: "The heads of the Departments are the persons through whom I must act," he wrote to his wife, "and unless the bureau chiefs are subordinate to the heads it makes government of an efficient character impossible." Whereas Pinchot had once been the "conscience" of the administration, he had now become "a good deal of a radical and a good deal of a crank."[46]

Despite Pinchot's campaign against Ballinger and his increasing insubordination, the President feared an open break with his chief forester. Taft realized that Pinchot had become a symbol of Roosevelt's conservation policies and that his dismissal would be a severe blow to the administration. He tried to persuade Pinchot to end his attacks upon Ballinger, but to no avail. "I anticipate that the time may come when I shall have to take some drastic action," the President admitted to Wickersham. "He is looking for martyrdom and it may be necessary to give it to him; but I prefer to let him use all the rope that he will."[47]

The President's perception of the campaign against Ballinger hardened his attitude toward the whole controversy. Taft believed that Pinchot's charges were part of an "organized conspiracy" by progressives to bring about an open rupture between himself and Roosevelt. He had no intention of sacrificing his secretary of interior to "an impressionistic school of reformers who regard laws as obstacles and only the higher moral tenets of a real reformer as limitations to be paid attention to." Taft determined to stand by Ballinger "at whatever cost."[48] He refused to submit to the "bugaboo" of public opinion which had no way of knowing the real facts, but which had already condemned Ballinger. Taft particularly objected to the tendency of progressive critics "to suspect the motives of those who are not willing to cut across lots and ignore legal limitations and vested rights."[49]Although unwilling to bend to public opinion, Taft found himself helpless to neutralize the progressive campaign against Ballinger. He realized that he did not possess the skills of his predecessor: "Of course, Roosevelt would have come back at those preferring the charges and would by now have them on the run, but I cannot do things that way. I will let them go on and by and by the people will see who is right and who is wrong. There is no use trying to be William Howard Taft with Roosevelt's ways."[50] When Congress convened in December 1909, Taft naively hoped that a congressional investigation, properly controlled by the party leadership, might absolve Ballinger and the administration of the Glavis charges. Pinchot, however, upset the President's hopes by sending Senator Jonathan Dolliver an explosive letter in which the chief forester acknowledged his insubordination to the administration in order to defend the public interest in conservation. The publicized letter was the last straw for the President. He fired Pinchot. The subsequent congressional investigation into the controversy occurred in such a charged partisan atmosphere that the public remained confused about the real facts of the case. Pinchot, however, was now a martyr.[51]

Whatever the merits of the charges against Ballinger, the secretary of the interior had outlived his usefulness to the administration. Taft might have neutralized the impact of Pinchot's dismissal by accepting Ballinger's resignation, but he was too stubborn and inexperienced. Ballinger had become a virtual albatross around the President's neck, signifying the President's alliance with the "interests" against the people. As Senator Lodge explained to the distant Roosevelt, "The general feeling in the country is that Pinchot represents the people and your policy of Conservation, which is true, and that Ballinger and the administration represent opposition to it, which is not true. But that is what the country thinks and you cannot get it out of the public mind."[52] Ballinger's retention in the cabinet for over a year after Pinchot's dismissal could not but contribute to the deteriorating relations between Taft and the progressive wing of his party.

Although aware of the damage Ballinger's presence in the cabinet was producing, Taft believed him innocent and stubbornly refused to yield to pressures for his dismissal. In answer to one critic demanding Ballinger's scalp, Taft replied: "If I were to turn Ballinger out, in view of his innocence and in view of the conspiracy against him, I should be a white-livered skunk. I don't care how it affects my administration and how it affects the administration before the people; if the people are so unjust as this I don't propose to be one of them." It was clear the President would not compromise his private morals for the sake of his administration: "[L]ife is not worth living and office is not worth having if, for the purpose of acquiring the popular support, we have to either do a cruel injustice or acquiesce in it."[53] Taft's stubborn integrity interfered with his duty as a democratic leader to save his administration and programs. He continued to refuse the resignation of his secretary until pressures within his own administration from Knox, Hitchcock, Meyer, and Charles D. Norton, the President's personal secretary, forced him to act. Knox, for example, bluntly told Taft that "by refusing longer to accept this resignation you are pulling at the beard of death!"[54] On March 7, 1911, one year too late, Taft finally accepted the resignation of Richard Achilles Ballinger. Even then, the President could not resist one last attack on Ballinger's enemies. In a highly publicized letter accepting the resignation, Taft reaffirmed his support of the secretary and bitterly condemned the unjust conspiracy which had forced Ballinger's removal.[55] Although the gesture assuaged Taft's conscience, it needlessly reopened old political wounds. The letter also offended the cabinet, which had not been consulted even though it had met shortly before the release of the letter. Attorney General Wickersham considered the timing and manner of issuance of the letter an "act of discourtesy" to the cabinet. His complaint impelled the President to write each member a note of explanation and apology! The cabinet had become such an essential part of the President's decision-making process that he genuinely feared slighting it. No doubt, had the cabinet been consulted, the President's bitter letter would have been tempered by cooler heads. Taft later confessed to Knox, "In spite of your advice I did pull the whiskers of death without changing the situation."[56] Only after a sobering electoral defeat in November 1912 did Taft acknowledge his mishandling of the Ballinger affair. "I might have let Ballinger go right away," he admitted to Otto C. Bannard. "But Ballinger's fate was the result of a deliberate conspiracy, and I can hardly hold myself responsible for the result of a malign combination as that which Gifford Pinchot and Jim Garfield set on foot."[57]

That the Ballinger-Pinchot row had not been without its political lessons for Taft was indicated by a relatively obscure incident in the spring of 1911. This time the potential furor revolved about progressive reformer Dr. Harvey W. Wiley, chief chemist of the Food and Drug Administration, who, according to Major Butt, the public believed, stood "between the people and a national belly ache."[58] Wiley's sin was a cavalier disregard for rules and regulations: he had hired a chemical expert in his department for a full year rather than on a per diem basis required by law. When charges against Wiley's illegal action, extremely mild in comparison to Pinchot's antics, were imprudently referred to the President by Secretary of Agriculture Wilson, Taft again asked Wickersham to investigate the matter. The attorney general, who Butt rightly thought "had about as much political judgment as an ox," recommended Wiley's dismissal.[59] Taft, however, realized that a political explosion over Wiley's dismissal would have broken all administration ties to the progressive wing of the party. Desiring no new martyrs, the President took no action against Wiley. One encounter with a symbol of the Roosevelt policies had left the President a far sadder but wiser man.[60]

IV

Important aspects of Taft's administrative style can also be glimpsed from his relationship with the Justice Department. Next to Secretary Knox, Attorney General Wickersham had become the strongest and most independent member of the cabinet. Because Taft and Wickersham had agreed upon a vigorous antitrust policy, Wickersham was allowed greater freedom in running the Justice Department than his Republican predecessors. At first Taft had felt that his attorney general was the "most brilliant member" of his cabinet and was destined to become one of his most popular lieutenants,[61] but Wickersham's dedication to trust-busting produced the opposite effect and made him, next to Ballinger, the most controversial member of the cabinet.

Although the Sherman Act was unpopular in the big business community, Taft intended to enforce the law despite its alleged deficiencies. There was no other choice open to a President so obsessed by the law. As Major Butt noted, "President Taft will do anything if he has the law on which to base his act. The law to President Taft is the same support as some zealots get from great religious faith. And the fact that the law is unpopular would not cause him to hesitate a minute."[62] The President did not hesitate to enforce the Sherman Act and even went further than Roosevelt in demanding the criminal prosecution of corporation officials responsible for violating the law. In a published interview in *McClure's Magazine*, Taft acknowledged that the "present need" of the country was to put a few trust-makers in jail. In his view, "nothing would stop this building up of monopolies more quickly than the conviction of some of the individuals who create them by their illegal acts."[63] The President's commitment to strict law enforcement impelled the attorney general to begin instituting antitrust suits at an unprecedented rate. The Taft administration eventually instituted ninety antitrust suits in four years as compared to Roosevelt's fifty-four in seven years.[64]

By the fall of 1911, Wickersham's zealous enforcement of the law had made him a very unpopular attorney general among big businessmen and had earned him the reputation of "the most radical man who has held that office for years."[65] Intoxicated by the President's unlimited support, Wickersham vigorously pursued his antitrust policies until disaster struck. On October 26, 1911, Wickersham brought suit against the United States Steel Company. The suit alleged that the company had purchased the Tennessee Coal and Iron Company during the panic of 1907 to decrease competition and had deceived Roosevelt about its motives. The suit specifically named the former President as a willing bystander in the takeover and made Roosevelt appear to be, in his own words, "either a fool or a knave." Roosevelt had acquiesced in the takeover because he had been informed at the time that if the Tennessee company failed, a number of brokerage houses holding the stock as collateral for various loans would fail, and there was no telling what effect the shock wave would have upon the stock market or the American economy. Roosevelt had to act without all of the facts in the midst of a financial panic. Only later did the truth emerge that United States Steel had been less than candid with the President in explaining its motives behind the takeover.[66]

The steel suit precipitated the final break between Taft and Roosevelt and led to their personal clash over the Republican nomination in 1912. Taft was understandably distraught at the mention of Roosevelt by name in the suit. Even though the attorney general had written the President (then traveling through the West) on the very day the suit was filed and was aware of the reference to Roosevelt, he made no mention of the fact to Taft. The question, moreover, had never been discussed in the cabinet.[67] The freewheeling attorney general had taken upon himself a task of great political sensitivity and had bungled badly. Even though Taft could plead ignorance, the political damage was irrevocable. "I don't think it helped the steel trust bill to put Roosevelt in," he lamented, "but I was not consulted at the time, and I can not do anything about it now."[68]

The bitter lesson of the steel suit did not go unheeded. When rumors reached his desk that Wickersham might try to indict criminally the directors of United States Steel under the existing law, Taft resolved to keep informed and dashed off a letter to his attorney general:

Constant rumors come to me that indictments are to be found against the directors of the United States Steel Company for violation of the anti-trust law. I do not credit these, and I rely upon you to confer with me before any such step is taken anywhere in the country.

In other words, I should like to be consulted before action of that sort is taken.[69]

Taft had been sorely embarrassed by his eager attorney general and could not afford another mistake. A president forced to plead for important information from a subordinate was hardly a model of effective executive leadership.

Although Taft had hoped at first that his antitrust policies would bolster his sagging popularity, they only produced more political headaches for his administration. Taft made no distinction, as had Roosevelt, between "good" and "bad" trusts and consequently indicted some companies merely because of their size. The policy alienated large segments of the business community, and Roosevelt himself, but the President had no intention of changing course. As he explained to his brother Horace shortly after the steel suit blunder, Wickersham "has the wheels of the Department of Justice working, and we are going to enforce that law or die in the attempt."[70] As the number of antitrust suits soared, business support of the administration plummeted without a corresponding rise in public support. Taft's policy began to disillusion even such a stalwart as Otto Bannard, president of the New York Trust Company, who could no longer remain silent amid the growing chorus of administration critics:

Your department of justice has offended big business, small business, stock holders and mechanics and poor people. Its moves and measures appear to have been made for political effect, without any political success. Indictments, irrespective of moral turpitude, will never appeal to Americans, and as they are rarely followed by incarceration, the masses consider them insincere. The Dept. of Justice should be semi-judicial in its attitude and helpful in time of perplexity; the Atty-General should not be merely a fanatical prosecuting atty. He has cost you the greater part of your popularity in the Eastern states, and the impression exists that he conducts an independent suzerainty, entirely far from your influence or control. If he fancies that he exercises any political wisdom in his method and moments for action, he is blind; if he acts without regard to political considerations he is tyrannical. His success will not be measured by the number of suits brought or indictments obtained but by the justification of them. A sense of duty should compel him to prosecute, and not a fanatical love of action. . . . You should prove yourself the master *of your* departments.[71]

Bannard's forthright criticism was indicative of the opinion of the business community and the conservative wing of the Republican party. As a result of such dissatisfaction with Taft's shotgun policy, the Republican party found many of its campaign finance sources dried up in 1912. Two of the largest trusts attacked by the administration, for example, the Standard Oil Company and the International Harvester Company, supported Roosevelt in his bid for the presidency in 1912. Roosevelt had been right when he had once admitted to Charles Evans Hughes that "conservatives object even more to an executive who invokes the law against them when they have violated the law than they do to a demogogue who seeks to excite the mob to plunder them."[72]

v

Although Taft was reluctant to dismiss any cabinet members for political reasons, he used the opportunities afforded by Ballinger's and Secretary of War Dickinson's resignations to change the political complexion of his cabinet by appointing more progressive Republicans. Goaded by advisers such as Hitchcock, MacVeagh, Meyer, and Norton, the President finally agreed to accept the long overdue resignation of Ballinger and to seek a prominent progressive as a replacement.

The selection of Walter L. Fisher, vice-president of the National Conservation League and co-conspirator of Pinchot and Garfield, as Ballinger's successor was a bitter pill for the President to swallow, but his coterie of advisers had impressed upon him the absolute necessity of repairing his public image.[73] Roosevelt, of course, was pleased at the belated effort of the President to move closer to the progressive wing of the party. "If two years ago he had done some of the things he has done now," he wrote to Garfield, "he would probably have saved himself from nine tenths of the blunders he has made and is making."[74]

The President was later horrified to discover that his new secretary of the interior was a firm believer in the progressive dogmas of the initiative, referendum, and recall. "Of course, I knew him to be somewhat of a reformer," Taft admitted to Charles Hilles, "but somehow it never occurred to me that he would accept a place in my cabinet if he held the views which it now develops he does hold."[75] Fisher, on the other hand, had assumed that the President was aware of his views and could live with them.

Although the new secretary aided Taft immensely in his conservation programs, he remained only nominally loyal to the President throughout the political wars of 1912. Fisher was strongly suspected of being a La Follette supporter for the presidency and even of harboring presidential ambitions of his own.[76]

When Secretary of War Dickinson resigned for personal reasons early in 1911, Taft was presented with another opportunity to reshape the image of his cabinet. He wavered, however, between his close friend and party stalwart Otto Bannard and attorney Henry L. Stimson, the unsuccessful gubernatorial candidate of New York in 1910. The cabinet was sharply divided on the choice, with most of the members leaning toward Bannard. The thankless task of boosting Stim-

son for the position fell to Secretary of the Treasury Mac-
Veagh, a man, according to Butt, "tinged with insurgent doctrines."⁷⁷ MacVeagh appealed to Senator Root for support.
The President, he wrote, "was in advance of his Cabinet and
needs to pull us up to his positions by an average." The secretary urged Root "to take the responsibility of holding the fort
against the positive and aggressive opposition to Stimson of
members of the Cabinet." MacVeagh felt that Stimson's appointment would "give an added mild flavor of liberal or progressive Republicanism to a Cabinet that in general regard is
held to be non-progressive."⁷⁸ Root's intervention was successful, and Stimson, despite stiff opposition from Wickersham and Horace Taft, was appointed secretary of war by
the President. The Stimson appointment represented another
belated effort by Taft and his moderate advisers to polish the
President's tarnished image as a progressive. By 1911, however, the Republican party was so divided that Taft's efforts
at reconciliation proved too little and too late.

The President's juridical style of administration, combined
with his weak coordination and control of subordinates, produced an organization that was, in many ways, far more un-
disciplined than the freewheeling Roosevelt administrations.
Taft's style slowly transformed the departments into nine independent kingdoms and bred bad politics. To a great extent,
Taft actually insulated himself from the flow of information
essential to his own political success by becoming overly dependent upon official lines of communication. To make such
an administrative style effective, a strong hand was needed at
the top, but Taft would not provide it consistently. Charles
Taft himself bitterly condemned his own brother for permitting his cabinet to "run riot with him. All he would have to
do is fire one of them," he admitted to Major Butt, "and the
others would be most wholesome. There is no coordination
among them. They want to run their own departments and

be let alone."[79] There were sound reasons why a number of cabinet members should have been replaced, but Taft lacked the tough-minded qualities necessary to make any controversial changes and, in some instances, did not even perceive the need for change. The major reason for his reluctance originated in his intense dislike of conflict. "I have never known a man to dislike discord as much as the President," Butt observed. "He want's every man's approval, and a row of any kind is repugnant to him."[80] Bannard also recognized the administrative deficiencies of the President when he complained to Taft after the 1912 election that the President had "always been unwilling to make removals for political reasons" and that "active political opposition in your own departments was a sad affliction to your party." The President replied that the personnel carried over from the Roosevelt administration "did not recognize the obligation on their part to change their loyalty from Roosevelt to me when I succeeded to the Presidency."[81] What remains clear, however, is that the President had failed to inspire that camaraderie and loyalty to the chief executive which had marked the Roosevelt administration. There were no "three Musketeers"[82] in the Taft cabinet, only nine D'Artagnans.

VI

Despite his serious deficiencies as administrative and political coordinator of his cabinet, Taft did succeed in introducing numerous organizational reforms which became permanent fixtures of the government and which earned him a national reputation as a good administrator. Taft entered office determined to systematize the operations of the departments, a task neglected by his more extroverted predecessor. Taft introduced modern business techniques in the departments in the hope of raising the quality and efficiency of government service. One of the first major steps toward reform was an attack upon the outdated budgeting procedures of the government. Each department was accustomed to drawing up its own estimates of needed expenditures, which were then perfunctorily forwarded by the secretary of the treasury to Congress for action. No provisions were made by law for review and revision of these estimates by any central executive agency. The federal government consequently did not know how much it was going to spend until all of the separate appropriation bills for the various departments were enacted into law by Congress. The departments, moreover, had no responsibility to gear their estimates to expected revenues or to propose new revenues to meet added expenditures. In short, the federal government operated without a budget.[83]

Taft attempted to centralize control of the budgetary process in his very first year. He believed that much budgetary fat could be trimmed if the executive could assume control over the appropriation requests of the various departments. He immediately notified his department heads that expenditure estimates should be reduced and cleared through the secretary of the treasury before being forwarded to Congress. Taft and the cabinet reviewed the departmental requests before they were finally approved and forwarded to Congress. After pruning a whopping $92,000,000 from the estimates, the President sent Congress what amounted to the first budget in modern American history.

The attempt to reduce expenditures through the use of a budget was disastrous, and Taft later admitted that his procedure had been politically naive. As he later described it, he had decided that a frank approach to Congress would produce better results than deception. "I will deal with Congress truthfully," he said. "I will tell them exactly how little we can get on with." He then went after the departmental requests "with an axe" when a more sophisticated weapon was needed. Congress was not impressed by truthfulness:

In the first place, Congress took the statement that we made in the same way that it takes every statement of an estimate. They think it is a good, healthy method with appropriations in which they are not particularly interested, to reduce them about twenty percent below the estimate, and thus it became the general understanding that the heads of the departments and of bureaus shall make their estimates twenty per cent more, so that when the reduction comes it will come to what they really think they need. But they treated my truthful statement that way, and so the appropriations were reduced, and when the next year came the cuts had so interfered with the operation of many of the departments that we had to have deficiency bills and the appropriations were increased. This is a lesson as to what can be done by an earnest desire to do something without the exact knowledge of how to do it.[84]

The result of Taft's strategy was a budget lower than that of the previous year, an event almost unprecedented since the Civil War.

Despite his initial setback in budget-making, Taft was determined to bring greater rationality to the whole budgetary process. At first he had sought to review and revise departmental estimates before they had been referred to Congress, but later he concluded that "the conditions attached by Congress have been such as to make effective review impossible."[85] In 1910, however, he secured from Congress an appropriation of $100,000 for the creation of a Commission on Economy and Efficiency to study the whole federal administration, including the problems of budgeting. Continuing his drive for greater executive control over his departments, Taft began to use the new commission as a clearing house for all of the departmental estimates. Even though Congress objected, Taft persisted in his plans to present the legislature with a budget cleared by the commission and conforming to its new standards. On June 27, 1912, he sent Congress a special message along with the commission report entitled "The Need for a National Budget." In his message, Taft placed himself squarely in the forefront of budgetary reform:

> So long as the method at present prescribed obtains, neither the Congress nor the country can have laid before it a definite understandable program of business, or of governmental work to be financed; nor can it have a well-defined, clearly expressed financial program to be followed; nor can either the Congress or the Executive get before the country the proposals of each in such a manner as to locate responsibility for plans submitted or for results.

The commission's report also recommended that Congress establish a budgetary system which would require the President, early in each session of Congress, to present the legislature with a comprehensive budget accompanied by a message "setting forth in brief the significance of the proposals to which attention is invited."[86]

The President was not content to wait for further action by Congress on his recommendation. On July 10, 1912, he directed the heads of all departments to prepare two sets of estimates, "one in accordance with the present practice and one in the report of the Commission on Economy and Efficiency, which was sent to Congress with my message."[87] Alarmed legislators attempted to forestall the President's plan and specifically incorporated into Section 9 of the legislative, executive, and judicial appropriation bill of 1912 a provision stating:

> That until otherwise provided by law, the regular annual estimates for appropriations for expenses of the government of the United States shall be prepared and submitted to Congress by those charged with the duty of such preparation and submission, only in the form and at the time now required by law, and in no other form and at no other time.[88]

The President was unwilling to budge on his plan. When some members of the cabinet questioned his power to flout the will of Congress by preparing a second budget, Taft reiterated his position. On September 19, he wrote a lengthy letter to Secretary of the Treasury MacVeagh in which he repeated his request that all department heads comply with his order of July 10 and explained his reasons for not complying with the congressional prohibition. Section 9, he informed MacVeagh, was "to be taken as a caution only . . . and can not be construed into an inhibition against the use by the President of the labor of his subordinates in the various departments in preparing estimates in accord with the new plan proposed by him for a budget, to be submitted by him to Congress in a message." Despite objections of John Fitzgerald, Democratic chairman of the House Appropriations Committee, to Taft's intended plans, the President refused to accept Section 9 as a legitimate limitation of his powers. To submit to Section 9

would be to permit the legislative branch of the Government to usurp the functions of the Executive and to abridge the executive power in a manner forbidden by the Constitution. I could not for a moment entertain, as reasonable, such a construction of Section 9. Under the Constitution, the President is entrusted with the executive power, and is responsible for the acts of heads of departments, and their subordinates as his agents, and he can use them to assist him in his constitutional duties, one of which is to recommend measures to Congress, and to advise it as to the existing conditions and their betterment.

As chief executive charged with the duty of recommending measures to Congress, Taft could not accept the underlying theory of Section 9 that the heads of the departments were purely "ministerial agents of the Congress," for

then as far as the business of Government is concerned, the President of the United States is shorn of most important executive power and duty. In my opinion, it is entirely competent for the President to submit a budget, and Congress can not forbid or prevent it. It is quite within his duty and power to have prepared and to submit to Congress and the country, a statement of resources, obligations, revenues, expenditures and estimates, in the form he deems advisable. And this power I propose to exercise.[89]

But Congress simply ignored the President's budget.

Taft's battle over the budget indicated that he was no Whig when it came to defending the administrative powers of his office. Indeed, his advocacy of an executive budget was one of his major contributions to the presidency. His plan, belatedly adopted in the Budget and Accounting Act of 1921, contributed more to the power of the modern presidency than almost any other administrative development of the period. His "usurpation" of budgetary powers, though only an obscure administrative issue at the time, foreshadowed the breathtaking view of executive power which he later expounded in *Myers* v. *U.S.* (1926) as chief justice.[90] Contrary to his critics, Taft did believe in a strong chief executive. He just believed quietly.

Although Taft could not convert Congress to the idea of an executive budget, he did succeed in eliminating an inherited deficit of $58,000,000 and he accumulated a surplus of $86,000,000 in his last three budgets. With annual budgets of nearly $660,000,000, this was no mean feat.[91]

In addition, Taft pressed for the reorganization of the Treasury, State, Navy, and War Departments. In the Treasury Department, superfluous jobs were eliminated and new auditing procedures and business methods were introduced by Secretary MacVeagh. In the State Department, new geographical divisions for the Far East, Near East, Latin America, and Western Europe were created along with a Division of Information. Legal and trade advisers were added to meet the growing needs of American commercial diplomacy. In accord with the recommendations of the Commission on Naval Reorganization, Secretary of the Navy Meyer also established four permanent bureaus concerned with naval operations, personnel, inspection, and material. Naval shipyards were reorganized and new cost-accounting procedures instituted in the department. Even the War Department was not immune from the reorganization fever of its former secretary. A regular Army Reserve was created and a comprehensive reorganization plan adopted as the tentative chart for future development. These reforms, however, represented only the most visible part of the President's overall program of modernization, for modern business methods were continuously introduced at all levels of the government throughout his four-year term. In his message of January 17, 1912, summarizing the administrative problems his Efficiency Commission had uncovered, Taft expressed the hope that the report of the commission would become a catalyst for continuing reorganization of the federal government.[92]

Administrative reform also included the extension of the merit principle to the federal service. The President discontinued Roosevelt's widespread use of executive orders to exempt federal employees from the civil service law and began a long-range plan to place as many federal positions under the merit system as possible. In his annual message of December 21, 1911, Taft boldly recommended that "all the local offices throughout the country, including collectors of internal revenue, collectors of customs, postmasters of all four classes, immigration commissioners and marshals, should be by law covered into the classified service."[93] Although Congress balked at eliminating these sources of patronage, Taft went ahead under his existing powers and incorporated 70,000 employees (including 36,000 fourth-class postmasters) into the civil service system. By executive order he also placed officials of the diplomatic corps, up to the grade of embassy secretary, under a merit system requiring examinations for appointment and promotion. If Taft could have had his way, he would have covered all government employees up to bureau chiefs under the civil service system.[94] "I think I have gone further into reforms than most Presidents," he wrote to his brother Horace, "especially those directed to the improvement of the civil service by the merit system and in economy."[95] Secretary of the Treasury MacVeagh could also boast, "I know of no Presidential record with respect to civil service reform, that equals that of President Taft; and yet nothing is said about it, and little is known about it by the public at large."[96]

Civil service reform, administrative reorganization, the introduction of modern business methods, budget-making—all these problems could not compete with more exciting issues and personalities for public attention. In contrast to Roosevelt who knew how to choose issues with a maximum impact upon the popular imagination, Taft appeared more comfortable dealing with highly technical issues. As he himself recognized,

Rarely, indeed, can the people, as a whole, be roused to the benefit of a policy the discussion of which involves a tedious recital of figures or a detailed explanation of a complicated plan of governmental reorganization.

Reforms of this kind are the result of the hardest kind of work in the closet. They cannot be exploited in the headlines. They tire the audience. Those who effect them must generally be contented with a consciousness of good service rendered, and must not look for the reward of popular approval.[97]

Taft realized that his reforms were beyond the grasp or perspective of the public. Despite the negligible publicity value of his work, Taft forged ahead. His mistake lay not in promoting such overdue reform, but in transferring his habits of "working in the closet" to other public issues requiring more aggressive and open methods of attack. Theodore Roosevelt might have successfully trumpeted such reforms before an apathetic public, but Taft had no skill or inclination to do so. He had labored as a judge and administrator too long to change his habits.

Cartoon by E. W. Kemble, 1912. The caption reads:
    "The peepul must rule, William."
    "Yes, Theodore, the peepul must rule."
    (in chorus): "But as we direct."

4. "The Policy of Harmony"

Always remember that you can catch more flies with molasses than on a club.

William Howard Taft,
May 29, 1910[1]

When Theodore Roosevelt left the White House on March 4, 1909, he left the presidency a changed institution. No longer was the president expected to sit in splendid isolation only to sign and administer laws passed by the Congress, rarely daring to suggest publicly what Congress should do. He had become a tribune of the people, a forceful spokesman for the public interest, an active leader of the legislative branch. In championing his own legislative proposals before Congress, Roosevelt had lobbied unceasingly with legislators, appealed over their heads to the people when necessary, publicly threatened vetoes, expanded the use of special messages, and generally employed his office as a "bully pulpit" to air his views on issues ranging from antitrust policy to phonetic spelling. By his efforts he had focused more public attention upon his legislative program than had any other president since the Civil War. Although his critics had charged him with "executive usurpation" of power, popular expectations about the presidency had been so altered by Roosevelt that his successor was obliged to exert strong legislative leadership. Roosevelt had transformed the presidency into an active though not yet dominant force in the legislative process. He had set high standards for his successor to follow.[2]

Largely as a result of his postpresidential writings, Taft has been associated historically with the "literalist" or "constitutional" theory of the presidency. Actually he shared Roosevelt's view of legislative leadership. After seven years of service under Roosevelt, Taft could see no danger of "executive usurpation" of congressional power "as long as Congress retains the power of appropriation and expenditure of money." Taft recognized that because the president has more responsibility than power in the American political system, he must use all the influence at his command to achieve his legislative goals, including his popularity and position as party leader. Presidents have been accused of usurping congressional powers because of their influence upon the legislative process, "but power acquired and informally exercised under these circumstances and dependent upon popular support, is never likely to be dangerous to the body politic or subversive of the liberties of a people." Such power, Taft felt, was "temporary" in character and would change with the election of a new Congress. "In view of his legitimate functions in securing legislation," Taft argued, "it is far-fetched to term his personal influence in securing the passage of useful legislation a usurpation."[3] "The truth is," he later maintained, "that there is a good deal more danger that the legislature will usurp some of the executive functions than there is that the executive will usurp some of the legislative functions."[4] In the light of such prepresidential support of Roosevelt, Taft could hardly be considered an opponent of strong legislative leadership. The difference between the two men stemmed not from their conception of the office or their goals, but from differences in temperament, political sophistication, and political realities in Congress. Both were committed to use all the power and influence at their command to achieve their legislative programs.

I

Taft's view of legislative leadership became more evident after his election as he grappled with the issues of tariff reform and "Cannonism." Taft was doggedly determined to redeem his campaign promises, especially his pledge to work for a lower tariff. Roosevelt had expediently avoided the issue during his presidency despite the growing sentiment across the country for reform. In 1904, for example, he had red-penciled one of Root's campaign speeches because of his own deep misgivings about the issue. "I find that [the tariff] needs more careful handling than anything else, because I do not want to promise the impossible, and I have to recognize the rather ugly fact that two opposite tendencies have been visible in the Republican party, namely a tendency in the majority to "stand pat," while in a large and fervent minority there is a growing insistence upon a reduction of duties." Always the realist, Roosevelt felt that he must "reckon with the temper of the party as a whole—not with the temper as it should be, but the temper as it is."⁵ After his election in 1904, Roosevelt dropped the idea of tariff reform upon the advice of Speaker Cannon. The political risks were too great. "We know from long experience," Cannon once related, "that no matter how great an improvement the new tariff may be, it almost always results in the party in power losing the following election. A man may do the brilliant thing in politics and personally get a lot of fun out of it, but for the sake of the party he had better do the safe thing."⁶ Roosevelt did "the safe thing" and never seriously raised the tariff issue. As sentiment for reform rose during the last year of the Roosevelt administration, Frank Kellogg suggested to the President that he send a special message to Congress demanding tariff reform. "No," shot back the President. "God Almighty could not pass a tariff bill and win at the next election following its passage.

The only time to pass a tariff is the first year of a new administration, and trust to have the effects counteracted before another Presidential election."[7]

Roosevelt had bequeathed Taft the burden of tariff reform. Taft did not dodge the issue despite Roosevelt's campaign advice to "move with great caution" on the issue. Taft had supported reform in his speech at Bath, Maine, in 1906. In 1908, he committed himself to calling a special session of Congress on the subject and continued to call for downward revision throughout the presidential campaign of 1908.[8] Roosevelt later admitted to his son-in-law Nicholas Longworth, "[I] told him when he was making these speeches that he was making pretty drastic promises, and that there might be difficulty in having them kept, and in meeting the mental attitude which he [was] himself causing; but he was perfectly breezy and cheerful, and declined to consider the possibility of trouble ahead."[9] For Taft, however, tariff revision had become a moral obligation of the Republican party to the nation.

"Cannonism" was a major obstacle to genuine tariff reform. Not only had House Speaker Cannon opposed the tariff plank in the Republican platform, but his autocratic rule of the House had become a national issue in the 1908 elections. The powers of the Speaker had reached their zenith during Cannon's reign. Cannon, for example, had the power to make all committee assignments, regardless of seniority. As Speaker, he was also the chairman of the powerful Rules Committee, which controlled the House agenda. He was unquestionably the most powerful party leader in the Congress. Without the approval of Cannon, few bills stood any chance of passage in the House.[10] By blocking most of Roosevelt's legislative program in the President's last two years in office, Cannon had won the undying enmity of the progressive wing of the Republican party. Both Taft and Roosevelt hoped for the election of a new House which would dethrone the Speaker. "I

shall be pleased if we can have such a Republican majority as
will take the power away from Cannon," Taft wrote to Roosevelt, "for I regard him as the burden that we have had in
the campaign and as obstruction to all legislation of a progressive character that we really need." Roosevelt agreed that
"the ideal result would be to have a Republican Congress with
a majority so small that neither Cannon nor Tawney [mem-
ber of the House Ways and Means Committee] can be made
Speaker."[11] Despite Taft's victory in November, Republican
strength declined slightly in the new Congress. The Republicans lost three seats in the House (219 R–170 D) and two in
the Senate (59 R–33 D). The setting was less than ideal for
dethroning the Speaker.

In view of the election results, Roosevelt began to express
misgivings about challenging Cannon. He felt there was no
solid candidate to replace the Speaker and recognized that
four-fifths of the Republicans in the House wanted Cannon.
Even if the overthrow of Cannon proved successful, Roosevelt recognized that it would be dangerous "to have him in
the position of the sullen and hostile floor leader bound to
bring your administration to grief."[12] Taft also had reservations about challenging Cannon, but they were temporarily dispelled when the Speaker and ranking members of
the House Ways and Means Committee dismissed the Republican tariff plank as campaign rhetoric. The President-elect
exploded privately at what he considered Cannon's "cynical
suggestion of indifference to public opinion" and his "intima-
tion that promises before an election looked a little different
after the election." He vented his anger in a letter to Senator
Root of New York, arguing that he would not permit Cannon
and the House leadership to "go ahead and fool the public
without a protest from somebody." Taft was ready to take
on the "standpatters" in the style reminiscent of his predecessor:

I think the attitude of Cannon, the cynical references that he has made in some of his speeches about promises and compliance with them, are enough to damn the party if they are not protested against. I have not said anything for publication, but I am willing to have it understood that my attitude is one of hostility to Cannon and the whole crowd unless they are coming in to do the square thing. If they don't do it, and I acquiesce, we are going to be beaten; and I had rather be beaten by not acquiesing than by acquiesing. You know me well enough to know that I do not hunt a fight just for the fun of it, but Cannon's speech at Cleveland was of a character that ought to disgust everybody who believed in honesty in politics in dealing with the people squarely, and just because he has a nest of standpatters in his House and is so ensconced there that we may not be able to move him is no reason why I should pursue the policy of harmony. I don't care how he feels or how they feel in the House; I am not going to be made the mouthpiece of a lie to the people without disclaiming my responsibility. If they will play fair I will play fair, but if they won't then I reserve all my rights to do anything I find myself able to do.[13]

There was no mistaking the dilemma facing the President-elect. "I am confronted in the beginning of my administration with what seems to be something of a party crisis," he acknowledged. "I do not wish to do anything rash, but neither do I wish to omit any legitimate effort as the head of the party to prevent a fatal reactionary mistake."[14]

Taft was careful not to condemn the Speaker and his cronies openly, at least not yet. He sent feelers out to friends and congressmen to test the sentiment in the new Congress for dethroning Cannon, but prospects appeared slim. When Vice-President-elect James Sherman and Congressman James A. Tawney, member of the Ways and Means Committee, informed Roosevelt of the odds against defeating Cannon, the President summoned Taft to the White House and advised him to come to terms with the Speaker. Both men agreed that "it would not do to try to beat Cannon unless we could succeed."[15] Taft subsequently sought conferences with Cannon and Tawney to assure their support for tariff reform and the Republican platform. A bargain was struck between Taft and Cannon: in return for the Speaker's legislative support, Taft pledged to remain neutral in the impending fight over the speakership. In addition to his understanding with the Speaker, Taft secured a gentleman's agreement from Senator Nelson W. Aldrich, majority leader of the Senate, to push the President's program in the Senate. "Mr. Aldrich," the President wrote his brother Horace, "has been to me a number of times, has constantly referred to the plan which I outlined in my Letter of Acceptance and in my Inaugural Address . . . and . . . has pledged himself and the leaders of the Senate to assisting me in fulfilling those pledges."[16] Taft had counted noses in the House and Senate and was forced to yield to the political exigencies of the moment.

Taft quickly began to invent constitutional reasons to justify his decision not to fight. "I would be very severely criticised if I should attempt to use Executive power to control the election in the House," he wrote to an anti-Cannon congressman.[17] And to another personal friend the President-elect explained, "The election of a speaker of the House is not within my consent. I have no jurisdiction in respect to the matter."[18] After Cannon's election as Speaker, however, Taft explained his real reasons for inaction to Senator Joseph L. Bristow of Kansas:

It isn't that I might not have beaten him [Cannon] if I had gone in hammer and tongs, but I think the example of a new executive attempting to beat a candidate for the speakership would form an ugly precedent, and by not carrying on the contest, I think I can accomplish what we desire, and that is such rules in the House as will prevent Cannon's blocking the legislation, and also such a thorough and genuine revision that the people will believe that the Republican party is complying with its promise.

Had I beaten Cannon, I should have had a factious and ugly Republican minority, willing and anxious to defeat all progressive measures, and with the power to defeat them; because you know as well as I that the Democrats in such a pinch are only too glad to leave the Republicans in a hole.[19]

In short, it was only *after* Taft had found it impossible to topple Cannon that he rationalized his decision on a legal basis. His constitutional scruples forbade interference in the legislative process only if he could not win! His invocation of the "jurisdictional" limitations of his office was not a self-imposed restraint, but simply a recognition of the actual power relationships between the President and Speaker which could not be changed without serious political damage to the new administration.

Taft's abortive campaign to dethrone Cannon produced a few beneficial side effects. The Speaker did agree to work with the new President to fulfill his campaign promises. The President-elect, moreover, had succeeded in arousing a "strong expression" of public opinion in favor of tariff revision by focusing attention upon Cannon and the House Ways and Means Committee. Taft had convinced the House leaders that "a compliance with the party promises is absolutely necessary to the future success of the party."[20] An angered Taft had become more committed to fulfilling his campaign promise of tariff reform and using a veto on any bill that fell short of his pledge. He wrote to his friend William Worthington,

I am hopeful . . . that we shall get good out of Nazareth, and I am certain that if we don't, I'll cook the gooses of the men who prevent it by vetoing the bill. It may be that it will ultimately defeat my administration, but I shall much prefer to go down upholding the proposition that we must comply with our party promises, than to go down, as we certainly would go down, if I were to yield by approving a bill which was nothing but a humiliating compromise with the reactionaries on the subject.[21]

But Taft was not yet in office. Collaboration with Cannon and Aldrich would change his tune. He was to discover that he needed more than anger and the threat of a veto to bring about a genuine revision of the tariff when dealing with experienced legislative foxes like Cannon and Aldrich.

Although Taft abandoned plans to unseat Cannon, he continued to hope for a reform of House rules which would transfer the absolute power of the Speaker over House business to a rules committee elected by the House "so that a majority of the Republicans may exercise control over the order of business."[22] He was even willing to see the Speaker deprived of his power of appointing the standing committees even though such a reform would reduce the Speakership to "an almost judicial position."[23] His hopes of securing a revision of the House rules collapsed, however, when Cannon informed Taft that if he, the Speaker, lost on the fight over the rules, his ability to promote the President's legislative program would be seriously jeopardized. When progressive congressmen (now increasingly labeled "Insurgents" for their rebellion against Cannon and the House leadership) called upon Taft on March 10 for support in the rules fight, the President gave them no encouragement. "I do not think it a good time to meddle," he later admitted. "I may have to use the very machinery they are denouncing to pass a tariff bill. And a tariff bill must be passed."[24] Despite his sympathy for their cause, Taft abandoned the "Insurgents," who numbered no more than thirty out of a total of 219 Republicans.

The Taft-Cannon understanding which had originally applied only to the fight over the speakership had now been broadened by the crafty old Speaker to apply to the rules themselves. When the crucial showdown over the rules came on March 15, Taft mobilized seven of his cabinet members as lobbyists against the Insurgent-Democratic move to amend the House rules. According to Champ Clark, the Democratic leader in the House, the Insurgents were "astounded and angered" at Taft's desertion. "We got a bloody licking," Clark admitted. "The insurgents never forgave him, and became more aggressive and grew in numbers."[25]

Taft was already aware of the price he would have to pay for supporting Cannon. In a prophetic letter to Roosevelt, about to depart for Africa, the new President tried to explain his legislative strategy.

I have no doubt that when you return you will find me very much under suspicion by our friends in the West. Indeed I think I am already so because I was not disposed to countenance an insurrection of thirty men against 180 outside the caucus. I knew how this would be regarded, but I also knew that unless I sat steady in the boat and did what I could to help Cannon and the great majority of the Republicans stand solid, I should make a capital error in the beginning of my administration in alienating the good will of those without whom I can do nothing to carry through the legislation to which the party and I are pledged. Cannon and Aldrich have promised to stand by the party platform and to follow my lead.[26]

The new President was confronted with a choice between the lesser of two evils—cooperation with Cannon and the congressional Republicans which was essential to the enactment of his program, or an all-out assault upon the Republican leadership in the hopes of arousing public opinion and eventually transforming the character of the congressional party. The first choice promised some legislative successes, but a minimum of personal popularity; the second promised much popularity, but a minimum of accomplishments. After all, Roosevelt had ended his term "giving and taking heavy blows" from members of Congress and constantly appealing over their heads to the public.[27] Since the new President could not wait two to four more years for his congressional party to be transformed—indeed, Roosevelt's preaching had not converted it in seven years—he chose the only viable alternative open to him, the "policy of harmony." "There is," he later wrote, "only one usual and natural way, under our form of government, for a Chief Executive to secure legislation: that is to work with and through the leaders of the majority party in Congress."[28]

II

In accord with his campaign pledge, the newly inaugurated President issued a call for the Congress to convene on March 15 to consider the tariff. The special session provided Taft with a unique opportunity to dramatize his leadership. But instead of sounding a call to battle, the new President issued an innocuous message stating merely that the business of the special session would be tariff reform. Progressive Republicans were disheartened as they listened in shocked disbelief to the brief message read to them. There was no attempt by the President to dramatize himself or his views. There was no sense of urgency in his words. There was no ringing declaration of principle around which supporters of lower rates could rally. There was no cry for redemption of campaign promises to keep faith with the people. There was no vision to inspire the people.[29]

Taft's phlegmatic message can be explained partly by his lack of political imagination and by his undramatic temperament, and partly by his calculated "policy of harmony." The President had no desire to alienate cooperative congressional leaders with empty rhetoric. On the advice of Cannon and Aldrich, he had adopted a hands-off strategy of allowing the congressional leaders to guide the tariff bill through the legislature. Only after the bill had been brought to the final conference committee would the President intervene at the promised invitation of the leadership. As Taft explained to his brother Horace:

> Speaker Cannon, Mr. Payne, and Mr. Aldrich all agree that the wise thing for us to do is to hold a conference when the bill gets into Conference and to make a bill which shall appeal to party support. They are going to confer with me, they say, and give my views great influence in the action of the Conference Committee. How much this means and how far they will be willing to go, I do not know. But I have not found Aldrich or Cannon in any way deceptive in the dealings that I have had with them, and I believe they are acting in good faith.[30]

Taft cannot be completely blamed for having adopted this strategy. After all, he possessed only superficial information about the tariff. To have intervened at the committee stage to do battle on over a thousand rates would have been impractical and would, moreover, have alienated many congressmen with vested local interests. Taft, however, was naive in leaving so much of the tariff-making to the established congressional leadership. They had convinced him that significant changes in the tariff could be made later in conference, but, according to Champ Clark, they had failed to inform him of a House tradition that "where the House proposed one rate on an item in the tariff bill and the Senate proposed another, the conferees could not go below the lower rate and could not go above the higher rate." By trusting his congressional leaders too much, Taft found that when the bill eventually reached conference, in Clark's words, "he was sewed up; that there were only six items in which he was interested and on which he could secure reduction."[31]

Despite the self-denying strategy inherent in "the policy of harmony," Taft did take the initiative in reducing United States tariff barriers on Philippine products. Where he clearly possessed superior information and a strong emotional commitment, Taft could pursue a more activist legislative strategy. For almost ten years, he had unsuccessfully lobbied for the reduction of tariff rates on sugar and tobacco to stimulate the Philippine economy. During the 1908 campaign, he had pledged to Judge Newton W. Gilbert of the Philippine Commission, "If I can be elected, I believe I can bring about a recognition of the obligation of the United States to give good trade to the Philippines, in such a way as to establish a permanent prosperity in those islands."[32] In December 1908, after his peace parley with Cannon, Taft visited the House Ways and Means Committee and "reached an agreement with them about Philippine sugar."[33] The President continued his paternal concern over the islands by sending three Philippine officials to Committee Chairman Sereno E. Payne to discuss free trade between the islands and the United States. "I would be glad if you would submit to them the part of your tariff bill relating to the Philippines," he wrote Payne.[34] The final Philippine schedules appeared to have originated in the White House itself.[35] However, when Congressman Oscar W. Underwood of Alabama threatened an amendment to eliminate Philippine taxes on the island's exports which threatened to nullify the beneficial effects of lower American rates on the islands, Taft urged administration spokesman Congressman E. J. Hill of Connecticut to refuse to compromise on the matter and "fight it out."[36]

When the bill went to the Senate, Taft attempted through Senator Lodge to pack a subcommittee considering the Philippine tariff with members favorable to free trade with the islands. Although Taft recommended Senators Albert J. Beveridge, Coe I. Crawford, and any friendly Democrat, he was subsequently content with Senator Weldon B. Heyburn and

Democratic Senator Joseph F. Johnston of Alabama. When Senator George C. Perkins attempted to amend the Philippine schedule by restricting island trade with other Far Eastern countries such as China and Japan, Taft warned Perkins that such an amendment would "destroy all the good results" of the bill.[37] When the Perkins amendment passed the Senate, Taft informed Congressman Hill that "we must attend to the matter in conference."[38]

The conference committee became the focal point of presidential pressure, which had previously been unsuccessful. In his determination to secure Philippine free trade, Taft sought help from Congressman John Dalzell on the conference committee:

I suppose you are occupied with a great many things, but I am very anxious that we should have upon the conference committee one fully charged with the details of the Philippine tariff question, so as to protect the interests of those people there. You have always assisted us in this matter and are so quick to catch the point of explanations, that I want to ask you to let Colton and Edwards of the Bureau of Insular Affairs come to see you and give you the points.[39]

During the month-long deliberations of the conference committee, Taft negotiated continuously with Congressmen Dalzell and Oscar W. Underwood and with Senators Aldrich and Reed Smoot of Utah for the elimination of objectionable amendments to the Philippine schedule. His patient persistence was finally rewarded when the conference granted the islands virtual free trade with the United States, except for a limitation on tobacco imports. "It has been a long, hard fight," Taft wrote to his wife, "and the possibility of great improvement arising from this feature of the present tariff bill is one of the reasons why I should be very reluctant to veto the bill."[40]

Taft's extraordinary success in effecting free trade for the

Philippines was the result of three factors. The President knew exactly what he wanted; he possessed expert advice on the Philippine rate schedules; and he doggedly fought for his ideas all the way from the original hearings of the Ways and Means Committee to the final report of the conference committee. Because the Philippine tariff bill was, in Taft's own words, "pretty dear to my heart,"[41] he displayed no scruples about interfering in the legislative process. When he finally signed the tariff act, Major Butt noted, "I think he feels it to be a greater triumph to secure the passage of the Philippines bill, giving free trade to the islands, than he does in the passage of the Payne-Aldrich [tariff] bill."[42]

The issues of a corporation income tax and a personal income tax also forced the President to abandon his "hands off" strategy in the special session. In attempting to fill the revenue gap which tariff revision would create, the House adopted a graduated inheritance tax favored by Taft in his inaugural address. The Senate, however, rejected the tax on the grounds that it conflicted with similar taxes already levied in thirty-six states. When Taft suggested to Aldrich the possibility of a corporation tax to fill the expected revenue gap, Aldrich laughed at the proposal and suggested that there was no need for any new revenue laws.[43] However, when the President privately confided to progressive Senator Albert B. Cummins of Iowa that he favored a personal income tax in theory, Cummins proceeded to persuade Senate progressives to ally themselves with the Democrats to pass an income tax measure. Nineteen Republican senators, combined with a disciplined Democratic party, threatened to pass an income tax in spite of a Supreme Court decision (*Pollock* v. *Farmers' Loan & Trust Co.*, 1895) that such a tax was unconstitutional.[44] When Senators Aldrich, W. Murray Crane of Massachusetts, and Lodge appealed to Taft to save them from the Insurgent-Democratic coalition and the income tax, the President knew he held all the trump cards. According to Taft, Aldrich had now "ceased laughing" at the idea of a corporation income tax.[45] The Senate leaders were confronted with a choice of either a personal income tax or, if the Persident intervened, a corporate tax combined with a constitutional amendment legalizing the personal income tax. Although Taft favored an income tax, the method of achieving it was all important. He sincerely feared that congressional passage of the tax in the face of the *Pollock* decision would damage the prestige of the Supreme Court. He chose to support a corporate tax along with an amendment legalizing the income tax. "If I had not intervened," he later explained, "the income tax would certainly have passed both houses of Congress and I would regard that as a great public injury, thus to involve the Supreme Court and injure its prestige, whatever its decision."[46] When Aldrich expressed a desire to place a two-year limit upon the President's corporation tax, Taft brushed the suggestion aside because of its unpopularity with the progressive wing of the party. Taft now held the whip hand. "The situation is not one of my yielding to Aldrich," he wrote to his brother Horace, "but of Aldrich yielding to me."[47]

Taft was elated over having outmaneuvered Aldrich. By winning the Senate leader's consent to a corporation tax, the President felt he had established the principle of national supervision over corporations which he had intended to press at the regular session of Congress in December. On June 16, he dispatched a special message to Congress asking for the immediate enactment of a corporation income tax and the adoption of an amendment to the Constitution legalizing the personal income tax.[48] The President's strategy pried enough Republican votes away from the personal income tax proposal to save the regular Republicans from a humiliating defeat. The hard-core progressives led by Senators Robert La Follette of Wisconsin and Albert B. Cummins of Iowa, however, were angry at Taft for deserting them on the verge of their success. The President, on the other hand, was puzzled by their anger and could marshal only scorn for their "personal and petty jealousy":

Had they the breadth of view and the keenness of insight, immediately upon the receipt of my message they would have arisen in their seats and said: "This gives us all we have been claiming and seeking only by another method, and we now claim to lead the procession because the President and the reactionaries have come to our side."[49]

It was clear from the conflict that the progressives were interested in immediate results; Taft was more concerned with the proper means of achieving those results.

The eventual passage of the corporation tax represented a more significant fulfillment of the Roosevelt policies than did the final Payne-Aldrich Act itself. The tax implicitly established the principle of federal control of corporations. Roosevelt himself was extremely pleased to hear of the new tax. He wrote to Senator Lodge:

I regard your success in putting on the corporation tax as most important; from the permanent and most important standpoint, as establishing the principle of national supervision; from the temporary standpoint, as scoring a triumph which the west will appreciate, and which may take the sting out of some of the inevitable grumbling about the tariff, by diverting attention to what is really of far greater moment.[50]

Taft's success was lost, however, in the debate over the tariff and charges by western progressives that he had sold out to the congressional leadership. Lacking Roosevelt's rhetorical skills, Taft was never able to divert public attention from the tariff to his successful sponsorship of the corporation tax or the income tax amendment.

III

In contrast to his active leadership on the Philippine and corporate tax issues, Taft generally pursued a "hands off" strategy toward the remainder of the tariff while awaiting his cue to intervene at the conference committee stage. The President's strategy was initially rewarded by House passage of the Payne bill which represented, in his estimate, "a genuine effort in the right direction."[51] The bill had eliminated the tariff on raw materials such as iron ore, oil, hides, coal, wood pulp, and included substantial reductions on scrap iron and lumber. The Senate, on the other hand, ignored the President's campaign pledges and produced a clearly protectionist bill raising the duties on all of the important items reduced by the House. As the House and Senate bills went into conference, the President sought to place the raw materials back on the House free list and thereby "reconcile the country to the view that a substantial step downward has been taken."[52] Taft had staked the outcome of the tariff battle on his ability to influence the conference committee.

Taft had privately threatened a veto of any tariff bill that did not comply with his promises before his inauguration, but public threats against a coequal branch of government were personally distasteful to him. Although it also suited his rather passive temperament, Taft had chosen a policy of harmony with the Republican leadership out of expediency. He sincerely believed he could be more effective in the long run by refraining from public threats and using a quieter approach to Congress. "I hardly think it wise to threaten a veto in advance of the passage of any pending bill," he once wrote. "It is hardly courteous and it is certainly not politic."[53] For Taft, public threats against Congress represented failure, not success in legislative leadership. If this meant that he would rarely dramatize himself as the righteous guardian of the public welfare, so be it. He was content to rely upon his ultimate legislative accomplishments for popular vindication.

After the Senate had passed the protectionist Aldrich bill, Taft was besieged with requests to veto it. The appeal of Professor J. D. Brannan of the Harvard Law School was typical of the pleas he began to receive:

If the Senate should prevail, in spite of your efforts, a veto would not only be approved by the people but would give you a popularity greater than that of Roosevelt. On the other hand to let such a bill go through and become law will be regarded as a reactionary step and a surrender to the selfish interests against whom you have been fighting with Roosevelt. It will be argued to you, I have no doubt, that a veto would divide the party. But we think that a veto would help the party politically. A party united for wrong is weaker than a party united for right. A veto would be applauded by the whole country and Congress would come back with a warrant from the people to stand by the President.[54]

Had the professor been able to read Taft's mind, he would have known that the President could simply not afford the luxury of a tariff veto so early in his administration. Two days earlier the President had written his brother Horace at length:

It may be also that I shall find Aldrich and the Senate Committee so stiff in the upholding of the Senate bill that I shall have to threaten a veto, or, indeed, which I sincerely hope not, really affix one to the bill. Of course, I could make a lot of cheap popularity for the time being by vetoing the bill, but it would leave us in a mess out of which I do not see how we could get, and the only person who would gain popularity would be your humble servant, and that at the expense of the party and the men who have thus far stood with me loyally. You can see, therefore, that it will take what I regard as almost equivalent to a breach of faith in their stubbornness about the Senate rates to make me veto the bill. The vetoing of the bill, of course, would throw me out with the leaders in the Senate and the House, and would make me almost hopeless in respect to effecting my reforms of next year, so you see how much more hangs on the question than the mere subject of the rates in the tariff bill. Of course, the position I have taken in respect to the tariff bill and downward revision may open me to a charge of inconsistency, and not standing to my promises, if I were to sign a bill that was distinctly at variance with those promises, and that is the only thing that puts me in a position where I can contemplate a possibility of a veto.[55]

Although Taft permitted the subtle threat of a veto to hang over the process of tariff-making, informed opinion in Washington considered a presidential veto unlikely.[56]

Taft's hopes for a lower tariff suffered a setback when Cannon and Aldrich packed the conference committee with members "above suspicion of insurgency."[57] Although he made an unsuccessful attempt to have Congressman E. J. Hill appointed to the conference, Taft ingenuously wrote to Albert Baldwin of the *Outlook*, "I did not attempt to dictate to Mr. Cannon, or suggest to him who should go on the conference committee."[58] The President's strategy cost him dearly, for Cannon, in defiance of low tariff sentiment in the House, proceeded to stack the committee with protectionist standpatters. The President was consequently forced to work through Congressmen Sereno E. Payne and Samuel McCall of the committee in influencing the House conferees. "I do not think it will be found that the House committee conferees are going to differ from Mr. Payne," Taft wrote to the editor of the *Outlook*.[59] Privately, however, the President felt that he had been duped by the Speaker who had not "played square" in selecting the conferees.[60] The Senate conferees, moreover, were scarcely less conservative. Taft worked principally through Aldrich to influence them. Thus, the stage was set. Confronted by a conference committee packed with standpatters, the President began his last-ditch battle to salvage his campaign promise.

When the conference committee convened on July 11, Taft was determined to get "as near to it as I can" and remain in the thick of the fight for reform. He felt inadequate, however, to the task of pushing for revisions which he himself knew little about. "Root thinks Aldrich will make a good bill on the tariff but I don't know," he wrote Mrs. Taft. "If I had more technical knowledge I should feel more confident. However, I shall have to struggle along with the assistance of such experts as I can find."[61]

While the conferees deliberated for almost a month, Taft engaged in an intensive personal lobbying campaign rivaling even his predecessor's in energy. Whereas Roosevelt had used social activities at the White House as a "reward" for service, Taft now employed them as a "means to an end." He hoped to breach the separation between the legislative and executive branches by an unprecedented degree of hospitality. "Indeed," commented Archie Butt, "it has seemed to me at times that he has entertained more Democrats than Republicans at entertainments of a purely personal character." Day after day, Taft's breakfasts, lunches, and evenings were spent with the members of the conference committee and other interested congressional leaders. The White House had become a central command post for lower tariff forces, and Taft had become their acknowledged general.[62]

Throughout the month of July, the conferees filed through the White House for consultations with the President. They found him determined to see iron ore, oil, hides, coal, wood pulp, scrap iron, and lumber placed on the free list or the rates on them reduced considerably. Taft wrote to Senator Albert J. Beveridge:

I feel that it is my duty to secure as far as possible a return to the free raw material feature of the Payne bill, which is its chief characteristic, and then with that as characterizing the new bill . . . we can go before the country and maintain with the reduction in the Senate bill . . . that we have made it a decided step in favor of downward revision and that it is a substantial compliance with our promise.[63]

To achieve his goal, Taft was willing to take the necessary personal abuse from high-tariff legislators. When Aldrich encountered difficulties from die-hard protectionists "bitterly opposed" to the President, Taft gave the Republican leader license to use the White House as a lightning rod in order for Aldrich to extricate himself from embarrassing political commitments. "I told him he could use me as he pleases," Taft confided to his wife, "and that I would threaten him if he wished me to, with a view to making some of these people come over."[64] Whereas strong Presidents have traditionally sought to use their subordinates as scapegoats for their unpopular actions, Taft willingly offered to act as Aldrich's scapegoat if that would help the Senate leader achieve the President's objectives.

The President found it unnecessary during the early course of the conference to threaten a veto. The House, despite the nature of its conferees, supported the President's desire for downward revision, and Taft publicly neutralized the major standpat opposition in the House by confronting twenty-two protectionist congressmen who had called at the White House to protest the presidential meddling. He firmly rejected their pleas and publicized his response to them. He asserted that his position as titular head of the Republican party and as president of the whole people provided him with "a broader point of view" on the tariff than the congressmen, and that he would consequently continue to regard the proper revision of the rates as a "question of fact" rather than of political interest.[65] The President's firmness resulted in a flood of congratulatory letters and favorable editorial comment. Although Taft had bolstered his bargaining position with the conferees with his public statement, his real strength lay in the extensive House sentiment for the lower rates of the original Payne bill. House feeling precluded the possibility of an embarrassing veto. "It is now, in my judgment, no question of veto at all," Taft wrote to his brother Henry, "for the House will never consent to adopting the conference report which I would not approve."[66]

Despite the President's strong bargaining position, a deadlock threatened between the standpatters on the committee and those supporting the President. Taft began to suspect the possibility of a sellout. "I am dealing with very acute and expert politicians," he wrote to his wife, "and I am trusting a great many of them and I may be deceived; but on the whole I have the whip hand."[67] The whole process of tariff revision had begun to disgust the President. In a moment of revealing anger, he admitted to Mrs. Charles Taft, "The tariff is an abomination, and if there is anything that makes a man feel in favor of free trade it is the attempt to secure the passage of a protected tariff bill."[68] Taft, however, suppressed his emotions and continued working for a better bill. "I am busy every day," he wrote Mrs. Taft, "and nearly all the time with members of the Conference Committee and others who come in to see me about it."[69] Despite his doubts, Taft remained outwardly optimistic about the outcome. "I am very certain," he wrote Arthur Vorys, "that the bill will be better for my interference in it and will be a nearer compliance with our promises than it would have been if I had stayed my hand."[70] Within the confines of House rules limiting the extent of compromises in conference, Taft of course was helping to improve the bill.

Excessive tariff schedules on lumber and gloves finally forced the President to issue a public ultimatum to Senator

Aldrich. The Senate leader had personally sought a tariff on undressed lumber of $1.40 per thousand feet and had over-ridden the President's desire for $1.25 in conference. In addition, Cannon had attempted to force a $4.00 per dozen rate upon the glove schedule in payment for a political debt and had angered the President, who considered it "the greatest exhibition of tyranny that I have known of his attempting."[71] When Taft learned that the committee had ignored his pleas on lumber and gloves, he drafted a public letter to Aldrich:

I have no disposition to exert any other influence than that which it is my function under the Constitution to exercise; but I can say that while there are some other parts of the bill which are not as satisfactory to me as they could be made, it has so many virtues and accomplished so much in the direction prom-ised by the party, that if the conference report could follow my recommendations above given in respect to lumber and gloves, I shall be glad to exert all the influence possible and proper to se-cure the adoption of the report in both Houses, and should give the bill my approval.

I write this with a full sense of the responsibility that the de-cision announced imposes on me, and with a full understanding that it may result in a report of a disagreement. This I should greatly regret; but after balancing the conflicting considerations, I am willing to face the disagreement and its consequences rather than to express concurrence in any higher duty on lumber than above stated, and in any increase in the duty on gloves for the purpose of establishing a new industry.[72]

The conferees capitulated on the two rate schedules. Taft considered the final report a personal victory over his con-gressional leaders. He wrote to his brother Charles, "I think the result on the whole is a substantial victory for me in bring-ing about a very considerable number of reductions beyond those which, if I had not accepted the invitation to take part in the conference, would not have been made."[73]

The acceptance of the conference report was assured by the Republican organizations in the two houses. The House agreed to the report on July 31, 195 to 183, and the Senate accepted it on August 5, 70 to 22. Although he signed the final bill, the President publicly qualified his approval: "The bill is not a perfect tariff bill or a complete compliance with the promises made, strictly interpreted, but a fulfillment free from criticism in respect to a subject matter involving many schedules and thousands of articles could not be expected." Taft characterized the bill, however, as a "sincere effort" at downward revision warranting his signature.[74]

The President had secured significant reductions in the tariff on iron ore, scrap iron, lumber, coal, oil, and hides, but he failed to obtain all of the House reductions on raw materials. Had the schedules on raw materials been the only issues involved, Taft might have vetoed the bill. But he was so pleased with the treatment of the Philippines, the authorization of a new tariff board, a maximum-minimum clause, and the corporation income tax that a veto would have jeopardized provisions which, collectively, were as important in his mind as the rates themselves. The Philippine tariff, as already noted, was the fruition of a decade of personal effort. The tariff board, although a temporary creation, was an opening wedge in the President's plans for a permanent tariff commission that would take "politics" out of tariff-making. The maximum-minimum provision granted the President wide authority to force trade concessions from other nations by imposing a maximum tariff on those countries deliberately discriminating against American products. The corporation tax was the first major step in Taft's program for the regulation of national corporations. Because of these provisions, most of which had escaped public attention, Tafe felt that he could not veto the final bill.[75]

Roosevelt reacted to the Payne-Aldrich Act with mixed

emotions. Senator Lodge and Major Butt, among others, had kept the former President informed of the progress of the tariff bill. Lodge, part of the congressional leadership himself, gave Roosevelt a flattering appraisal of Taft's role in the tariff fight:

The President refrained from saying anything or doing anything while the bill was passing through the Houses, which I thought was wise and I told him so and I am still of that opinion, but when the conferees met they went to him and said they would like to know what his views were and he gave them his views very freely. He stood very firmly for what he demanded and forced a number of reductions which ought to have been made. I think his influence has been salutary in a high degree and his action has strengthened the Party with the Country, strengthened him and, I think, has made a bill which is really a very good one and contains some very valuable provisions and is much better liked than it would otherwise have been.[76]

Archie Butt was even more ecstatic in his praise for his new chief. "He used the White House as a great political adjunct in the battle," he informed Roosevelt, "and tried to coax when it was possible. But when he failed he used methods which reminded me of some of the methods which made the Executive feared in the past."[77] Roosevelt, however, had also received letters from progressives critical of Taft's handling of the tariff. Although he considered Taft's legislative strategy rather weak, he was surprisingly philosophical about the final bill:

I am not at all sure that it was possible under the old methods to get any other result. I am very much afraid that the trouble was fundamental; in other words, that it is not possible, as Congress is actually constituted, to expect the tariff to be well handled by *representatives of localities*. I am beginning to believe in the truth of what Root continually said while he was in the Cabinet; that it was useless to hope to do good work on the tariff if we adhered to the way which Cannon, Payne, Dalzell, and even as able a man as Aldrich, declared to be the only way, and that a complete change, into the details of which I need not go, ought to have been made in the methods of achieving the result.[78]

Roosevelt subsequently supported the tariff upon his return to the United States. He hid any doubts about the bill or the President's leadership for the sake of party unity throughout the fall of 1910.

A combination of reasons lay behind Roosevelt's disappointment in Taft's handling of the tariff. First, Taft had vacillated in his support of Insurgent Republicans and, by supporting the final bill, had alienated them from the administration. Second, Taft had imprudently adopted a legislative strategy of waiting until the conference committee stage to exert maximum influence when it was, for the most part, too late. Roosevelt undoubtedly would have intervened at an earlier stage to guarantee a better bill or would have publicly threatened Congress with a veto. Third, the President had allied himself too closely in the public mind with Cannon, Aldrich, and the whole crowd of regular Republicans with whom Roosevelt had fallen out in his last years in office. Taft had simply not displayed the political sophistication required for revising the tariff without splitting the party more deeply.

Whether Taft could justly be condemned for having cooperated with the Republican leadership remains an open question. Roosevelt too had been compelled by circumstances to work with the same leaders in his early years in office and had expressed admiration for their ability.[79] Taft cannot be faulted for having come to a similar conclusion in his first year in office. He never wavered in his belief that the "policy of harmony" had been his only choice. "Looking back now on the record of those first few months," he later explained, "I do not see that I could have done otherwise; for however far the results may have fallen short of an ideal standard, it is on the Regular Republicans I have had chiefly to lean for support."[80] Neither Roosevelt nor Taft could alter the built-in antagonisms of a constitutional system which guaranteed perpetual conflict between the executive and legislature. The major differences between the two presidents lay, finally, not in their cooperation with the established leaders, but in the degree of their public identification with them.

The Insurgent Republicans, on the other hand, believed that Taft had broken his campaign promises on the tariff. As the tariff bill had made its way through the legislative maze of the two houses, progressive Republicans led by Senators La Follette, Cummins, Joseph Bristow of Kansas, and Dolliver had increasingly heaped scorn and abuse upon the bill, and eventually upon the President himself. Taft had painfully watched them desert their party and vote against the final bill. Part of their differences with the President lay in the interpretation of the Republican platform. Once Taft had become aware of the dim prospects for a reduced tariff, he began to measure the rates with a yardstick that would help cushion the shock of the final bill. Whereas Taft measured the effects of the bill upon the total amount of goods consumed in the United States, regardless of their origin, the progressives measured the effects of the bill upon the total amount of goods imported into the United States. According to the President, tariff rates could be lowered but not affect importations into the United States and still represent a fulfillment of the party's pledges.[81] The progressive Republicans, inclined toward the free trade doctrines of the Democratic party (except on items of importance to their own states), were bound to object to the token reductions of the Payne-Aldrich Act. This, however, does not mean that the revisions were worthless. The Bureau of Trade Relations, for example, tried to assess the impact of the new law and concluded:

The net result of such a review of the law is to make it evident that when all of the necessities of the situation are considered, the conflicting claims and interests, the former inequalities and incongruities of rates, fairly demanding correction, the necessities of revenue—the new law, while representing a compromise between strong antagonistic forces, and containing the disappointments inevitable in all such compromises, is undoubtedly a distinct advance in the direction of tariff reform and reduction, and is not only to be justified but commended for what it has achieved in that direction.[82]

Regardless of the merits of the Payne-Aldrich Act, the fact remains that Taft was victimized by his own campaign rhetoric. He had led the public and progressive Republicans into believing that there would be a substantial revision of the tariff, reducing duties on total imports. He had aroused public expectations which were too great for him to fulfill under the tariff-making procedures of the Congress.

To counteract the widespread public criticism and misunderstanding of the Payne-Aldrich Act, Taft decided to tour the United States explaining his position. Realizing that the success of his legislative program depended upon the support of the congressional leadership, the President also began to cultivate the good will of those congressional leaders necessary for the enactment of his programs. In Boston he delivered a "gorgeous eulogy" of praise for Senator Aldrich and at Winona, Minnesota, publicly flattered Congressman James A. Tawney, chairman of the House Appropriations Committee.[83] In Montana, he praised Senator Thomas H. Carter, chairman of the Committee on Irrigation and Reclamation of Arid Lands, and concluded his journey with a lavish show of affection for Speaker Cannon. By such deliberate courting, the

President hoped to ensure the success of his legislative program. Taft, of course, needed Tawney's support for his policy of naval expansion and for the creation of a permanent tariff commission. Senator Carter was considered the key to the administration's conservation policies. Aldrich and Cannon were acknowledged powers in Congress whose support was essential for every administration measure. Thus, Taft's policy of harmony had increasingly compelled him to identify himself with the congressional leadership. Privately, he respected Aldrich, tolerated Tawney, despised Carter, and hated Cannon. At the very moment he was praising Cannon to the skies he was plotting with Secretary Knox to secure the Speaker's retirement.[84] Taft's abhorrence of conflict naturally reinforced his own legislative strategy. Persuasion and conciliation rather than open threats remained hallmarks of his political style. His relations with Congress remained deferential, at least formally so, not because Taft held a more limited conception of the presidency than Roosevelt, but because of his belief that, in the long run, such tactics would be more effective. As he later advised Republican House Whip John Dwight, "Always remember that you can catch more flies with molasses than on a club."[85]

The President's open collaboration with the conservative congressional leadership and his support of the Payne-Aldrich Act began to discourage many of his progressive supporters in the West. The Ballinger-Pinchot affair, moreover, added insult to injury to those Republicans who already believed that Taft had betrayed them. When William Dudley Foulke of Indiana heaped scorn upon the President for his association with reactionaries like Cannon and Aldrich, Taft replied with an impassioned defense of his strategy:

During the next three years I expect to be President, if I live at any rate, and during that time I expect to carry out what I believe in, whether it meets the views of those whose friendship I would like or not. The alliance between Mr. Cannon, Senator Aldrich and myself is one of the easy accusations to make; but as I am engaged in trying to lead a party to take up certain measures and pass them, which we have promised to do, I can not avoid the charge of cooperation with those who are in leadership in each House. If those who are very free in their criticism could for a moment in a judicial way put themselves in the position of one charged with responsibility for affirmative action, they might be able to make useful suggestions to help one laboring upon a considerable burden; but the millennium is not reached, and those of us with responsibility must struggle on and do the best we can.[86]

Taft could not afford the luxury of progressive self-righteousness. He had no intention of remaking Congress to his own image and likeness by declaring war on the very men he needed. "I am trying to do the best I can with Congress as it is, and with the Senate as it is," he admitted to critic Lucius B. Swift, "and I am not to be driven by any set of circumstances into an attack upon those who are standing faithfully with me in attempting to redeem the pledges of the party."[87]

The President had expected such attacks upon his methods. As he explained to Mrs. Taft during his nationwide tour,

This disposition to use Roosevelt's reputation and popularity as a club to beat me is not of course very agreeable, but it is something which I might have expected and did expect, but I hope to be able to demonstrate to the country that I am consistent in the course that I am following, and after a while to obtain from a reasonable number of my constituents support because of myself and not because I happened to have adopted anybody else's policies, though the latter of course is the source of my strength at present, and I am quite willing to recognize it.[88]

Taft realized that his "policy of harmony" would not achieve results overnight, but he was willing to weather the temporary

ire of the press, public, and progressives as long as he was ultimately successful. "The muckrakers think Aldrich has captured me," he maintained, "and I think I have captured Aldrich. The results will show which is right."[89]

Criticism of Taft's association with the congressional establishment continued throughout the course of his first two years as president. Even the belated appointments of Fisher and Stimson to the cabinet in 1911 failed to assuage the bitterness that Taft's identification with the leadership had wrought. Roosevelt's rhetorical ability and political expertise had kept him unsullied by his association with such men, but Taft was too principled and consistent to match his predecessor's performance. His cooperative policy had produced merely a draw on the tariff. The regular December session of Congress now presented the acid test for his strategy, a strategy Roosevelt had been forced to abandon in his last years in office.

IV

The December session was fraught with danger for Taft's program. Not only had the special session increased the factionalism within the Republican party, but the Insurgents, particularly in the Senate, had grown personally hostile to Taft for his alleged apostasy from the progressive faith. The continuing struggle within the House against "Cannonism," moreover, threatened to tear the congressional party asunder and render constructive cooperation among Republicans impossible. The outlook for a productive, businesslike session was not bright.

The President was determined to make the most of the session and, in his message of December 7, presented a specific legislative program calling for the redemption of Republican campaign pledges. He placed high priority upon three measures: a law to strengthen the regulatory powers of the Interstate Commerce Commission, a law to create a postal savings bank system, and legislation to legalize the extensive withdrawals of public lands for conservation purposes. Other items on the agenda called for a bill to curb the abuse of injunctions by federal courts in labor-management disputes, enabling legislation to admit Arizona and New Mexico as states, a bill requiring the publicity of campaign contributions and expenditures in congressional elections, the maintenance of Roosevelt's two-battleship policy, and an increase in rates on second-class mail affecting newspapers and magazines. With the surprising exception of the postal rate hike, all of these measures had been promised by Taft and the Republican party in 1908.[90]

The issue of "Cannonism," however, remained a stumbling block for the President. Although Taft publicly had suggested revitalizing the Republican caucus as a decision-making organ of the party, he remained prudently aloof from the Insurgent struggle against Cannon. Once the Speaker had agreed to support the President, Taft discovered that the centralized machinery of the House could be immensely useful in pushing Republican measures through. The Insurgents, on the other hand, did not object as much to the centralized organization of the House as to the reactionary ends for which it had been employed. Since they were not in control of the House machinery, they viewed it as a threat to their progressive objectives.[91]

Despite Taft's support of Cannon and the House rules at the special session, the Insurgents did not give up hope of stripping the Speaker of his extensive powers. On March 17, 1910, through a series of intricate parliamentary maneuvers, Insurgent House leader George W. Norris of Nebraska unexpectedly moved the adoption of a resolution eliminating the power of the Speaker to appoint the Rules Committee and calling for the election of the committee by the House. The

Insurgent move caught Cannon completely off guard. The President, moreover, was trapped away from Washington en route to Chicago. At first, Taft believed that Norris' move had been deliberately timed to prevent Cannon from appealing to the President for assistance. Later he learned that the timing had been determined by the exigencies of the parliamentary situation. Although he was not concerned about the personal fate of the Speaker, Taft did worry about the effects of the conflict upon his legislative program. He wrote to Mrs. Taft:

If this fight in the House results in the humiliation of Cannon and his removal from the Rules Committee, I don't know what may happen in respect to the organization of the House, and whether we can keep a Republican majority sufficiently loyal and disciplined to pass the legislation which we promised. Cannon would feel himself vindicated by a failure to do so. So you see my lot doesn't promise to be a happy one for the next two months. It would please me very much if they could effect a compromise by which the old man should not be eliminated from the Rules Committee even though they enlarge the Rules Committee and allow a number of other Representatives in the House on it.[92]

While Taft made no effort to aid either side, the Insurgent-Democratic alliance broke Cannon's iron grip by adopting the Norris resolution on March 19 by a vote of 191 to 156. Cannon, however, was magnanimously asked to remain as Speaker, thereby assuaging some of his bitterness at the defeat.

The passage of the Norris resolution was the beginning of the end of "Cannonism." The Speaker's powers of recognition were eventually limited, a discharge rule was passed to permit a majority to force bills out of committee, and ultimately the Speaker's power to appoint the standing committees and their chairmen was stripped from him and given to the party caucus.[93] Cannon understandably termed the new

128 *William Howard Taft*

procedures "the recognition of anarchy under the color of law" which would ultimately destroy party government in Congress.[94] The principle of majority rule which Cannon defended, however, had been the majority rule of the majority party. The Insurgent-Democratic coalition, on the other hand, had fought for the principle that a majority of the whole House should be able to rule. The Insurgents, by successfully destroying the centralized power of the Speaker, unwittingly weakened effective party government in the House. Subsequent congresses would pay for the zeal of the progressive reformers. Throughout the course of these internal legislative changes, so momentous for the future of party government in the United States, Taft remained on the sidelines, watchful only over the progress of his legislative program. The President's personal dislike of Cannon and his recognition of the Speaker's waning power dictated a course of prudent silence.

The President, of course, remained concerned about his program. A constant parade of legislators visited the White House during the regular session of the Sixty-first Congress as Taft continued to toil behind the scenes for his objectives. During the regular session, he made no sustained effort to generate public support for himself or his program. Moreover, by March 1910, he had turned his back upon the Insurgents who had begun to obstruct some of his legislative proposals. Taft became convinced that the Insurgents were "determined to be as bitter as they can against the administration, and to defeat everything that the administration seeks." The President, however, refused to abandon his "policy of harmony." "If I can beat them in the legislation I am trying to get, I shall not be at all troubled that they have aligned themselves against me," he admitted to his brother Horace.[95] By opposing much of the President's program, however, the Insurgents continued to furnish the Democrats with ammunition against the administration for the approaching mid-term congressional elections.

As the session progressed, Taft began to call in political debts from the congressional leadership whom he had been deliberately courting. After persuading the reluctant Speaker to work for Roosevelt's two-battleships-a-year policy, the President appealed to Tawney, an inveterate opponent of naval expansion, for help in implementing this policy and for funds to strengthen the tariff board created by the Payne-Aldrich Act. Although Taft could use no "club" on a powerful legislator like Tawney without jeopardizing his whole program, he was able to wheedle the battleships and the tariff board funds out of the old chairman.[96]

However, Taft could crack the whip over recalcitrant legislators under the right circumstances. When Senator Julius C. Burrows of Michigan, anxious for the President's help in his campaign for reelection, phoned to inform the President one day that he might vote with the Insurgents against an administration amendment to the postal savings bank Bill, Taft angrily told the senator over the phone that his reasons were "a mere excuse." "I thought you were an Administration Senator," the President asked. "I am an Administration Senator," replied Burrows, "but—." "There is no 'but' in it," retorted the President angrily. "The way to be an Administration Senator is to vote with the Administration." And while Burrows was trying to explain, the President hung up.[97]

When he held the upper hand, Taft had no compunction about using pressure for his own purposes. Since he was more of a liability to Republican congressmen than they were to him, however, Taft generally could not afford to use desk-pounding tactics even if he desired to. The "policy of harmony" limited the tactics he could employ to attract congressional support. Had Teft cultivated personal popularity more as an end in itself rather than as a fortuitous by-product of his accomplishments, he might have been able to pressure vulnerable legislators more frequently. Since few legislators desired to be identified with a losing cause, Taft usually found that threats were less effective upon them than the more subtle techniques of flattery, persuasion, or appeals to party unity.

Chances of passing the President's program were not as hopeless as the press would have it. Early in March, Taft wrote to his brother Horace, "The situation in Congress is uncertain, but with the assistance of my wicked partners, Cannon and Aldrich, I am hopeful that I can pull off the legislation that I have most at heart."[98] Prospects for success brightened considerably in June. When twenty-five western railroads filed 20-per-cent rate increases with the Interstate Commerce Commission to avoid the pending regulatory provisions of the Mann-Elkins bill, Taft immediately instructed Wickersham to invoke the Sherman Act against them. After extensive consultations with the attorney general and representatives of the railroads, the President, in return for a temporary suspension of the increase, promised the railroads to support an amendment to the bill giving the I.C.C. immediate jurisdiction over the proposed rate hikes.[99] This compromise satisfied the railroads.

Public support of the administration improved dramatically. Whereas the press had been highly critical of Taft, they now began to praise his leadership in the railroad controversy. According to the press, the prospects for congressional action on the President's program had begun to brighten. Senator Chauncey Depew of New York expressed his amazement at the overnight transformation of opinion. "Never in my acquaintance with administrations have I seen such a change for the better as has occurred in the last four weeks for Taft," he wrote to Root. Although Taft could count on "no reliable administrative majority in either House, within a few days the President had a firm majority in both Houses." "The whole atmosphere of the Capitol," Depew continued, "was charged with the idea that the people were behind President Taft as they had been behind Roosevelt and that it was exceedingly dangerous to defeat his program, or any part of it."[100] The Washington correspondent of the *New York Tribune*, George Hill, acknowledged also that "No more sudden or remarkable change of sentiment has been witnessed at the national capital within the memory of the oldest legislators than that which has occurred during the last two weeks."[101] Taft's stand against the railroads had captured the imagination of the press, which had succeeded in creating the impression that public opinion was strongly behind the President. What few people realized is that Taft had been relatively confident that the congressional leaders would deliver on his high priority bills. He was able to capitalize upon superficial public support only because the preliminary spade work had already been done to put his bills in shape for final action. In other words, the presidential victory over the western railroads provided an added impetus to the President's bills which were already on their way toward final passage.

Although Taft had worked intensively behind the scenes for his program, his leadership surfaced in the final stages of the legislative process as amendments were offered or deleted and as conference committees ironed out the differences between House and Senate bills. For example, when progressive Republicans succeeded in sending a rather strong railroad bill (the Mann-Elkins Act) to conference, Taft openly pressed his views upon the conferees. He fought to make the bill effective immediately to accord with his agreement with the western railroads. He sought to have railroad stocks and bonds regulated by the I.C.C. and to reduce the commission's power to delay cases from ten to six months. Although he failed to delete a provision allowing the I.C.C. to suspend rate increases for up to eleven months, he emerged from the conference committee with a stronger bill. Taft gladly signed the Mann-Elkins Act, which embodied one of the most important Roosevelt policies to which he had been pledged.[102]

When an Insurgent-Democratic coalition of senators, led by Senator Albert B. Cummins of Iowa, attempted to filibuster the postal savings bank bill in the closing days of the session, Taft moved quickly to save the measure. He sent for the Senate leaders and informed them that he would "think nothing" of staying in Washington until December to break the filibuster rather than be defeated by, in his own words, "irresponsible insurgents" who had nothing better to offer by way of opposition than "a contemptible little grouch." He also made it clear that he was opposed to any amendments which would delay passage of the bill and reaffirmed his commitment to the measure as one of his "highest duties" as party leader. He also called in a number of senators inclined to support the filibuster and persuaded them to back the administration's bill. When the senators returned to the capitol, they spread the word that "the old man had blood in his eye," and that was enough to break the filibuster. In addition, Taft dispatched personal telegrams that evening to all absent senators likely to support the bill and requested their presence and support for the final vote.[103] With the filibuster dead, the Senate fell into line and voted 44 to 25 for the House bill, with only insurgents Cummins, La Follette, and Bristow voting with the Democrats against the bill. Taft was very pleased with his legislative success so far. He confided to Otto Bannard:

The truth is that the leaders of the House and the Senate did not intend to pass either bill, and would not have done so if I had not made a fuss about it and insisted and I think you will find they will admit—certainly Aldrich does—that they were not in favor of either bill and only passed it because I urged it upon them.[104]

The President's legislative strategy had finally begun to pay off.

As the legislative log jam began to break, Taft was confronted with the unexpected issue of whether labor unions should be exempted from the Sherman Act. He responded clumsily. The House had attached an amendment to a minor housekeeping bill prohibiting the use of funds to enforce the Sherman Act against labor unions. The President immediately summoned Congressman Tawney and a group of other congressmen to breakfast to urge the defeat of the amendment. Although not openly threatening a veto, the President explained that he wanted the amendment deleted, even "if it cost him the support of every laboring man in the country."[105] Instead of waiting for the Senate to strike out the amendment in conference (the Senate was known to be strongly opposed to it), Taft denounced the labor exemption in a public letter to the president of the Brotherhood of Locomotive Firemen and Engineers:

I am entirely opposed to such class legislation. If it were proposed to amend the language of the Sherman anti-trust law itself so as somewhat to narrow its scope, that would present a proper question for consideration, but so long as the present anti-trust law remains upon the statute books an attempt to modify its enforcement so as to render immune any particular class of citizens, rich or poor, employers or employees, is improper legislation and, in my judgment, ought to be opposed by your brotherhood. The laboring man and the trades-unionist . . . asks only equality before the law. Class legislation and unequal privilege, though expressly in his favor, will in the end work no benefit to him or to society.[106]

Here was the President, who allegedly never looked for a

fight, wading in to do battle with labor over an issue which he could have avoided by merely stiffening the backs of the Senate conferees. Despite the warnings of his cabinet and personal friends, according to George Hill, he "could see no reason why he should not take a decided stand against legislation that was bad." Hill described Taft's behavior as "at least reckless."[107] But when labor was involved, the former injunction judge could not hold his tongue.

By the time Congress adjourned on June 25, the Republican congressional machine in the House and Senate had ground out virtually all of the President's legislative program, and then some. Taft's conservation bill validating the withdrawal of public lands which Roosevelt had authorized by executive order was passed along with a $20 million bond issue for the Reclamation Service for irrigation projects already undertaken in the West. Funds for two new battleships and the tariff board were appropriated. Secretary of the Navy Meyer's reorganization plans were approved. Even Taft's proposal for publicizing campaign contributions and expenditures was enacted. The only important party pledge which was not redeemed was the antiinjunction bill. Taft's controversial call to eliminate the magazine subsidy, however, was sidetracked until after the November elections. Although threatening to veto a similar measure in the future, Taft reluctantly signed a "pork barrel" river and harbors bill out of gratitude to the numerous congressmen who had stood loyally by him.[108]

Barring only the 1889–1890 and 1905 sessions, the legislative session was the most successful since the Civil War. According to the *New York Tribune*, "The lions share of the credit for what was accomplished must go to the President."[109] Uncle Joe Cannon also expressed satisfaction with the work of the Congress. He issued a press statement condemning the muckrakers and praising the record of the session:

The work of this Congress has been greater than any with which I have been identified as a member, and it has been constructive legislation in the face of destructive tactics and efforts to create factional strife. These efforts, I regret to say, have received more attention in the public press than the real work of legislation, and, having given so much space to these revolutionary efforts at the expense of the record of work, it is not surprising that some of the editors should suddenly discover in the last days that the Republican Congress has enacted laws to carry out the pledges of the Republican platform.[110]

Taft's sentiments were quite similar. Although he occasionally had doubts about the wisdom of his policy of harmony, his legislative victories banished them. "I did this greatly to the surprise of the country," he wrote to his brother Charles, "which had been led to believe by correspondents who could not see beyond their noses, and by other correspondents who were anxious to defeat the purposes of the national administration, that nothing would be accomplished."[111] The legislative results showed indeed that Taft had chosen the only realistic strategy open to him.

v

As substantial as the Taft accomplishments were, they failed to alter those deep tides of public opinion which were reflected in the congressional elections of November 1910. Despite Roosevelt's return from Africa and his subsequent campaigning for Republicans across the country, nothing could save the party from the effects of the Payne-Aldrich tariff, the Ballinger-Pinchot row, the President's close association with the congressional leadership, and a year of bad press. The House went Democratic for the first time in sixteen years by a sixty-eight-vote majority, 228 Democrats to 160 Republicans. Although the Republicans still retained control of the Senate 51 to 40, they lost eight important seats. The pronounced mid-term swing of the pendulum toward the Democratic party presaged a Republican defeat in 1912.

With a Democratic House in the offing, Taft's only chance to complete his legislative program lay in the short lame duck session which convened in December 1910. The President decided to place top priority on securing congressional approval of a reciprocity agreement negotiated with Canada which drastically lowered trade barriers between the two nations. The reciprocity agreement had been conceived by Taft as part of his long-range policy of trade expansion and had been secured by Knox and the State Department through secret negotiations. The President and the Canadian Prime Minister, Sir Wilfred Laurier, both pledged to recommend to their respective legislatures tariff rates which they had mutually agreed upon. The agreement had the same legal standing as any ordinary tariff bill and did not require the two-thirds Senate majority of a conventional treaty. (The use of an executive agreement implemented by statute was rather unusual for an allegedly Whig president.) On January 26, 1911, Taft presented the Congress with the agreement which called basically for freer trade on agricultural products of the West and mid-West in return for sizable tariff reductions on manufactured exports from the East.[112] It was hardly a proposal designed to heal the growing rift between the President and the western progressives.

Taft was acutely aware of the explosive nature of the agreement, but decided to press on with it to fulfill his campaign promise of tariff reform and also mitigate criticism of the high Payne-Aldrich rates. Having already fought a costly, indecisive battle for tariff revision in his first year, Taft realized that the agreement would open up old political wounds and possibly split the party further. "I think it may break the Republican party for a while," he confessed to Roosevelt. To Otto Bannard, he was even more blunt:

My judgment before I sent in the message (and even now it hasn't changed), was that this will blow me up politically, but I think that ultimately there will come a realization that it will help the country; and the question of parties is not quite so important, and still less the question of personal political fortunes.

Roosevelt shared Taft's hopes of securing approval of the agreement in spite of its effects on the party:

It seems to me that what you propose to do with Canada is admirable from every standpoint. I firmly believe in Free Trade with Canada for both economic and political reasons. As you say, labor cost is substantially the same in the two countries so that you are amply justified by the platform. Whether Canada will accept such reciprocity I do not know, but it is greatly to your credit to make the effort. It may damage the Republican Party for a while, but it will surely benefit the party in the end, especially if you tackle wool, cotton, etc as you propose.[113]

Like Roosevelt, Taft believed that the long-range political and economic considerations involved in the agreement would far outweigh the temporary political disadvantages to the party or himself. He saw the agreement as "a great step toward a commercial union with Canada" which had to be grasped while the opportunity existed. He described Reciprocity to Senator William O. Bradley of Kentucky as "the most important measure" of his administration.[114]

With time running out on the lame duck session, the President had to work quickly. He beseeched Congressman Payne, chairman of the Ways and Means Committee, to lend his personal prestige to the agreement by sponsoring it in the House. He was forced, however, to settle for Congressman Samuel McCall because of Payne's opposition. Taft continued to prod

Payne to hold an "early hearing" on the bill regardless of his personal opinions on the issue. When Payne responded by reporting the bill to the House, Taft then exerted pressure upon the unsympathetic John Dalzell, chairman of the Rules Committee, to issue a rule for the bill immediately.[115] Taft's lobbying behind the scenes paid off in quick House passage of the bill on February 14 by a vote of 221 to 92. Eighty-seven Republicans deserted the administration to vote against the bill. Only 78 supported it. The Democrats voted overwhelmingly 143 to 5 in favor of the agreement.

Prospects for action in the Senate appeared uncertain. The most serious difficulty Taft faced in the upper House was a lack of leadership capable of filling Senator Aldrich's shoes. Aldrich, whose assistance would have been invaluable as the chairman of the Senate Finance Committee and majority leader, had left the Senate to recuperate from illness and fatigue. The task of Republican leadership fell to standpatter Eugene Hale of Maine, who strongly opposed reciprocity. The President was consequently forced to work with Senators Root, Lodge, and Crane to push his bill through. He sought, however, any support the ailing Aldrich could give. "How I wish you were here, to lead the confused and dazed members of your body," he wrote Aldrich. "A blast upon your bugle was worth a thousand men." Taft tried to persuade the Republican leader to support the agreement, arguing that if the agreement were not adopted, "I feel sure we are going to be beaten in the next presidential election and then the Democracy without restrain will play havoc with our industries and create chaos in business from which we shall be a long time recovering." Taft's appeal for support was met by Aldrich's subsequent public endorsement of the agreement.[116] With Aldrich's support, Taft was able to get the agreement out of the hostile Senate Finance Committee even though the committee did not endorse it.[117]

Realizing that reciprocity might be sidetracked in the closing moments of the session by his own party, Taft began to
issue veiled threats of calling a special session of the new
Congress. He bluntly warned Senator Theodore E. Burton:

If I find . . . that the movement is defeated by men who change
their views, as they have given them to me, then I will call an
extra session at any rate, even if the reciprocity agreement is
beaten; because I will have six more votes in the next Senate, and
the American people are entitled to a vote on the merits, which
shall not be affected by the personal engagements of Senators
for going abroad or for any other purpose than their legislative
duties.[118]

Few Republicans took the President seriously. They scoffed
at the notion that a president would commit political suicide
by calling a Democratic House into session to harass his own
administration nine months sooner than necessary.[119] Taft,
however, conferred with Democratic House leaders Champ
Clark and ranking Democratic member of the Ways and
Means Committee Oscar W. Underwood, who acknowledged
that they would pass the reciprocity agreement at a special
session as well as, in Clark's words, "any other bills that we
thought proper, including tariff bills."[120] By the time startled
Republicans realized the seriousness of the President's threat,
their opportunity to force a vote on reciprocity had slipped
by. When Republican legislators protested against the calling
of a special session, the President replied, "I do not care a
tinker's dam whether it injures my political prospects or not."
When informed that the agreement was economically un-
sound, Taft retorted: "It may be economically rotten. But I
regard it as good statesmanship."[121] Amid bitterness, frustra-
tion, and filibuster, Congress adjourned on March 4 without
action on the bill. Taft immediately called for a special session
of the Sixty-second Congress to meet on April 4. He was not

to be thwarted so easily, even in the face of extensive opposition by his party.

Presidential lobbying became even more feverish at the special session as Taft tried to rally his disintegrating party behind the agreement. Recognizing the importance of the Senate Finance Committee to his success, the President tried to prevent his enemies from being appointed to the committee. He was angered by Republican leader Hale's "devilish ingenuity" and "utter lack of decency" in attempting to have both La Follette and Cummins, avowed opponents of the agreement, appointed to the committee. Taft appealed to the retired Aldrich for help. "I sincerely hope," he wrote, "that you will confer with Penrose and with other leaders of the regulars to see to it that that committee shall have some friends of reciprocity on it, and that the finance committee shall not be surrendered entirely to the insurgents and Bailey."¹²² Taft's appeal was partly successful, for Cummins was prevented from being appointed to the committee by the regular Republicans.¹²³

The President had carefully counted his votes in the new Congress and worked hard to assure that his support would not evaporate. When Senator George P. Wetmore of Rhode Island, for example, wavered in his allegiance, Taft appealed to Aldrich to do what he could to secure the senator's vote. The President noted that "with the proper measures, we can get reciprocity through the House and the Senate, and defeat either in the Senate or by veto any improper tariff legislation." Taft believed he could muster a majority in the Senate to eliminate all tariff amendments to the agreement and "compel the treatment and consideration of the tariff revision separately."¹²⁴ His calculations proved to be correct.

Taft's leadership extended beyond the influencing of committee assignments and lobbying; he also tried the subtle method of stimulating "grass roots" sentiment. At the personal invitation of the President, Democratic Senator Augustus O. Bacon of Georgia accompanied Taft on one of his speaking trips to New York City. En route, Bacon had explained that the Democrats strongly desired to link the so-called "farmer's free list" bill to the reciprocity bill in the Senate in order to guarantee a vote on the free list bill, a tactic Taft believed would have killed both measures. Taft suggested that, rather than see both measures defeated, the Democrats move to discharge the free list bill from the Finance Committee and, in that manner, force a vote on the bill. He then explained his predicament to Governor Hoke Smith of Georgia and asked his assistance on behalf of reciprocity. "May I not ask you to write Senator Bacon and present the matter to him in this light?" wrote Taft. "I would like to have this view get into the newspapers so as to influence our Democratic friends," he added. "I should like to reach the Atlanta newspapers and have them take the same view, but I do not know exactly how to do it." Presumably Smith did. Then, adding a personal touch to his appeal, the President included a letter of introduction for the governor's daughters instructing American embassy officials to show them every courtesy on their European trip.[125]

The President needed all the "grass roots" support he could muster for his agreement, for the Insurgents, heartened by their defeat of reciprocity in the Sixty-first Congress, had regrouped for the second, more difficult battle at the special session. Opposed to the Payne-Aldrich Act because it had not reduced tariff rates enough, the Insurgents now objected to reciprocity with Canada because it lowered tariffs on agricultural goods too much. Taft found his Insurgent opponents from the West increasingly "desperate" to prevent the passage of the bill, while his congressional maneuvering floundered for lack of able Republican leadership in Congress:

I labor under very serious disadvantage in not having any very earnest supporter to take the lead. Some of my supporters disgust me more than I can say. Lodge never misses an opportunity to say things that heap ridicule on the bill, and even Root prophesies great political disaster to those who are supporting the bill, although he is going to support it.[126]

Nevertheless, the President remained confident that he had the votes to pass the bill.

When criticism of the agreement continued from the lumber, paper, and agricultural interests of the country, Taft launched a counterattack. In major speeches in New York and Chicago, he explained the need for reciprocity and bitterly criticized the vested interests opposing his bill. "This seems to have been taken with a good deal of anger by certain gentlemen who are opposed to the bill," Taft later noted, "but I can not help it—I have to talk out—and while I will be hammered on the floor of the Senate, I am content to leave the matter to the public if only we can secure enough votes to pass the bill."[127]

Heedless of immediate political consequences, Taft doggedly pursued his goal of reciprocity. When representatives of the National Grange trooped to the White House to protest against the impending economic disaster from the bill, Taft courteously listened to their complaints but exploded after they had left:

Their daring to come to me and threaten me with their miserable votes! I want this country to know that I will do nothing I do not think to be right if my reelection depends on it. We must all play politics, and I am willing to play my part so long as it does not involve any sacrifice of principle, but there my politics ends.[128]

Such opposition to the agreement only forced the President to increase his feverish pace of persuading, cajoling, flattering, and encouraging his legislative forces for the final vote. When friends expressed anxiety over his pace of work, Taft brushed aside their concern. "I have done so," he explained, "because I am determined to leave no stone unturned in an effort to secure the approval of the reciprocity measure. It is one of the most important pieces of legislation that has been under consideration in a decade, and the opportunity to make this favorable trade agreement will have passed, probably forever, if we do not strike at this time."[129]

The best testimonial to the President's effectiveness in marshaling his legislative strength came from former Speaker Cannon, who found it necessary to condemn openly the secrecy under which the agreement had been negotiated and the steamroller tactics of the President in pushing the bill through Congress. "I have so voted in the past and God helping me," he cried on the floor of the House, "I shall so vote in the future, according to my judgment, whatever Presidents may recommend. His duty is to veto my action, not to dictate it before it reaches him."[130] But Cannon's desperate stand against presidential leadership and the agreement failed. On April 21, the House passed the bill by an overwhelming vote of 265 to 89. One hundred ninety-seven Democrats combined with a mere 67 Republicans for the bill, while a majority of the Republicans (78) voted against the measure. On July 22, under continuing threats from Taft to remain in Washington all summer long until reciprocity was passed, the Senate finally approved the measure 53 to 27. Twenty-one Republicans voted for the bill, twenty-four were opposed. The Democrats overwhelmingly supported the measure 23 to 3.

Taft had achieved his most significant legislative victory of the Sixty-second Congress, and possibly of his whole presidency, with the majority of his party aligned against him. His prediction that the measure would temporarily "break" the party had been prophetic. Nevertheless, he signed the agreement on July 23 and praised it as marking "a new epoch" in Canadian-American relations. With an eye upon the Democratic majority in the House and their increased strength in the Senate, he expressed gratitude to the Democratic party:

> In a sense, the bill passed was a non-partisan measure, though the Republicans who voted for it, probably did so, on one economic theory, and the Democrats who voted for it, on another. I should be wanting in straightforward speaking, however, if I did not freely acknowledge the credit that belongs to the Democratic majority in the House, and the Democratic minority in the Senate for their consistent support of the measure, in an earnest and sincere desire to secure its passage. Without this, reciprocity would have been impossible. It would not have been difficult for them to fasten upon the bill amendments affecting the tariff generally in such a way as to embarrass the Executive, and to make it doubtful whether he could sign the bill, and yet to claim popular approval for their support of reciprocity in its defeat. In other words, the Democrats did not "play politics," in the colloquial sense in which these words are used, but they followed the dictate of a higher policy.[131]

The high praise for the Democrats contrasted sharply with the President's deliberate silence about his own party, which had deserted him.

The anticipated benefits of reciprocity, however, were never realized because of internal Canadian politics. The Liberal government of Sir Wilfred Laurier, forced to dissolve Parliament over reciprocity, was defeated at the polls on September 21 by the Conservative party, which had raised the specter of American annexation of Canada as a major campaign issue. The President was literally stunned by the Liberal defeat, for it dashed his hopes for eventual economic union with Canada. "We were hit squarely between the eyes," he confessed to his brother Horace, "and must now sit tight."[132] Taft's dream of a free trade area encompassing all of North America was shattered. The defeat was a blow to the President's place in history. Nothing remained from the reciprocity battle but a demoralized and embittered Republican party.

VI

The short lame duck session of the Sixty-first Congress also brought defeat to other elements of the President's program. Although the construction of two more new battleships and plans to fortify the Panama Canal were approved by the Congress along with a crucial Japanese-American commercial treaty, Taft's plans for a permanent tariff board and an increase in second-class postal rates on magazines and newspapers were lost in the closing rush of the session.[133]

One of the President's most cherished aims was to see a tariff board created that would take tariff-making out of legislative politics. Such a board would gather evidence regarding the cost of goods produced at home and abroad, thereby making tariff adjustments more scientific. Taft had signed the Payne-Aldrich Act partly because it had created a temporary tariff board. Desiring to make the board permanent, Taft persuaded Congressman Nicholas Longworth, Roosevelt's son-in-law, to introduce the administration's bill creating a permanent board of five members with extensive powers of investigation. The President cautioned Senator Lodge against introducing a similar measure simultaneously so that the Longworth bill would not be jeopardized. "Afterward there is no objection to your introducing a bill, if you desire," the President explained to Lodge, "but I think it would be unwise to have you and him introduce the same bill at the same time. It would be regarded as an administration matter, and would weaken the whole case, in my judgment."[134] Taft was worried that the Insurgents might oppose the bill if they felt it had originated in the White House. In explaining his interest in the Longworth bill to Congressman William A. Calderhead of Kansas, a member of the Ways and Means Committee, Taft maintained, "This is not the Administration bill, because the Administration has no bill. It is a bill, I understand, whch has been drafted by Congressman Longworth after a conference with a good many different elements in respect to the bill."[135] Taft had to soft-peddle his role in the drafting of the measure to prevent its defeat.

Although the Longworth bill died as the clock ran out on the session, an additional $225,000 was appropriated to aid the temporary board to continue its inquiries into the Payne-Aldrich rates. With the added funds, Taft appointed two more members to the three-man board, both Democrats, in the hope that this display of belated nonpartisanship might reconcile the Democrats to a permanent board. Later the President was very disappointed when the new Congress eliminated the tariff board altogether by refusing to appropriate funds for its continuance.[136] Tariff-making would remain the special preserve of the legislature for some time to come.

The President's third major defeat at the lame duck session occurred when the magazine publishers, through a concerted lobbying effort, forced the President to postpone his proposed raise in second-class postal rates. In a temporary about face, Taft was forced to compromise with the publishers and support an amendment to the Post Office bill calling for a judicial inquiry into the merits of the whole issue. The House, however, rejected the President's proposed amendment which Taft had negotiated with the publishers. When news of the House action reached the President at 3:00 A.M. on the day of adjournment, he immediately sent for Congressman John A. Moon of Tennessee, who had just forced the amendment out of the postal bill, and asked him to reconsider his action. The two men quickly worked out an agreement whereby

Taft would visit the congressman's district on his behalf if Moon could get the amendment back into the bill. Although this proved impossible in the rush for adjournment, Moon successfully sponsored a joint resolution calling for the creation of a commission to investigate postal rates which achieved the same objective. The President eventually abandoned the postal rate increase as he became more sensitive to the requirements of a good press.[137]

The fourth presidential defeat at the lame duck session came on the seating of Senator William Lorimer of Indiana. When charges of fraud and corruption in Lorimer's election in 1908 were raised, Taft decided to try to unseat the senator. He could not sit idly by and see the office of United States senator purchased, especially when the senator was of little help to the administration. Since the disciplining of a senator was an internal legislative matter, the President had to work very carefully behind the scenes to exert influence. He called in Senators Root, Theodore E. Burton of Ohio, Knute Nelson of Minnesota, Coe Crawford of South Dakota, and William E. Borah, among others, and quietly encouraged them to work for the ouster of Lorimer. "I am doing everything I properly can do in this Lorimer business," he admitted privately. "I believe we are going to win, but I can not take an open stand on the subject for the reason that it would be regarded as executive interference, and I do not wish to transfer the issue from one simply of corruption to that of the prerogative of the Senate and Executive usurpation." Although Taft had quietly encouraged Republican senators to deliver speeches against Lorimer, news of his behind-the-scenes activities began to leak out. "I fear that it has not helped the situation generally," Taft wrote to Roosevelt, "because of that strong feeling of clubdom in the Senate and that resentment against outside interference which nobody who is not intimately acquainted with the situation can understand the weight of."

Taft consequently urged Roosevelt to refrain from publishing an article on Lorimer until the Senate had aired the issues in debate. He had no desire to see Lorimer's supporters "shift the subject from the tainted character of his seat to the independence of the Senate in acting as judge of the qualifications of its own members."[138]

Taft was unsuccessful in depriving the Senator of his seat. On March 1, 1911, the Senate voted 46 to 40 to uphold Lorimer when eleven Democrats remained unconvinced of the charges against him. It was not until July 1912 that the Senate finally unseated Lorimer by a vote of 55 to 28.[139] Roosevelt might have ignored charges of "executive usurpation" and spoken out against Lorimer to dramatize his opposition to corruption in government, but Taft's reputation as President had fallen so low that his public opposition to a United States senator would have been self-defeating.

VII

The special session of the Sixty-second Congress, which convened on April 4, 1911, promised only headaches for the President. Sensing victory in 1912, Democrats were in no mood to cooperate with the troubled President except, as in the reciprocity struggle, where they could indirectly contribute to Republican troubles. The Democrats sought to embarrass the administration by instituting numerous congressional investigations. Taft noted that twenty-five House committees were "engaged in minute muckraking" in an attempt to pull down the tottering Republican regime.[140] In addition, the Democratic-Insurgent coalition had decided to pass a number of low tariff bills for the purpose of, according to Taft, "putting me in a hole."[141] Even the Republican-controlled Senate could offer little resistance to the passage of such bills in the face of the coalition. "We hold on by our teeth there," Taft confessed to the retired Aldrich, "and then our hold is not very secure."¹⁴² Despite the administration's lack of a firm majority in either house, Taft was determined not to bend to the political pressures generated by the Insurgent-Democratic opposition. "I am here with a veto to prevent any foolishness," he explained to his brother Horace.¹⁴³

Vetoing Democratic tariff bills was not a question of political expediency or popularity for the President: it was a question of his continued commitment to tariff revision by means of a tariff commission. Although the reciprocity agreement had been negotiated without the benefit of the "scientific" findings of a tariff board, the President would accept no further revisions until the tariff board had concluded its studies of the Payne-Aldrich Act. Progressives in Congress had also been committed to the principle of "scientific" revision, but when an opportunity to reduce rates on items of interest to their constituents in the West arose, they abandoned their position to cooperate with the Democrats on a number of bills. When the coalition sent him three major low tariff bills —a so-called farmer's free list bill revising tariffs on farm implements and assorted commodities, a tariff on wool and woolens, and a bill on cotton textiles, chemicals, and steel—Taft vetoed all three without hesitation. After his veto of the second bill, he wrote to his brother Charles, "I can not see how I can do otherwise than to kill them, if I am to be consistent or to live up to any standard which I have advocated."¹⁴⁴ Although many Republicans, Insurgents and Regulars alike, felt that the President would not act on the recommendations of the tariff board, Taft was determined to live up to his promises. He would make specific recommendations, he explained to Otto Bannard, and

then we can watch and see what the Insurgents and Democrats will do about it. My stand pat friends may look aghast and think

I have gone back on them. But such experience would not be new, for I find that most of the world would wake up with surprise and indignation to find me attempting to keep my promises, the making of which they fully approved but solely for political purposes.[145]

When railroad financier James J. Hill expressed concern over the public repercussions of the President's expected veto of the wool tariff bill, Taft brushed the advice aside:

I can not help what the public think,—I am not going to injure the industries of this country by cutting down the tariff that is needed to protect them, and I don't care whether it hurts me or not. I have the responsibility of protecting them, and I am going to do that. If the people of the country want to go into the business of destroying the industries, why they can do it through some other President than me.[146]

Taft was determined to be consistent in his policy of securing tariff revision according to the standards—imperfect as they might be—laid down by the tariff board, and no threat of personal political disaster could make him change his mind.

The President, however, was willing to help draft legislation in accord with the tariff board recommendations, even if that meant breaking a few precedents regarding traditional executive-legislative relations. When he learned that it might be possible to call a formal executive-legislative conference to break the impasse over pending tariff legislation, he quickly made soundings through Senators Root and Lodge on the matter.

I observe there is some suggestion that possibly tariff legislation might be agreed upon between the Executive and the two Houses of Congress if a conference was had. On the other hand, I observe that objection is made to such a conference, on the ground that it violates precedents. I write to say to you that I do not feel that such a resolution would violate any precedent that has been clearly established, or that it would be a precedent that would be detrimental. Should the Houses of Congress see fit to take the course suggested, I should be very much gratified to meet the representatives whom they would send.[147]

Although the congressional resolution calling for a formal conference between the legislature and the executive was never passed, Taft's offer of cooperation symbolized his deep desire to break down the barriers between the legislative and executive branches of government. One of Taft's last serious recommendations to Congress was his proposal to give cabinet members seats in both houses of the legislature with the right to introduce bills and to speak or be questioned about any issue arising before Congress. "It was never intended," the President maintained, "that they should be separated in the sense of not being in constant effective touch and relationship to each other. The legislative and the executive each performs its own appropriate function, but these functions must be coordinated."[148] Although by no means novel, Taft's proposal was an attempt to introduce some of the advantages of the British cabinet system into the United States without really tipping the constitutional balance of power between the executive and legislative branches. Taft had come to realize that personal persuasion and intensive socializing could not bridge the gap between the two branches of government, and that new machinery was necessary to coordinate the growing responsibilities of the two branches.

The deadlock between Taft and the badly divided Sixty-second Congress produced little significant legislation. The major controversies centered on tariff bills, financial conventions with Nicaragua and Honduras, arbitration treaties with France and England, ship subsidies, and the Panama Canal Act. The treaties along with the ship subsidies were scuttled by congressmen suspicious of the administration's "Dollar Diplomacy."[149] Although a Children's Bureau and an Industrial Bureau were established, parcel post and federal corrupt practices acts passed, and the Food and Drugs Act strengthened, the legislative session was a disaster for the President, who failed to place his personal stamp upon any major piece of legislation. The absence of strong, centralized Republican leadership in both Houses and Democratic control of the House produced a stalemate between the two branches. No wonder Taft grew melancholy as he viewed the indecisiveness, bitterness, and tactical blundering of the 1912 session:

When we lost Aldrich and Hale and the old leaders in the Senate and the House, we then only came to understand what leadership meant. Now we have no leaders, and, with the exception of a dozen in each House, all the rest are mediocre, poor things, indicating a day of small things and a transition period to another when I hope men will be larger.[150]

The President was merely lamenting the de facto shift of power from the rather centralized party organizations under Cannon, and to some extent Aldrich, to numerous committee chairmen. Eventually, the decentralization of power in the legislature would pave the way for presidential dominance of the legislative process. Taft's varied legislative tactics, though not always effective, had already become customary thanks to the precedent-shattering performance of his predecessor. As Roosevelt had also shown, presidential leadership would increasingly require more direct appeals to the public for legislative support, something which Taft had learned too late.

When the Sixty-second Congress adjourned on March 4, 1913, it was remembered more for what it had not done than for its accomplishments. No major tariff bills had been passed over the President's vetoes. None of the financial or arbitration treaties crucial to Taft's foreign policies had been approved by the Senate. Although Arizona and New Mexico had been admitted as new states and the Panama Canal Act had been passed, no landmark legislation stood out for succeeding generations to remember and praise. Only the reciprocity agreement with Canada remained as a silent reminder of what might have been.

5. "The Discipline of Defeat"

The Republican party needs the discipline of defeat.
William Howard Taft,
July 14, 1912[1]

Had William Howard Taft been elected to office in a tranquil period of American history, his record as president and party leader would probably have compared favorably with those of most other presidents. It was his misfortune to have been elected in a period of rising social protest—the progressive era. Public-spirited citizens, journalists, public officials, and office-seekers had begun to recognize the growing threat to representative democracy posed by the increasing power and wealth of corporate America. They called for increased public regulation of corporate activities and advocated such reforms as direct primary, direct election of senators, woman suffrage, and the initiative, referendum, and recall, believing that the best cure for the ills of democracy was a stronger dose of it. Theodore Roosevelt had recognized the growing, sometimes hysterical sentiment for change and had tried to defuse the extremism of the progressives by preaching moderate reform of American economic and political institutions. He was so successful that, upon his retirement from the presidency, he left the nation ready for a burst of creative reform and a new crusader. Instead, he gave the country Taft.

The task of maintaining a united and effective party was far more difficult for Taft than it had been for Roosevelt. Personal and ideological divisions among Republicans had grown wider during the party's long reign and had been exacerbated by the influx of progressive reformers. The growing progressive movement forced the President and his party to reckon deeply with their conscience in deciding their future course of action. Given the intensely ideological nature of progressive doctrines and the President's reverence for the Constitution, conflict between Taft and the Insurgents was inevitable. At first, the President tried to work with both the congressional leadership and the progressives, but soon aligned himself with the leadership on the tariff. By the spring of 1910 an embittered President had decided to purge the party of Insurgent leaders through the use of patronage and by encouraging opposition to them in primary elections. When the attempt failed, Taft quickly reversed himself, but too late to salvage the November 1910 elections. Finally, when Theodore Roosevelt sought to capture the Republican nomination in 1912, Taft decided to rid the party of extreme progressives in order to maintain the party as a sanctuary for sound constitutional principles. As he grappled with these internal party problems, it became increasingly evident that he had been ill equipped to inherit Roosevelt's mantle of party leadership.

I

The manner in which Taft was selected as the Republican nominee in 1908 guaranteed trouble for the party. As we have already noted, the function of the American political convention—the selection of a candidate with the political skills and personality that are needed by the nation—was frustrated by Roosevelt's strong support for Taft. Had Roosevelt remained truly neutral regarding a successor, the Republican party might have turned to a candidate with the skill and determination necessary to win broad convention support on his own, perhaps Charles Evans Hughes. Roosevelt knew well that Taft looked out "too little for his own interests" and would be apt to lose to more determined and self-interested candidates. Although Roosevelt had once criticized Andrew Jackson for hand-picking Martin Van Buren as a successor, he thought the need for continuing his policies justified his selection of Taft. Roosevelt, consequently, chose a statesman rather than a skilled politician as his successor. By September 1910, after his return from Africa, he had recognized his mistake. "I think he is a better President than McKinley and probably Harrison," Roosevelt admitted, "but the times are totally different, and he has not the qualities that are needed at the moment."[2] By disrupting the inherent logic of convention politics, Roosevelt had paved the way for four long years of unspectacular government by an honest but inept politician.

After twelve years of uninterrupted control of the White House and sixteen years in complete control of Congress, the Republican party found itself shaken to the core by the influx of idealistic progressives. The Republican National Convention of 1908 had reflected the growing cleavage between the progressively oriented West, which had supported Roosevelt and Taft, and the more conservative eastern wing, which was more closely tied to the industrial and financial interests of the country. The 1908 campaign made Taft acutely aware of the increasing strength of what he called the "La Follette-Bryan" wing of the party throughout the West. He attributed its growth to the length of Republican dominance at the national level. "When a party has been in power as long as the Republican Party had been," he admitted to Elihu Root, "the factional feeling is likely to grow intenser than the party feeling against the Democrats."[3] During the campaign, Taft continued to complain that "there are very few Republican States in which factionalism has not risen above party feeling so as to make a division that is hard to close."[4] He later blamed most of his ineffectiveness as president on such factionalism:

I came into the presidency March 4, 1909, under conditions in the Republican party that made any controlling leadership by me, the redemption of platform pledges and the maintenance of party discipline most difficult. The two divisions in the party after fifteen years of power were such that one faction much preferred the defeat of the other to the continuance of party success or the performance of party pledges.[5]

Public opinion had also begun to shift away from the Republican party. Republican strength had reached its peak with Roosevelt's victory in 1904. In 1906, Roosevelt himself began to fear that the pendulum had begun to swing away from his party.[6] Republican strength in the House dropped twenty-five seats in 1906 and another four in 1908, despite Taft's respectable electoral showing. The passage of a tariff bill was bound to speed the decline in Republican fortunes. It was not the most propitious moment to become party leader.

II

Taft brought to the presidency a modern belief in principles of responsible party government. In 1906, and well before he ever confronted the Insurgent Republicans in Congress, he outlined his commitment to party government in a series of lectures at Yale University entitled *Four Aspects of Civic Duty*. He argued that popular government could not exist without political parties to transform private opinions into meaningful alternatives of public policy. He felt it was necessary for party members to subordinate their "less essential" principles for the more important ones embodied in the party program:

A useful party cannot be formed unless those who are members of it, with a sense of responsibility for the successful and unobstructed continuance of the administration by that party, yield their views on the less important and less essential principles, and unite with respect to the main policies for which the party is to become responsible. The resultant solidarity of opinion is necessary to secure unity of action. The sense of responsibility for the successful operation of the Government must furnish a power of cohesion which shall prevent the breaking off from the party of a sufficient number of its members to make its arm nerveless and to take away from it its power of initiative and action. That party is the more efficient party, therefore, in which the members are more nearly united on the great principles of governmental policy.[7]

Although aware that many persons preferred to remain "independent" of parties, Taft felt strongly that their influence upon public policy and good government would be minimal as individuals. The "only avenue" a person could follow to obtain "permanently useful results" lay through his influence in a political party:

As this is a party government, and as measures are controlled by party decisions, the real progress must be made along party lines; and if a man separates from his party he loses altogether any influence he may exert in determining those policies. I do not at all advocate that a man should adhere to party against high principle and conviction, but this life is all a series of compromises by which little by little, and step by step, progress toward better things is made. All the good in the world cannot be attained at one breath. We must achieve what we can at the time we can, and must let other aims and objects of the highest good abide a different opportunity for their attainment. While, therefore, we may not agree with all the principles adopted into legislation or into executive policy by a party with which we are affiliated, we should ordinarily not destroy our usefulness and power for good in influencing the party in the right direction, by withdrawing from it on issues not the most important, if, on the whole, we believe that more good can come from its success than from that of its opponent.[8]

It was Taft's dedication to party government, his commitment to working within the existing rules and institutions rather than against them, and his willingness to subordinate his "less essential" principles "for the greatest good to the greatest number" that characterized his philosophy as party leader.[9]

Taft's belief in party government was complemented by an almost ruthless integrity which led him to view the fulfillment of his campaign promises of 1908 as his highest priority. Whereas many Republican legislators were content to ignore campaign promises, Taft was doggedly determined to see them enacted into law. He was willing to pay almost any personal price to redeem them, even if it meant an alliance with the devil himself. When it appeared that he would have to support the reelection of Cannon as Speaker, William Allen White, editor of the *Emporia Gazette*, warned Taft that sentiment in the West was strongly in favor of the Insurgent cause. Taft responded:

I have your telegram that sentiment in Kansas is with the insurgents. I know it is, and I expect it is generally so. But I have got a good deal more responsibility, or at least have to look a good deal farther ahead, than the public who are sympathizing with the insurgents. I have a definite program before me as to securing certain legislation, and can not lean on a broken reed like the Democracy. I have to regard the Republican party as the instrumentality through which to try to accomplish something. When, therefore, certain Republicans decline to go into a caucus, and stand out 30 against 190, it would be the sacrifice of every interest I represent to side with the principle in respect to the House reforms that they seek to carry out. . . . I can not afford, merely to accomplish one good purpose, to sacrifice all the others, when those others are, as compared with the one, much more important.[10]

This response reflected Taft's cavalier unconcern, expressed throughout his presidency, for popularity or reelection. He did not need the plaudits of the crowd to retain his self-esteem, nor did he seek reelection as an end in itself. "I shall not be believed when I say that all I am praying for is to come through one term with credit, and that the second term plays no part in my contemplation," he wrote to Henry S. Brown of the *New York Herald*. "If I can survive the troubles of one and not be swamped, I shall be content."[11] Taft continued to express such sentiments in his correspondence and at social gatherings of friends and party leaders. Growing Insurgent hostility toward him only strengthened him in his course:

One thing I have decided to do, that is to play no politics. I am going ahead as if there were no second term and pay no heed to the demands of this element. If the party comes to my point of view, well and good; if it doesn't, I am content to step down after four years.[12]

By the spring of 1910, Archie Butt had concluded: "I don't believe he ever thinks about a second term, or, if he does, merely as something not even to be desired."[13]

Although difficult to accept, the record points to Taft's marked disinterest in pursuing popularity and reelection as ends in themselves. It was his outstanding fault as a democratic politician. He was more willing to fight for a principle, a policy, or another person than for himself. This had been an admirable trait in a lieutenant, but it was a major vice in a president expected to promote the cause of the Republican party through his own personality. For most Americans, trust and confidence in the president as a person is their only link to the complex policies for which he stands. Taft's personal humility actually undermined public confidence in himself and his administration. Lacking the desire for popularity or reelection, Taft consequently lost touch with his party and the country and set the stage for the disaster of 1912.

III

It was inevitable that so principled a man as Taft should ultimately have split with the progressive Republicans. The "Insurgents," as they were dubbed by congressional leaders, were western and midwestern congressmen and senators swept into office on a wave of agrarian discontent in 1906 and 1908. They came to Washington imbued with a strong sense of social consciousness and self-righteousness and committed to placing control of government back in the hands of the people. Most western and midwestern progressives shared the old populist suspicion of the industrial East and feared the growing power of accumulated capital and wealth. They favored stronger government regulation of the railroads and the "trusts" and also conservation policies designed to preserve American natural resources from the ravages of big business. They were more interested in the results than the techniques of reform. The eleven hard-core "Insurgents" in the Senate were led by Senators Robert M. La Follette of Wisconsin, Albert J. Beveridge of Indiana, Jonathan P. Dolliver and Albert B. Cummins of Iowa, Joseph L. Bristow of Kansas, and Moses E. Clapp of Minnesota. They were frequently joined by Norris Brown and Elmer J. Burkett of Nebraska, Coe Crawford of South Dakota, Knute Nelson of Minnesota, and William E. Borah of Idaho. A lesser-known House contingent of about thirty Insurgents was led by Congressman George W. Norris of Nebraska. These progressives gave Taft his most difficult hours while President.

Once the seeds of distrust had been planted in the minds of Insurgents during their struggle for a lower tariff, they could find little merit in the President's subsequent handling of legislative or party issues. A more astute politician might have avoided an irrevocable split within the party, but Taft was psychologically incapable of straddling political fences. He was unable to hold the party factions together by force of personality, program, or rhetoric. Because of his initial mistakes, the burden of proof of his progressivism now shifted to him, and try as he might he was unable to dispel his reactionary image among the Insurgents.

An important factor in the Taft-Insurgent split lay in the principled character of the protagonists. Although Taft could be classified as a political moderate in his day, his reverence for the Constitution was uncompromising. He was understandably upset by the self-righteousness and the contempt for constitutional procedures displayed by the Insurgents and found it very difficult to cooperate with them. As his constitutional conservatism unfolded in office, he was soon viewed as an apostate from the progressive faith. Apostates are frequently more bitterly hated by the faithful than infidels who supposedly know no better.

The Insurgent temperament was epitomized by Senator La Follette. In sharp contrast to the American political tradition of compromise, La Follette's doctrinaire ideology was characteristic of mass social movements like progressivism. Whereas Roosevelt and Taft had operated according to the traditional American principle that half a loaf of bread is better than none in politics, the senator was uncompromising:

I believe that half a loaf is fatal whenever it is accepted at the sacrifice of the basic principle sought to be attained. Half a loaf, as a rule dulls the appetite, and destroys the keenness of interest in attaining the full loaf. A halfway measure never fairly tests the principle and may utterly discredit it. It is certain to weaken, disappoint, and dissipate public interest. Concession and compromise are almost always necessary in legislation, but they call for the most thorough and complete mastery of the principles involved, in order to fix the limit beyond which not one hair's breadth can be yielded.

La Follette believed that the industrial and financial interests of the nation had captured and corrupted the federal government and the Republican party. Drastic steps were needed immediately to curb the insidious power of corporations: "It is against the system built up by privilege, which has taken possession of government and legislation, that we must make unceasing warfare." The very legislative establishment which Taft had chosen to use for reform had become the object of La Follette's scorn and attacks. Committed dogmatically to his own principles, La Follette could never subject himself to any political organization wholeheartedly. "Party loyalty is still a fetish in Congress," he could write in explaining his opposition to the Tariff.[14] Since the President still believed in the "fetish"—indeed, his political success depended upon it— Taft and La Follette were inevitably to clash.

A thin-skinned Taft was sorely hurt by vitriolic progressive attacks against his program and believed that the Insurgents were unwittingly contributing to the destruction of the Republican party in the 1910 and 1912 elections. "They have probably furnished ammunition enough to the press and the public to make a Democratic House," he wrote to Roosevelt in 1910. "Whether they will bring on a Democratic administration in three years remains to be seen." "It is impossible for a faction in a party to attack the leaders of it, to misrepresent their motives, and to charge them with everything dishonorable without its having effect upon the people,"[15] Taft maintained. Just as the Insurgents could not tolerate apostasy from progressivism, Taft could not tolerate disloyalty to the party.

The President's handling of patronage contributed to Insurgent hostility toward him. At first Taft thought he could work with Cannon and remain on relatively good terms with progressives, particularly since he intended to grant them their patronage requests. In his drive to garner sufficient Republican support for the Payne-Aldrich tariff, however, Taft was forced early in his administration to consider the use of patronage to discipline uncooperative congressmen. Vice-President Sherman had urged Taft to withhold patronage from the Republican opponents of the tariff. "Mr. President," he pleaded, "you can't cajole those people. You have to hit them with a club. My advice is to begin to hit. I would send for Hitchcock and shut off the appointments of postmasters until the bill is passed." Taft answered, "I have already sent for Hitchcock for this very purpose, but I only want to use this lever on the members and Senators who are recalcitrant." Sherman replied: "You had better send for him again, and shut them all off so that the innocent can get to work on the guilty and it can all be done without any personal threat. Simply have it announced that the party is committed to this reform bill and that everything must give way before it, and that any person who tries to defeat the party wishes must necessarily be considered as hostile to the national party and his opinion will not govern with the government." "I hate to use the patronage as a club unless I have to," Taft replied. "It is your only club," Sherman answered. "You have other weapons, but the appointing power is your only club."[16] Although Taft refused to use the club during the special session of Congress, the Insurgents were nevertheless made "apprehensive" about their patronage, and many of their postal appointments were delayed.[17]

The regular December 1909 session of Congress brought the issue to a head. Taft had decided to do more than make the Insurgents "apprehensive." He waited only for the most propitious moment to strike, and then he proposed "to separate the sheep from the goats."[18] The process of separation, however, further strained relations between the President and the Insurgents. When some of the Insurgents became alarmed at rumors that Taft intended to cut off their patronage, Taft denied the rumors and reaffirmed his desire to consult congressmen on appointments. He wrote to Congressman George Norris that "there should be party action to discharge the promises of the party platform, and those who feel no obligation in respect to it can not complain if their recommendations are not given the customary weight." Professing loyalty to the party, Norris expressed his fear that Taft was using patronage to force his program through Congress. "I never had used, and do not intend to use patronage for the purpose of either making a machine or influencing legislation," Taft replied, "but I do not propose, on the other hand, to have it used against the Republican party." Although Taft would have preferred to place virtually all patronage under civil service, he could not allow patronage to be used "to fortify opponents of the administration and opponents of the declared policies of the Republican party."[19]

Taft justified the withholding of patronage as an attempt to strengthen the party, but there was little distinction in his mind between party aims and his own legislative program. On January 13, shortly after his response to Norris, he confessed to a puzzled Albert Baldwin, editor of the *Outlook:* "I have only said that where a man elected as a Republican is taking steps to defeat the legislation recommended by me, in performance of party promises, he is no longer a Republican, and to give weight to his recommendations for patronage would be to furnish him means in the future of defeating the administration policies."[20] That same day, while attempting to heal the widening breach in the party, Taft publicly acknowledged that he could no longer consider as real Republicans those Insurgents who opposed administration measures merely because Cannon supported them. The next day, at a White House conference with feuding congressional leaders, Taft helped temporarily to neutralize opposition to Cannon by producing an agreement among the leaders pledging more extensive use of the party caucus as a decision-making organ in the House.[21]

Taft continued to use his patronage powers to punish Insurgent leaders like La Follette and Cummins who vindictively opposed the administration's program. As the President admitted to Postmaster General Hitchcock, "Iowa and Wisconsin are the only States where I cared anything about deliberation with respect to the recommendations of certain of the insurgents." Congressman Frank P. Woods of Iowa was another object of presidential wrath. "Woods is so much of an insurgent," Taft admitted to Hitchcock, "that I do not feel under any obligation to respect his recommendations unless he makes it known to me that they are not men engaged in attacking me and my administration." Congressman Miles Poindexter of Washington was also included on Taft's list, for the President believed him "nothing more than a Democrat" who "ought not to be gratified in any degree" with patronage.[22]

The attempt at party discipline was a complete failure. Not only did it increase Insurgent bitterness toward the President, but it turned them into martyrs for the progressive cause and increased their popularity back home.[23] Later, before the 1910 congressional elections, the President was forced to reverse himself for the sake of party harmony. Personal faith in responsible party government or the selective use of patronage were not enough to enforce discipline.

The clumsy way in which Taft altered his policy only increased his differences with the Insurgents. The President's personal secretary Charles Norton sent a letter to one of the Insurgents trying to explain the President's change of policy without acknowledging there ever had been such a policy. Norton admitted what the President had been denying all along:

While Republican legislation pending in Congress was opposed by certain Republicans, the President felt it to be his duty to the party and to the country to withhold Federal patronage from certain Senators and Congressmen who seemed to be in opposition to the Administration's efforts to carry out the promises of the party platform. . . . The President feels that the value of Federal patronage has been greatly exaggerated, and that the refusal to grant it has probably been more useful to the men affected than the appointments would have been. In the preliminary skirmishes in certain States, like Wisconsin and Iowa and elsewhere, he was willing in the interest of what the leaders believed would lead to party success, to make certain discriminations; but the president has concluded that it is now his duty to treat all Republican Congressmen and Senators alike without any distinction. He will now follow the usual rule in Republican Congressional districts and States, and follow the recommendations made by Republican Congressmen and Senators of whatever shade of political opinion, only requiring that the men recommended shall be good men, the most competent and the best fitted for the particular office.[24]

The letter contained the humiliating admission that the President was now discontinuing the withholding of patronage, not because the policy had been wrong, but because it had been ineffective. The blunder of the letter, however, lay in Taft's willingness to delegate responsibility to Charles Norton on a matter so pregnant with political controversy. The President had not seen the letter before his secretary made it public, and admittedly would not have approved it if he had. The letter marked the end of the President's ill-conceived attempt to enforce party discipline by means of patronage.[25]

IV

The President's policy of patronage toward regular Republicans revealed him as a president unconcerned about his personal power within the party. Taft described his policy as one of generally "adopting the recommendations of Congressmen, subject, however, to where a man has been in one term, or two terms, and sometimes three terms, of continuing a good incumbent."[26] Although Taft would have preferred to eliminate all patronage, he said that he would use his power to improve the level of government service rather than his personal dominance of the party.

This was especially true of the federal judicial appointments. The President closely scrutinized such appointments in an effort to revitalize the federal courts. As a former judge, he was acutely aware of the deficiencies of previous presidential appointments to the bench. Realizing their impact on constitutional development for decades to come, Taft considered his appointments to the judiciary as "the most sacred duty I have to perform."[27] Once, while discussing a southern appointment in the Roosevelt administration, Taft advised Roosevelt that "the question of judgeship is to be settled not with respect to the particular faction of the Republican party to which the candidates belong, but solely with respect to their judicial qualifications."[28] Taft's concern with the judiciary of the South was especially evident in his own administration. He confessed to Archie Butt:

The Judiciary has fallen into a very low state in this country. I think your part of the country has suffered especially. The federal judges of the South are a disgrace to any country, and I'll be damned if I put any man on the bench of whose character and ability there is the least doubt.[29]

Taft maintained this position throughout his term in office.

The President's concern for the judiciary led to his confrontation with the custom of "senatorial courtesy" which required the President's patronage appointments to be acceptable to the senior Republican senator from the state in which they were made. Taft did not accept the basic constitutional theory underlying "senatorial courtesy," for he believed that the custom placed arbitrary distinctions in the Constitution between Republican and Democratic senators.[30] Although the record does not indicate any serious clashes between Taft and Congress on the issue, Taft did successfully ignore the custom on some of his judicial appointments. In February 1910, for example, he wrote to Colonel Cecil A. Lyon that "in respect to the selection of Federal judges I act on my own initiative and do not feel bound to follow the recommendations of Congressmen or Senators."[31] Also, to Senator Burton of Ohio, whose views he had occasionally ignored, he wrote:

> In regard to judicial officers, of whom I have appointed five from Ohio, I have consulted you, but have not necessarily followed your recommendation, and this for the reason that I have claimed with respect to all judicial appointments that, while I listen with due respect to the recommendation of the Senators, I must exercise my own judgment in regard to judicial candidates.[32]

The President's policy was pursued with no fanfare or belligerence and drew little attention from the press or the public. The fact remains, however, that Taft did not rubber stamp the choices of Republican senators and succeeded in placing 109 highly qualified men on the federal bench.[33] His successful low-key challenge to the prerogatives of the Senate can be explained only by his impressive judicial credentials, which allowed him to interfere more with "senatorial courtesy" than any other twentieth-century President.[34]

By stressing merit, the President deemphasized the political consequences of his appointments to his own career. He did not follow Frank Kellogg's advice to offer patronage only to those men who would aid him in his quest for reelection. He would not appoint a known political opponent to office, but, according to Major Butt, "he would rather not have the question raised."[35] Taft's policy, however, clashed with that of his

more politically sensitive postmaster general. When Senator
Crane and Charles Norton bitterly criticized Hitchcock for his
propensity to take "all the glory for the appointments which
are satisfactory and dumping on the Administration all the
appointments . . . which were in a snarl and a tangle," Taft
admitted his utter disregard for the personal consequences of
his policy:

> The trouble with Hitchcock is he does not understand me or
> my aims. He is always looking to the future for some petty ad-
> vantage to be gained, whereas I want to stand still and, if not
> actually look back, at least to look around, pick out the most
> decent man, and try to make the service good and let the future
> take care of itself. . . . He does not the least bit try to under-
> stand what I want him to do in the South, and it is a constant
> wrangle with him to give to the South decent postmasters, even
> though they do not have any influence with some organization
> which will one day nominate delegates to a national convention.[36]

Hitchcock, more than Taft, had his eye upon the 1912 Republican convention. Taft was willing to let the future take
care of itself. No politically astute president would have so
carelessly ignored the personal political factor involved in his
appointments. The President's attitude clearly revealed his deficient understanding of the realities of presidential power in
a democratic system.

v

The congressional elections of 1910 provided Taft with an
opportunity to purge his party of obstructionists. Although
he did not actively campaign in the primaries or general elections, he intervened clandestinely in a number of states to try
to defeat Republican opponents. When pressured in April to
support progressive Senator Beveridge of Indiana for reelection, Taft declined because the senator "has attempted to kill

my legislation in such a way in the Senate that I do not feel under any obligation to him."[37] One month later, when Secretary of the Treasury MacVeagh imprudently promised presidential support to Beveridge, Taft again balked at the idea; he feared Cannon and his friends would retaliate by refusing to push his legislative program, which they were not enthusiastic about. "I am putting these bills over all personality and politics," he explained to MacVeagh. In Iowa, Taft enlisted Aldrich's help in financing political opposition against the Insurgent Cummins-Dolliver faction in the primary and general elections. Taft was careful not to allow Hitchcock to enter the fight, for he desired that the opposition to the Insurgents appear to originate within the state itself. After a White House conference in which Taft and Aldrich agreed on the financing of the regular Indiana faction, Taft admitted to Butt:

Well, Archie, I had to descend to politics this afternoon. I believe in fighting the devil with fire. I don't propose to have my administration a failure simply because of the hostility of Dolliver and Cummins. After I write my bills on the Statute Books, they can then do their worst, for the record will have been written and the law will be there.[38]

The President also intervened in the state of Washington to try to prevent the nomination of Insurgent Congressman Miles Poindexter to the Senate. In Tennessee, he tried to eliminate opposition to his preferred candidate Congressman Richard W. Austin.[39] Although Austin was successfully renominated and reelected to Congress, Taft could not prevent the nomination of Poindexter.

Despite covert presidential support for the party regulars, progressive Republicans throughout the country continued to roll up impressive primary victories against regular Republicans identified with the Taft administration. By the end of September forty regular Republican congressmen had been defeated in the primaries by Insurgent challengers and every Insurgent up for reelection had been victorious. The President's indirect attempts to purge the party of malcontents had backfired disastrously. Although the efforts highlighted Taft's foxlike qualities, they also revealed his general inability as a leader to capture the imagination of his party and make such indirect methods of intervention unnecessary. Only in failure had Taft discovered that the enforcement of party discipline was a hazardous, almost impossible task in the American political system.

It should be noted here that Taft possessed little taste for internal party combat. He preferred to remain aloof from state politics and act as a mediator in party disputes when called upon. Occasionally he was drawn into state politics to prevent either the Old Guard or progressive factions from completely dominating the party, but even then his intervention was reluctant.

As a native of Ohio, Taft was naturally interested in the 1910 Republican nominee for governor of that state. Rather than back any particular faction or candidate in the state, the President tried to mediate the internal disputes, hoping thereby to prevent either the Old Guard Cox faction or the progressive Garfield wing of the party from completely dominating the June convention. That summer, in a strategy session with Republican leaders from Ohio, he succeeded in securing an agreement among them to prevent any prior deals which would make the convention meaningless. To the obvious delight of the President, the convention finally compromised on Warren G. Harding.[40]

The reentry of Theodore Roosevelt into New York politics eventually drew the President into another fierce factional struggle. Taft's appointment of Governor Charles Evans Hughes to the Supreme Court precipitated an internal struggle for control of the September 1910 Republican convention. As in Ohio, Taft tried to steer a middle of the road course. However, Roosevelt's endorsement of the direct primary, one of the hottest issues in the state, and his announced candidacy for the temporary chairmanship of the state convention forced the President off the political fence. Since Taft had decided to oppose the more conservative and unpopular Woodruff-Barnes faction, he was not averse to supporting Roosevelt's bid for the chairmanship. But when Vice-President "Sunny" Jim Sherman used the President's name on behalf of his own candidacy, the executive committee of the state Republican party endorsed Sherman instead of Roosevelt, and Taft was blamed for having humiliated Roosevelt. Though the President claimed his name had been used without authorization, Roosevelt supporters remained unconvinced.[41]

After Roosevelt's defeat within the executive committee, Taft tried to stay out of the factional battle shaping up at the state convention. "I intend to keep out of the fight altogether," he wrote his brother Charles, "and let Griscom and Loeb and the rest of them do what they can with Roosevelt against the machine, but I shall not directly interfere."[42] On September 19, however, Taft and Roosevelt did confer at New Haven, Connecticut, about the impending convention and agreed that "the candidate should not be the result of a victory by the machine, and the platform should not be dictated by the machine."[43] Despite this agreement, the festering differences between the two men were not resolved by their meeting, but Roosevelt's conference with the President contributed to his election as temporary chairman of the convention and the success of the more progressive Griscom-Bannard faction.[44] The President was greatly pleased by the nomination of progressive Henry L. Stimson for governor and expressed no regrets at having aided Roosevelt against the old machine leaders.[45] Taft's behavior in New York, however, was basically a reaction to Roosevelt's initiatives in trying to carry the state for the Republican party. The President had no love for internal party combat and was content to let Roosevelt set the pace of battle in the most populous state of the Union.

As the fall elections approached, Taft withdrew his hostility toward the Insurgents for the sake of expediency. He wrote to Senator Charles Curtis of Kansas that some form of presidential endorsement for all Republican candidates would be made:

I am going to write a letter advising strongly that all the regulars support insurgents and that all the insurgents support regulars, and that a Republican majority is a good deal better than a Democratic majority. I have received some letters from the West indicating that the insurgents would like to have some such assistance as that, and I am quite sure the regulars would. It is quite possible that in this slough of despond (*sic*) in which we have found ourselves we may acquire such a contrite and loving spirit toward each other that it will lead to ultimate victory.[46]

Taft wrote a letter to Congressman William McKinley of Ohio, chairman of the House Congressional Campaign Committee, supporting both regular and Insurgent Republicans, and defending the record of his administration.[47] The fall elections, as we have seen, were a disaster for the party reaching landslide proportions. The Republicans would have to reconcile their factional differences or face certain defeat in 1912.

VI

Theodore Roosevelt held one of the keys to the future of the Republican party. While vacationing and hunting abroad, he had been informed of political events through a variety of informants. When he returned home already dissatisfied with Taft in June 1910, Roosevelt became the catalytic agent within the party that helped widen the split between Taft and the progressives. By the spring of 1910, the former President was already prepared to admit to Lodge his mistake in having chosen Taft as his successor:

I finally had to admit that he had gone wrong on certain points; and I then also had to admit to myself that deep down underneath I had all along known he was wrong, on points as to which I had tried to deceive myself, by loudly proclaiming to myself, that he was right.

Although Roosevelt believed Taft had shown a "certain adherence" to his goals, "these objects have been pursued by the present Administration in a spirit and with methods which have rendered the effort almost nugatory," and he felt that Taft had not appreciated the "needs" of the country or "the way the country felt." As he complained to Lodge, "To announce allegiance to what had been done, and to abandon the only methods by which it was possible to continue to get it done, was not satisfactory from my standpoint."[48]

Roosevelt was also sorely embarrassed by progressive criticism of his support of Taft as a genuine progressive at the 1908 convention. Since these progressives held Roosevelt to "sharp account" for Taft, Roosevelt believed that he could no longer continue his deception about Taft. He was particularly distraught at what Taft had done to the Republican party. "I do think we had the Republican Party in a shape that warranted the practical continuance of just what we were doing," he complained to Lodge.[49] After a firsthand view of party affairs upon his return to the United States, the former President concluded:

One of the heaviest counts against Taft is that by his actions he has produced a state of affairs in which the split is so deep that it seems impossible to heal it, and the most likely result is that the people will say: 'A plague on both your houses,' and will turn to the Democrats.[50]

Roosevelt soon confronted the dilemma of whether to support Taft or the President's Insurgent critics. In his own inimitable manner, Roosevelt chose to do neither. He refused to endorse the record of the Taft administration. Taft was genuinely distressed by Roosevelt's silence but refused to take the initiative in bringing about any kind of reconciliation. "I shall let matters shape themselves in his mind and give him every chance to whip around if he sees he is making a mistake," Taft said to Butt. "I shall take no notice of it until it absolutely forces itself on me or the Administration."[51] When Roosevelt began to hold court with administration critics almost daily at Oyster Bay, Taft advised his cabinet to follow a "wait and see" policy toward the former President.

I think it very important that nothing should be said on the subject one way or the other by either myself or any member of my Cabinet, for the present. It is just as well to wait until the situation shall open itself; at least we do not desire to create any situation. We may very well content ourselves with standing upon our record until circumstances arise calling for further action.[52]

Taft also appeared too proud to take the first step toward Roosevelt. He explained to Major Butt:

I am deeply hurt by his attitude and have been. If he was hurt with me, the proper thing for him to have done was to give me the opportunity to explain my position and to thrash it out as we had done many times in the past. He has closed my mouth by his seeming indifference to my administration, and it is inconceivable that I, the President of the United States, should go to him on my knees, so to speak, and ask his approval.

Taft remained ignorant of the reasons behind Roosevelt's silence. "If I only knew what the President wanted," he remarked to Butt, "I would do it, but you know he has held himself so aloof that I am absolutely in the dark. I am deeply wounded, and he gives me no chance to explain my attitude or learn his."[53]

Despite increasing pressure, at least at first, Roosevelt declined to support either the "ultra-Taft people" or the "wild" Insurgents who desired a clean break between the two men.[54] He made no real effort to reconcile the differences with his successor. Although Taft at first could not understand Roosevelt's behavior, he slowly began to convince himself, with the aid of his family and cabinet, that Roosevelt was interested in his old job. Aware of his predecessor's combativeness and love of power, Taft watched with growing misgivings Roosevelt's enthusiastic receptions in the West during the 1910 campaign. With every rousing reception, the President thought he perceived a corresponding increase in Roosevelt's dissatisfaction with the administration. "I think he occupies his leisure time in finding reasons why he is justified in not supporting me," Taft wrote to his brother Horace. The reason seemed obvious. "I have it on authority that can hardly be disputed that he has determined to become a candidate for 1912."[55] After his brief meeting with Roosevelt at New Haven, the President admitted to Major Butt:

The fact of the matter is if you were to remove Roosevelt's skull now, you would find written on his brain '1912.' But he is so purely an opportunist that should he find conditions changed materially in another year and you were to open his brain, you would not find there 1912, and Roosevelt would deny it was ever there.[56]

The President had already resolved not to be pushed out of the way by Roosevelt, even if his nomination meant defeat in 1912. "Having once been nominated and elected I am under obligations to accept another term if it comes, and if only the nomination comes to accept that and go through the campaign and be beaten like a gentleman."⁵⁷ Taft was too stubborn to make way for his predecessor.

The allegedly "wild ideas" of Roosevelt's western speeches strengthened the President's resolve to seek reelection. Particularly in his Osawatomie and Denver speeches, Roosevelt criticized the judiciary for its ultraconservative defense of property and maintained that human rights were more important than property rights. "I think the 'New Nationalism' proclaimed in the Osawatomie speech has frightened every lawyer in the Untied States," Taft explained to his brother, "and has greatly stirred up the indignation and fear of the thinking part of New England and the Middle States."⁵⁸ It was not so much Roosevelt's substantive criticism of the decisions of the Supreme Court which alarmed Taft, but the "tone" of the speeches and the "conditions" under which they were given. The President believed the speeches were designed to "stir up" the "bitterness of feeling" of the western progressives against the federal courts.⁵⁹ In particular, he considered Roosevelt's criticism of the power of judicial review as "an attack upon our system at the very point where I think it is the strongest."⁶⁰ Taft, moreover, considered the policies of the "New Nationalism" as "utterly impracticable, because they could never be gotten through without a revolution or revisions of the Constitution, either of which is impossible." Taft's reaction was "to sit tight and let him talk."⁶¹

The Republican losses of 1910 only increased Roosevelt's ambitions. The former President saw a Republican defeat in 1912. "It looks to me if, ultimately, the best thing that could happen to us now would be to do what we can with Taft, face probable defeat in 1912, and then endeavor to reorganize under really capable and sanely progressive leadership."⁶² When Henry Stimson suggested that Roosevelt become a candidate for renomination in 1912, Roosevelt admitted what he later forgot when convention fever gripped him: "My present impression is that to nominate me would not save the Party, but, on the contrary, would split it even wider than would the renomination of Taft, and would render it utterly impossible for me to be of any use whatever in the future."[63] Roosevelt felt that the party needed strong reform-minded leadership to save it from becoming a party of reaction. "I want to see a radical party," he wrote to William Allen White. "I want to see the Republican Party as radical as in the days of Lincoln."[64] As the outstanding progressive leader in the country, Roosevelt could hardly prevent himself from becoming the rallying point for all those Republicans dissatisfied with Taft.

Taft's role as party leader became even more difficult. Progressives grew colder, and even regular Republicans became increasingly disenchanted with the administration. By calling the disastrous special session of Congress in 1911 and pushing reciprocity, Taft had risked his stature as party leader for economic union with Canada. In the new Congress the President began to alienate a few regulars by disassociating himself from the faltering congressional leadership with which he had been allied for two years. The standpat elements within the party strongly reacted against the rigorous enforcement of the antitrust laws. Finally, Roosevelt became more outspoken against Taft. The United States Steel suit so outraged Roosevelt that, according to Root, "it dethroned his judgment."[65] Whereas in November 1910 Roosevelt had felt that Taft merely lacked "the gift of leadership," was "too easily influenced by the men around him," and did "not really grasp progressive principles," by December 1911 Taft had become a "flubdub," "puzzle-witted," and a "floppy-souled creature."[66]

When Republicans, increasingly anxious about the 1912 elections, pressed Taft for a more militant stand toward civil disorder in Mexico, the President refused to risk bloodshed and finally had to admit his inability to combine his role as president with that of leader of the Republican party. "I am a constant disappointment to my party," he explained to Mrs. Taft. "The fact of the matter is, the longer I am President the less of a party man I seem to become." When Mrs. Taft inquired whether he had become a Democrat, he replied, "Hardly that, but it seems to me to be impossible to be a strict party man and serve the whole country impartially." Despite his confessed inability to combine presidential roles, Taft stubbornly refused to make way for Roosevelt. He admitted to his wife that he was "chiefly interested" in the nomination rather than the election. "If we lose the election," he maintained, "I shall feel that the party is rejected, whereas if I fail to secure the renomination it will be a personal defeat."[67]

VII

As 1912 approached, Roosevelt's attacks upon Taft's policies grew in intensity, especially after the unfortunate steel suit. Taft remained somewhat bewildered by his predecessor's increasing attacks. "I don't know what he is driving at except to make my way more difficult," he admitted to Major Butt. "I could not ask his advice on all questions. I could not subordinate my administration to him and retain my self-respect, but it is hard, very hard, Archie, to see a devoted friendship going to pieces like a rope of sand."[68] In February 1912, he wrote to his brother Horace:

I hate to be at odds with Theodore Roosevelt, who made me President of the United States and towards whom I shall always feel a heavy debt of gratitude on that account. But, of course, he made me President and not deputy, and I have to be President; and I do not recognize any obligation growing out of my previous relations to step aside for him and let him become a candidate for a third term when he had specifically declined a third term and repeated it a number of times.[69]

Taft was too proud to attempt an ignominious reconciliation by walking the extra mile. He feared the public impression of undue subordination to Roosevelt such a move might produce. According to La Follette, Taft's fears were legitimate. "While Taft made some effort at reconciliation," he wrote in his autobiography, "he was not willing wholly to subordinate himself to his former chief. Nothing less would have satisfied Roosevelt."[70]

La Follette also nursed presidential ambitions. He had created the National Progressive Republican League to serve as a political base for his own presidential boom in 1912. Roosevelt had been asked to become a charter member of the league and to subscribe to its principles—the direct election of senators, the direct primary, the direct election of party convention delegates, the initiative, referendum, and recall, and corrupt practices legislation—but he declined allegedly because of his interest in more practical problems involving the regulation of corporations, conservation, and labor-management relations. Although such figures as Gifford Pinchot, James Garfield, Hiram Johnson, Ray Stannard Baker, and William Allen White became charter members, Roosevelt was unwilling to commit himself to what might be interpreted as an endorsement of La Follette for president. Support of La Follette would have precluded Roosevelt's candidacy and have destroyed his ability to unite the Republican party if he were nominated.[71]

Roosevelt did not declare his active candidacy until February 21. Nine days earlier, sensing the mounting pressures upon him and aware of his love of power, Root warned him to remain firm in his pledge of noncandidacy. "No thirsty sinner ever took a pledge which was harder for him to keep than it will be for you to maintain this position," he wrote to Roosevelt. Regardless of whether Roosevelt or Taft won a contested nomination, Root concluded, "In either case I am satisfied no Republican candidate would be elected."[72] Roosevelt, however, succumbed to political pressures, forcing Taft into an unequal struggle for the support of rank and file Republicans. Taft had suffered deeply throughout his presidency from constant comparisons with Roosevelt. Now he found himself forced to do battle with the most gifted campaigner of the period. He was understandably distressed at the news.

A few days before Roosevelt's announcement, the President had written to his brother: "He is surrounded by so many sycophants and neurotics who feed his vanity and influence his judgment that his usual good political sense is at fault in respect of the election."[73] This judgment was proven all too true. There was no steadying hand of a Taft, Root, Knox, or Lodge near Roosevelt, only progressives like Pinchot, Garfield, and White. What Roosevelt's old associates failed to realize was that Roosevelt no longer desired the counsel of the very men he knew would advise against his candidacy. A thirsty sinner rarely consults the preacher before he begins to drink again.

Roosevelt's announcement was not unexpected, but his progressive manifesto delivered before the Ohio Constitutional Convention shocked many conservatives across the country. Roosevelt proclaimed the idea that "human rights are supreme over all other rights; that wealth should be the servant, not the master of the people," and endorsed the popular recall of judicial decisions.[74] Taft's worst suspicions were confirmed. He perceived Roosevelt's speech as the beginning of a progressive campaign to undermine the right to private property and the independence of the judiciary, the most fixed principles of the President's political philosophy. Taft's fear of

Roosevelt grew almost pathological. He saw the specter of revolution arising:

He has leaped far ahead of the most radical leaders of the Progressive party, and his heart is not with them, but he deludes himself that he will be able to guide it and stem it when he gets in power. He can't do it. He has gone too far. He will either be a hopeless failure if elected or else destroy his own reputation by becoming a socialist, being swept there by force of circumstances just as the leaders of the French Revolution were swept on and on, all their individual efforts failing to stem the tide until it had run itself out.[75]

Although not as alarmed as Taft about revolution, Root shared the President's view of Roosevelt's opportunism and shallow commitment to progressive ideas:

He is essentially a fighter and when he gets into a fight he is completely dominated by the desire to destroy his adversary. He instinctively lays hold of every weapon which can be used for that end. Accordingly he is saying a lot of things and taking a lot of positions which are inspired by the desire to win. I have no doubt he thinks he believes what he says, but he doesn't. He has merely picked up certain popular ideas which were at hand as one might pick up a poker or chair with which to strike.[76]

Roosevelt's opportunism was a classic quality of the democratic politician. It was a quality which Taft, so philosophically dedicated to the Constitution, sadly lacked.

The President decided to concentrate on political issues and delegates in his preconvention campaign and avoid a mudslinging personality contest which he felt he would surely lose. "Personal abuse is not likely to control ultimately in this campaign," he explained to Senator Bradley, "and I certainly don't want to be responsible for it if it does. I believe the arguments pro and con will force themselves upon the electorate without the use of denunciation and personal attack."[77] In

March, Taft warned his campaign staff to refrain from directly attacking or answering Roosevelt at every opportunity. As he explained to his brother Horace, his own campaign was most likely to succeed "if I can keep my people from talking too much."

You have to have headquarters, and those in charge think it necessary to give out something every day. They are tempted to do this by the loquacity of Teddy, who is master of the art of presenting his views to the public and getting them printed. He has a faculty, if he makes a mistake, of diverting the public the very next day to something else, so as to keep them all right.[78]

Taft reiterated his warning to Congressman William McKinley, his publicity manager, against trying to answer Roosevelt's parade of charges:

Your bureau of publication should confine itself to giving encouraging views of our canvass so far as the correspondence and facts justify, and should utterly ignore the attacks either made by Senator Dixon or by Colonel Roosevelt upon me or the Administration or on our friends whom it seems wise to them to attack.

The President had assumed the role of censor over the news releases of his publicity bureau. He was beginning to appreciate the importance of public relations to his own political fortunes. "I want to be consulted about every paragraph that goes out of a critical or hostile nature," he ordered McKinley, "and especially of a personal nature, with respect to Colonel Roosevelt or the canvass."[79] The President's strategy was to remain "as quiet as possible" and continue collecting convention delegates.[80]

A personality contest was the last thing in the world he wanted, but Taft found it increasingly difficult to remain silent in the face of Roosevelt's pounding. "I see my opponent, the Colonel, is making a fight against a straw man whose position in regard to the people he formulates himself and can not base on any statement of mine; and then he proceeded to knock him out of the ring," he lamented to a personal friend. But Taft refused to be drawn into a personal fight. "I do not care to be dragged into a series of controversial and constantly recurring speeches," he continued, "attempting to follow him and show his perversion of my language and meaning."[81] In such a campaign of crimination and recrimination, Taft recognized that Roosevelt "would have a great advantage over me because that is the kind of weapon he knows how to use and I don't."[82]

Roosevelt's increasing radicalism on the campaign trails hardened Taft's resolve to be renominated. The impending contest at the Republican convention had become "a very critical one in the history of the country" for conservatives.[83] The President feared that, if Roosevelt were nominated, the fall campaign between the parties would degenerate into "a chase to see which candidate can put his flag on the most extreme battlement of radicalism."[84] The basic constitutional principle of the progressive movement—"It must be constitutional because it is right, and what ever is right is constitutional"[85]—simply horrified him. He saw the growing radicalism of the progressive movement as threatening the foundations of American government.

Taft viewed his renomination as the best method of saving the Republican party from the heretical dogmas of Roosevelt and his followers. As he explained to William Worthington:

If I run as the regular Republican nominee, I may go down to defeat if a bolt is started by Roosevelt, but I will retain the regular organization of the party as a nucleus about which the conservative people who are in favor of maintaining constitutional government can gather, both from the Democratic and Republican parties, and we will have two radicals and one conservative.

I do not think that that means success, but it means one champion at least of our present system of government . . . against two champions of things that are not and never will be, and who have only a nebulous theory of how to reach the glorious result that they paint to their followers.[86]

Taft recognized the legitimacy which the party title would give his conservatism and fought all the harder for delegates. "I want only justice," he explained regarding the delegate contests in various states, "but I insist on getting that, and I will take the nomination if I can get it by only one vote."[87] Sane constitutional government had become more important to Taft than party harmony or a November victory.

A major crisis to confront the President in his bid for renomination arose over the loyalty of his postmaster general, Frank Hitchcock. By ignoring questions of personal loyalty in his patronage appointments throughout the country, particularly in the South, the President had scandalously allowed Hitchcock to build up a bloc of convention delegates personally loyal to the postmaster general.[88] When rumors first began to circulate throughout Washington that Hitchcock would swing his bloc of delegates to Roosevelt, the President scoffed at the stories. Senator Crane, Charles D. Hilles, Taft's personal secretary, and Secretary of Commerce Nagel, however, urged Taft to approach Hitchcock and reach some type of an understanding with him regarding his loyalty and the delegates under his control.[89] Taft confronted his postmaster general in a cabinet meeting and asked him bluntly, "Frank! Are you for me or against me?" Hitchcock, surprised, answered, "I am for you, Mr. President."[90] Hitchcock did support Taft for renomination and reelection, but his enthusiasm never equaled that of 1908, nor Taft's trust of him.

Despite the scare over Hitchcock's desertion, Taft refused to alter his basic patronage policy of considering merit rather than personal loyalty as the criterion for appointment. When he refused to remove a collector of customs at Salem, Massachusetts, because of the official's support for Roosevelt, Taft explained to the local congressman:

I have removed no one in this campaign because of his political views, and I do not intend to begin to do so now. The truth is there has never been a time, with which I am familiar, in the history of politics in this country when the political support of the Federal officeholders, such as it is, has been so divided, and at no time has the Federal patronage exercised less influence in the National convention than it will in the one to be held at Chicago.[91]

Taft was flagrantly violating a basic rule of strong party leadership—that patronage should be used to strengthen the president's personal hold upon the party. Roosevelt would never have allowed the Hitchcock or Salem situations to have developed, but would have placed his appointees in personal debt to himself.

The contest for delegates between Taft and Roosevelt became one of the most fearsome and bitter spectacles of American party history. Prior to Roosevelt's announced candidacy, Taft had counted upon practically solid delegations from New England, New York, Pennsylvania, Ohio, Indiana, Illinois, Kentucky, Maryland, and all of the southern states—over 700 convention votes, with only 540 needed for nomination.[92] Roosevelt's more aggressive personal attacks, however, began to pay off. He delivered a heavy jolt to the Taft bandwagon by winning the presidential primary in Illinois by a margin of two to one. When, on April 14, Roosevelt administered another stunning defeat to the President by winning sixty-five out of a possible seventy-six delegates in Pennsylvania, the President's complacency was shattered. Fearful of a stampede for Roosevelt in other states, Taft was forced out onto the stump to wage Roosevelt's kind of war.

The toe-to-toe battle on the campaign trail further illuminated the differences in style and temperament between the candidates. Roosevelt had not lost his old touch with crowds. His aggressive methods of attack only drew attention to the President's acute deficiencies as a campaigner and image-maker. According to Root, Roosevelt's rhetorical radicalism "had the effect of throwing Taft into high relief in the public mind as the representative of conservative constitutionalism."[93] Indeed, the President began his counterattack in Massachusetts already on the defensive answering charges hurled by his skillful challenger. He began his fight apologetically.

I am bound to come out. I can not help it. I am to come and refute those charges. I don't like to fight. I am a peaceful man. I would a good deal rather go around the corner and avoid trouble, but he has got me up against the wall and if I have any manhood at all I have got to fight, and I have to show the American people as best I can that he does not know what a fair deal is in his criticism of me.[94]

Few presidents, however, could win the sympathy of the crowd with such rhetoric. The public desired a strong, dynamic leader, not a cringing apologetic.

At Boston, Taft refuted Roosevelt's campaign charges point by point as only a lawyer could do. He denied Roosevelt's charges that he was allied with the Old Guard political bosses or that he favored an oligarchical form of government. He exposed Roosevelt's deliberate deceit on reciprocity, defended his own vigorous antitrust policy, and condemned Roosevelt for seeking to violate the two-term tradition of the presidency.[95] The President had finally begun to answer Roosevelt's half-truths and outright lies, but Roosevelt already held the upper hand, for Taft was on the defensive. He had failed to blunt Roosevelt's classic campaign technique of attack! attack! attack!

Taft was distraught at having sunk to the level of person-alities in the campaign:

I greatly deprecate having to trail the office of the President in the mire of politics, but I can not help it. I am fighting for a cause, and I have got to win, not for myself, but to prevent this attack on the independence of the judiciary and to prevent the triumph of the dangerous demagogue.[96]

To Republican national committeeman George J. Diekema, Taft also admitted, "The most serious indictment I have against Roosevelt is that the character of his campaign has made my campaign necessary."[97] Stepping down into the gut-ter to match epithets with Roosevelt, one of the greatest phrase-makers of all time, was a soul-searching trial for the President, but preserving the American constitutional system had become more important to Taft than maintaining a high moral posture. This head-on but unequal clash exposed the meager campaigning skills of the President. He lacked the temperamental aggressiveness, rhetorical skill, and moral flexi-bility that permitted Roosevelt to utter deliberate lies and half-truths, engage in a personal campaign of charge and countercharge, and create and demolish straw men. Taft would not resort to the demagoguery of his competitor.

Roosevelt's popularity among the rank and file Republicans continued to emerge. With the exception of Massachusetts, Roosevelt carried every primary against Taft, sweeping the states of Illinois, Pennsylvania, California, Ohio, New Jersey, and Nebraska, winning in the process 281 delegates to the President's 71. Such an impressive string of popular victories only added to his bandwagon appeal and threatened Taft's renomination. Rank and file Republicans had clearly repudi-ated Taft, but established leaders like Boies Penrose of Penn-sylvania, William Barnes of New York, Henry Cabot Lodge of Massachusetts, Jim Watson of Indiana, and Harry Daugherty of Ohio remained loyal to the President. With the regular party organization solidly behind him, Taft refused to step aside.

Roosevelt remained about 80 votes shy of a majority when the convention opened on June 18th. The Taft forces were grimly determined to hold their approximately 550 delegates in line. The President planned to keep in direct contact with the convention by telephone at three different hours of the day in order to confer with his leaders "direct on the exigencies of the situation as they arise."[98] Charles D. Hilles, Taft's campaign manager, acted as the personal spokesman for the President at the convention and distributed the authorized versions of the President's planks for the platform.[99] Taft, moreover, was assured control of the Republican National Committee and the Credentials and Platform committees. His strength on the all-important Credentials Committee, charged with evaluating challenges to many Taft delegates, was 32 to 21 in his favor.[100] In addition, Taft had chosen Elihu Root as the temporary chairman of the convention and was confident that Root would "ring true" for sane constitutionalism in his opening address.[101] The Taft forces were in control of the convention machinery and were ready to do battle.

As the convention opened, talk of a Roosevelt bolt from the party was pervasive. Taft was inclined to believe the rumors, but he did not care. When another rumor began to spread that Taft would step aside for a compromise candidate, Taft debunked the gossip as "wholly unfounded."[102] Although he might have withdrawn if he could have guaranteed the nomination of Hughes or Root, he realized that a retreat now would spark a move by some of his own delegates to Roosevelt and that he could not accept. As he explained to Hilles on the opening day of the convention, "Personally, I have no desire to continue as a candidate. I had no desire to do so when I went out on the stump, but the fear of Mr. Roosevelt's success made it necessary."[103]

The election of Root as temporary chairman provided the first major test of strength between the contending forces. Root won election by a vote of 588 to 502, but some delegates pledged to Roosevelt had supported Root. Taft's apparent strength was only 536 delegates, or four short of an absolute majority. However, on the next day, June 20, the President's real strength became evident on a motion to prevent challenged Taft delegates from voting on their own contests before the convention. The motion was tabled by a vote of 564 to 510—a clear victory for Taft. When the contests were taken to the floor of the convention, the Taft forces beat back the challenges as the President's strength on each ballot increased gradually from 558 to 605 votes. Once the Credentials Committee had ruled against the Roosevelt challenges and been upheld by the convention, the contest was all over. On June 22, the convention renominated Taft with 561 votes, Roosevelt winning only 107. Under instructions from Roosevelt, three hundred forty-four delegates refused to vote at all. Vice-president Sherman was also renominated despite some previous flirtations with the Roosevelt camp. A relieved President issued a statement from the White House:

The Chicago Convention just ended is . . . in itself the end of a pre-convention campaign presenting a crisis more threatening and issue more important than those of the election campaign which is to follow between the two great National parties.

The question here at stake was whether the Republican Party was to change its attitude as the chief conservator in the Nation of constitutional representative government and was to weaken the constitutional guarantees of life, liberty, and property, and all other rights declared sacred in the Bill of Rights, by abandoning the principle of absolute independence of the judiciary essential to the maintenance of those rights.[104]

Taft, of course, was jubilant at the outcome of the convention. "We are all happy over the result at Chicago," he wrote to Mabel Boardman, "and we don't care what happens in November—at least we don't care enough to minimize the pleasure we have in the accomplishment of so great a result as the suppression of such an evil as Roosevelt."[105] Although Roosevelt had criticized Taft for his alliances with many of the Old Guard bosses, Taft could not have won without their support, support which Roosevelt would have welcomed if it had been available. "The truth is," the President wrote to James A. Hemenway of Indiana, "that I owe my nomination to such veterans as you and Jim Watson, Penrose, McKinley, Root, Olmstead, Hilles, and a number of others who understood what real politics were and met the fury and foam of the Rooseveltian attack with cold steel."[106] The organization politicians had beaten back a candidate who Taft felt had become a dangerous demagogue. As Otto Bannard wrote to Taft, "We hold the fort, and he is the guerilla."[107] The party was well on its way to becoming the "citadel of conservative orthodoxy."[108]

VIII

Roosevelt and a large contingent of delegates bolted the Republican party and, on August 7, nominated Roosevelt as the Progressive party's candidate for the presidency. Composed of the crusading remnants of the progressives beaten by Taft, the new "Bull Moose" party was tailor-made to promote the progressivism and social justice of Theodore Roosevelt. To Taft, however, the party had attracted a conglomeration of social types: "Every crank, every academic enthusiast, every wild theorist with any proposition for the solution of any social problem has been gathered there by invitation."[109] Although many Republicans refused to risk their political futures by divorcing themselves from the party, enough did to provide Roosevelt with sufficient support to run a strong campaign.

The President recognized that the creation of the Bull Moose party would mean "a long hard fight with probable defeat" in November, but it would also end all future chances of Roosevelt's nomination by the Republican party.[110] The President believed that Roosevelt had so discredited himself at the convention that "many who followed him before . . . will now fall away from him and yield to the calls of regularity." In any case, Taft felt that victory in November was not as important as preserving the party as the defender of "conservative government and conservative institutions."[111] He almost welcomed a purifying defeat. To Mrs. Buckner Wallingford of Cincinnati he wrote:

The Republican party needs the discipline of defeat, and the great object that I have in carrying on this campaign is saving the parts of the party which can be saved, and making a solid disciplined force which will have sloughed off, as members of importance at least, these wild-eyed populists who insist on being Republicans, without obeying any of the rules of conformity that ought to obtain in a party which is to accomplish anything.

More was involved for Taft than the preservation of constitutional principles: the two-party system itself had to be saved. Taft feared the emergence of a fractionalized multiparty system and ineffective government in which public policy would degenerate into a "compromise between extremists, which always means little progress." In the parliamentary systems he saw emerging in Europe, politics had become a process of merely "fooling the voters by promises." Taft felt that if American politics became more fragmented, they would become "more and more of a game in which the real public interest is lost sight of, and the question of soliciting or alluring popular support becomes the sole purpose of attempted or actual legislation." The "object of a real statesman" was to preserve "the solidarity of his party" in order to maintain a "consistent, uniform support of really useful measures until they be enacted into law and demonstrate their usefulness."[112] Although there was little "solidarity" among Republicans now, Taft hoped that a defeat would help the mavericks "recognize the tremendous value there is in the compactness and discipline of a party for the accomplishment of good in popular government."[113] He hoped that the lessons of defeat would force the party to select a sound statesman in the future rather than an opportunist like Roosevelt.

IX

In contrast to his energetic fight for the nomination, Taft decided to remain aloof from the fall campaign. Neither Roosevelt nor Taft was likely to defeat the Democratic nominee Woodrow Wilson, reform-minded governor of New Jersey. The President recognized his impossible situation and virtually eliminated himself from the campaign. "I am not going to make any speeches in this campaign if I can help it," he explained to Edward Colston of Cincinnati. Taft planned only to deliver his speech of acceptance, and "when that is done I hope I shall be done, so far as speaking activity in the canvass is concerned."[114] After his speech on August 1, Taft decided to make no further speeches. He explained to an anxious supporter:

I am very sorry, but my time has been so much taken up, and I have had no vacation of any sort for so long, that I must reserve the month of October, so far as possible, to myself. I expect to be in Beverly during that month, and feel as if I ought not make public addresses. I do not expect to take any part in the campaign, following in that respect the tradition of former Presidents.[115]

Badly scarred from his struggle for renomination, Taft preferred to leave the campaign to the Republican National Committee and its new chairman, Charles Hilles.

The speech of acceptance added little to the President's notably inert campaign. Despite the reactionary image with which Roosevelt had tarred the President, the speech was moderately progressive in tone. Taft recognized that the old Jeffersonian rhetoric would no longer do: "Time was when the least government was thought the best, and the policy which left all to the individual, unmolested and unaided by government, was deemed the wisest," Taft argued. "Now the duty of government by positive law to further equality of opportunity in respect of the weaker classes in their dealings with the stronger and more powerful is clearly recognized." Taft felt that the Constitution was flexible enough to permit the federal government to assume more paternalistic functions if necessary. The President also warned of the dangers of extreme progressivism. Although in favor of the short ballot and the reduction in the number of elective offices on the state and local level, Taft could not accept the other tenets of the progressive faith. He condemned Roosevelt for threatening the right to private property and an independent judiciary and criticized such progressive panaceas as the initiative, referendum, and recall:

These gentlemen propose to reform the Government, whose present defects, if any, are due to the failure of the people to devote as much time as is necessary to their political duties, by requiring a political activity by the people three times that which thus far the people have been willing to assume; and thus their remedies, instead of exciting the people to further interests and activity in the Government, will tire them into such an indifference as still further to remand control of public affairs to a minority.[116]

Although Taft's warnings about the deficiencies of progressive dogma proved astonishingly correct in subsequent decades, his moderate appeal to the American people was lost amidst the populist rhetoric of the campaign.

What plagued Taft during the fall campaign, indeed, the whole dramatic year of 1912, was the disloyalty of his cabinet and close friends. Hitchcock, as noted earlier, had apparently wavered in his support of the President prior to the nomination and never really played a significant role in Taft's reelection campaign. Taft also became aware of Vice-president Sherman's willingness to desert the administration for Roosevelt if he could secure renomination as vice-president. The whole cabinet, moreover, proved reluctant to work for Taft's renomination. According to Charles Taft,

Knox does not even stay in Washington. Meyer is holding on until he sees what Roosevelt is going to do. Stimson can't afford to fight the Colonel or be a party to it. Fisher is seeking reputation for Fisher. Wickersham has done nothing but embarrass the President since he entered the Cabinet. Nagel is the only member who seems anxious to assist the President. MacVeagh means well, but he ought to be given a bottle of milk and allowed to crawl on the lap of Mrs. MacVeagh and sleep.

The lethargy of the cabinet did not change appreciably after Roosevelt's formal announcement of his candidacy. Secretary of the Navy Meyer, former postmaster general under Roosevelt, was placed in a position of "genuine distress" by Roosevelt's candidacy, but pledged Taft his support.[117] When asked to speak on behalf of the administration during the fall campaign, however, Meyer declined, alleging illness and fatigue.[118] Secretary of War Stimson also promised to support the President for renomination, but he was willing to make only two speeches for Taft that fall. Stimson remained so indifferent and inactive that Hilles relegated him to his list of "sunshine soldiers." Hilles was ready to place Fisher and MacVeagh on the same list.[119] Although Fisher had received pleas for aid from both Taft and the national committee, he declined to give any speeches because of the press of official business. Of course, he had no sympathy for the campaign against Roosevelt.[120] Secretary of State Knox, on the other hand, delivered a few perfunctory speeches for Taft, but was reluctant to campaign extensively for what he must have considered a lost cause.[121]

The dilemma facing Elihu Root was similar to that of many of the President's friends. When Roosevelt had formally announced his candidacy, Root had written to Robert Bacon in Paris of the anguish and gloom which hung over Lodge, Meyer, Stimson, and himself. Roosevelt had thrown the party into such a distressing predicament that Root confessed, "I wish to fall upon your neck and weep."[122] In the preconvention campaign, Root refused to campaign for Taft because of his close friendship with Roosevelt. He had accepted the job of temporary chairman of the Republican convention and helped head off the Roosevelt bandwagon for nomination, but he declined to make any speeches for Taft that fall, pleading illness and fatigue.[123] Root's illness, for the most part, was merely an excuse to avoid speech-making which, he admitted to Bacon, "I hate always and which I positively loathe now."[124] Root too had become a "sunshine soldier."

Although Harry M. Daugherty, chairman of the Ohio Republican State Executive Committee, sent pleas to Taft to "lay down" on Root, Knox, Wickersham, Stimson, and Nagel, and send them into Ohio to campaign if possible, Taft could budge only Nagel.[125] Amid the backsliding and desertion of his associates, Taft tried to remain philosophical.

You know I have a heart for any fate, and that I am not making myself sick over the present situation. Although the treachery of a good many people might make me a misanthrope, I hope I am above allowing it to do so. I don't know that there is any more treachery now than there always has been, only the peculiar situation has developed it all at once.[126]

Only Nagel and old James Wilson of the Agriculture Department lent political support to the administration. For the most part, Taft and Hilles were forced to rely upon "passive advertisement" to put their message across.[127] The President's closest friends and associates deserted him in his hour of need. And yet, since Taft himself had failed to inspire anyone by his example, who could blame them?

Although inactive as a candidate himself, Taft remained concerned about the outside chance of a Roosevelt victory. Taft expected his former boss to grow even more radical as a candidate because of the followers he had attracted. "He has been radical to the last degree in state socialism," the President wrote to Hilles. "He has not advocated the appropriation of rich men's property to distribute among the poor, but that is only another step and perhaps is one involved in the really successful accomplishment of those steps which he proposes."[128] In one of his more optimistic moments, however, Taft thought there was little to fear. He believed Roosevelt would draw many progressive Democrats away from Wilson, drive the regular Republicans back into the party, and, with the aid of Wilson's candidacy, force all of the conservative Democrats into the Republican party.[129] As the President admitted to Hilles, Roosevelt "is gradually helping us to a position I should like to occupy—that is, he is going to have third parties everywhere."[130]

The desired benefits of a third party did not materialize. The Bull Moose movement only exacerbated Republican factionalism across the country. In some states, the Bull Moosers succeeded in selecting Republican electors who were pledged to vote for Roosevelt even if Taft carried the state. Much of the initial energy of the Republican campaign was diverted from electioneering toward the elimination of Bull Moosers disguised as Republican electors in the states of Pennsylvania, West Virginia, Michigan, Illinois, Missouri, South Dakota,

California, and Oregon. Although Taft had hoped to create the impression that a vote for Roosevelt was a wasted vote, he came to believe that Roosevelt had succeeded in turning the tables and convincing the public that "there was not the slightest chance for Republican success."[131] Thus, many Republicans refused to waste their votes on Taft and supported either Wilson or Roosevelt. Finally, to crown the misfortunes of the President, vice-presidential candidate Jim Sherman died suddenly on October 30, six days before the election.

The result of the November 5 election was a resounding defeat for Taft. He won only the eight electoral votes of Utah and Vermont and was relegated to an ignominious third place by the voters. Wilson polled 6,301,254 (41 per cent) votes, Roosevelt 4,127,788 (27 per cent), Taft 3,485,831 (25 per cent), and Socialist Eugene Debs 900,672 (6 per cent). Roosevelt was far more successful in winning the 88 electoral votes of California, Michigan, Minnesota, Pennsylvania, South Dakota, and Washington. Taft believed that Roosevelt had picked up many votes from Wilson of the "labor, socialistic, discontented, ragtag and bobtail variety," but he concluded that hundreds of thousands of Republicans, afraid of wasting their votes, had supported Wilson in order to escape the danger of Roosevelt. The 25 per cent of the popular vote for Taft represented "the irreducible minimum of the Republican party that was left after Roosevelt got through with it and after Wilson drew from it the votes of those Republicans who feared Roosevelt."[132] Republican chances for victory in 1912 had been slim, but the combined votes for Taft and Roosevelt had given the two a 9-percent edge in the popular vote over Wilson. The question of whether a vigorous campaign by Taft leading a united party would have produced a November victory will always remain a matter for speculation.

The postelection statement of the President conceding defeat provided the finale to Taft's campaign for constitutional government:

The vote for Mr. Roosevelt, the third party candidate, and for Mr. Debs, the Socialist candidate, is a warning that their propaganda in favor of fundamental changes in our constitutional, representative government has formidable support. While the experiment of a change in the tariff is being carried out by the Democratic administration, it behooves the Republicans to gather again to the party standard and pledge anew their faith in their party's principles and to organize again to defend the constitutional government handed down to us by our fathers. We must make clear to the young men of the country who have been weaned away from sound principles of government by promise of reform, impossible of accomplishment by mere legislation, that patriotism and common sense require them to return to a support of our constitution. Without compromising our principles, we must convince and win back former Republicans, and we must reinforce our ranks with Constitution loving Democrats.

We favor every step of progress toward more perfect equality of opportunity and the ridding society of injustice. But we know that all progress worth making is possible with our present form of government, and that to sacrifice that which is of the highest value in our governmental structure for undefined and impossible reforms is the wildest folly. We must face the danger with a clear knowledge of what it is.

The Republican party is equal to the task. It has no nobler cause. Let us close our ranks and march forward to do battle for the right and the true.[133]

6. "The Pathology of Hysteria"

If I were to try to read, much less answer, all the attacks made on me, this shop might as well be closed for any other business. I do the very best I know how—the very best I can; and I mean to keep on doing so until the end. If the end brings me out all right, what is said against me won't amount to anything. If the end brings me out wrong, ten angels swearing I was right would make no difference.

Abraham Lincoln[1]

For the major part of his presidency, Taft kept a framed photograph of Lincoln's words on his White House desk to symbolize the spirit of his office. Whereas Lincoln had been President in time of Civil War, Taft had merely succeeded Theodore Roosevelt in a period of rising social protest. Words which reflected greatness in Lincoln turned to wormwood for Taft, for they reflected his stubborn unconcern for his public image as president. Taft's indifference toward his public image was the prime cause of his failure as president. His attitude adversely affected his relations with the news media of the nation and led to serious tactical blunders in his advocacy of public policies.

I

When Roosevelt bequeathed the office of president to Taft, he willed more than a list of public policies; he left an expanded role for the President at home and abroad. From his personal intervention in the anthracite coal strike of 1902 to his bold dispatch of the navy around the world in 1908, he stamped his personality indelibly upon the minds and hearts of Americans as the righteous guardian of the public good. More than any other man of the period, Roosevelt had aroused the nation to the dangers of growing corporate power and imbued the public with a sense of confidence in the ability and integrity of their government to bring about meaningful reform. The president was now expected to be an energetic spokesman for the disparate, unorganized voices of the public and the national interest. As Roosevelt himself recognized in the twilight of his presidency, "I believe that whatever value my service may have comes more from what I *am* than from what I *do*."[2] When he finally bowed out as president, he left the American people with one notable legacy—the expectation that the next president *would* and *should* be like Theodore Roosevelt.

Temperamentally the two men were direct opposites. Roosevelt was moralistic, opportunistic, aggressive, and energetic; Taft was legalistic, consistent, reflective, and passive, some even said lazy. Roosevelt was the acknowledged master of the art of rhetoric; Taft merely a junior apprentice whose training as a judge and administrator had left his oratorical and publicity skills severely atrophied. As a member of the Roosevelt administration, Taft had gained national attention, not through his own publicity efforts, but because, as Charles Hilles later put it, "He had the finest press agent ever a man had in Teddy."[3] When Taft became president, however, he was suddenly forced to become his own press agent and generate his own publicity. "He will have to find his own fuel now," Major Butt noted after the inauguration, "and, like a child, will have to learn to walk alone."[4] Butt's assessment was extremely perceptive, for the new President appeared to be leaning psychologically upon his predecessor. When Taft explained his initial actions as president to the departing Roosevelt, he acknowledged Roosevelt's influence upon his own political judgment: "I want you to know that I do nothing in my work in the Executive Office without considering what you would do under the same circumstances and without having in a sense a mental talk with you over the pros and cons of the situation."[5] Although Taft would eventually discard this psychological crutch and simply be himself, the attitude indicated the new President's political immaturity.

II

Already noticeable during the election campaign, Taft's deficiencies as his own publicity agent were mercilessly exposed after his inauguration. With little talent for dramatizing himself or his policies, Taft soon found himself on the defensive trying to explain his indifference toward publicity. When editor William Allen White expressed concern over the relative silence of the President regarding his policy objectives, Taft replied:

I am not constituted as Mr. Roosevelt is in being able to keep the country advised every few days of the continuance of the state of mind in reference to reforms. It is a difference in temperament. He talked with correspondents a great deal. His heart was generally on his sleeve, and he must communicate his feelings. I find myself unable to do so.[6]

The very next day, in anticipation of the criticism which he knew would be forthcoming, Taft wrote to Roosevelt:

I have not the facility for educating the public as you had through talks with correspondents, and so I fear that a large part of the public will feel as if I had fallen away from your ideals; but you know me better and will understand that I am still working away on the same old plan and hope to realize in some measure the results that we both hold valuable and worth striving for.[7]

This shortcoming would not have been so disturbing had Taft

not been so inflexible regarding his own style of publicity. "After I have made a definite statement," he wrote White, "I have to let it go at that until the time for action arises, when I seek as sincerely and earnestly as I can to live up to my previous declaration." Taft acknowledged the pitfalls involved in such a strategy, especially when applied to his tainted cooperation with the legislative leadership. "I expect to have my position questioned," he admitted to White, but he hoped his legislative success would vindicate his strategy.[8]

A week after Roosevelt's departure for Africa, Major Butt noted the glaring deficiency in the new President's sense of public relations. Roosevelt had possessed an uncanny instinct for making headlines and would often distribute news items to keep himself in the national spotlight, but Taft, according to Butt, had "no conception of the press as an adjunct to his office." "Neither the President nor his secretary gives out anything of any real interest," he noted, "nor do they understand the art of giving out news." The result of the presidential news blackout was the increased circulation of rumors. When some of the press became very angry at Taft for withholding news, Butt tried to explain to them that the nation would just have to readjust to a president with a less dramatic style than Roosevelt.[9] Conditioned by Roosevelt to expect attention and help in making news, reporters found it difficult to adjust to Taft's self-effacing style. Thus, ignorant of the art of news management, Taft began his presidency without any real public relations policy.

Taft's handling of the Payne-Aldrich tariff highlighted his indifference toward the press. When he pledged a downward revision of the tariff in 1908, little did he realize how important reductions on print paper and wood pulp would become to the news media and how his moderate position would poison their attitude toward his administration. As early as January 1908, the newspaper publishers had begun to pressure

Congress for free print paper and wood pulp in the new tariff law to break the alleged monopoly of the domestic paper manufacturers. When the Associated Press held its general meeting in April 1909, it passed a resolution asking Congress to "grant immediate relief from the exactions of combinations of paper makers." When the American Newspaper Publishers' Association joined the fight for free paper and pulp, virtually the whole news media became committed to lowering the tariff.[10]

Considering their expectations, the publishers fared poorly in the new tariff bill. The existing rate on print paper had been six dollars per hundred pounds, which the House initially lowered to two dollars. The Senate then raised it to four dollars. Although the press strongly criticized the Senate bill, Taft believed it was "by no means so bad as has been represented."[11] He was, however, shocked at the "deliberate misrepresentation" and "misconception of the facts" which the press displayed toward the Senate bill, much of it due, he felt, to their desire for lower rates on print paper.[12] Despite press opposition to the Senate bill, Taft made no strong effort to mobilize public opinion behind the House bill or explain his views on the Senate bill. He did not want to rock the boat and jeopardize his policy of harmony. When he eventually compromised in conference on a rate of $3.75 for print paper, an unfriendly press was assured for the bill. When press criticism of the tariff increased, Taft blamed the high print paper rates for much of it. "I can not help attributing a great deal of bitterness of this controversy to the counting room of the newspapers which have been affected by the failure to reduce the tariff on print paper in the tariff bill."[13]

This early impolitic course of neglecting the vested interests of the opinion-making organs of the nation guaranteed the President an unsympathetic, almost hostile press when he needed it most to counteract the inevitable disaffection with a new tariff and to build his own independent image as president. Taft eventually realized his mistake. After his defeat in 1912 he wrote to Otto Bannard, "I think I might have secured a tariff on print paper at $2.00 per one hundred pounds, and if that had been brought about we should not have had the bitterness of spirit in reference to the Payne Bill."[14] But the damage had been done.

In order to dispel widespread misconceptions about the Payne-Aldrich tariff, Taft left Washington on September 15 for a month-long political tour of the country. The tour became a trial. Taft admittedly had no facility in addressing crowds. "I am expected to make a good many speeches, and that frightens me; for I do not know exactly what to say or how to say it. I shall stagger through the matter some way, but not in any manner, I fear, to reflect credit on the Administration."[15] Taft's fears were well founded. Not only did he imprudently associate himself with many standpat leaders of Congress, but he praised the tariff at Winona, Minnesota, as "the best tariff bill that the Republican party ever passed."[16] The Winona remarks contradicted Taft's guarded language at the signing of the act and, according to Senator La Follette, "in effect challenged the Progressives in Congress who had voted against the measure, and the progressive judgment of the country, which had already condemned it."[17] Despite progressive outcries across the country, the President continued to defend his Winona speech wherever he went. Privately, he had convinced himself of the soundness of his position. He confided to his son Robert, "My impression is that the speech is the best thing I have done."[18] When William Dudley Foulke complained about the rising criticism of his remarks, Taft replied, "I do not know that I can do anything to prevent this, in view of the fact that I can not myself see that I have done anything to call for such severe criticism. I meant every word of my Winona speech."[19]

The nationwide tour failed to bring Taft any closer to an

appreciation of the public mood. He mistook the natural curiosity and receptivity of the people for support of the tariff and the new administration. He concluded that the criticism of the tariff represented only the vocal outcry of a small progressive minority:

They have become desperate . . . and their cry is heard above the quiet chant of contentment that exists everywhere in this country where I have been in view of the remarkable conditions of prosperity and comfort that surround the people. It is a case in my judgment where the "shallows murmur and the deeps are dumb."[20]

A few days later, Taft wrote to his son Robert, "The theory that the people are discontented or are waiting to make a breach in the Republican party is in my judgment all nonsense."[21] With this misguided air of confidence, Taft continued to praise the tariff long after his return to Washington in October. Roosevelt might well have created a diversion and concentrated on such issues as the corporation income tax or the income tax amendment, but not Taft. "I am in favor of continuing to discuss the tariff bill . . . and everything else," he maintained, "because that is where the fight is to be and that is where the misrepresentation has taken place."[22] When Horace Taft complained that the President's laudatory references to the tariff were like a surgeon needlessly turning a knife around during a necessary operation, Taft retorted, "I am sorry you think that my reference to the tariff law is to be compared to the operation you describe, but I am going to keep turning the knife around if that's what it is."[23]

It was not until June 1910 that the President finally clarified his Winona remarks in a published interview in *McClure's Magazine*. Months of progressive criticism had begun to sink in:

I finally signed the bill. Not because it was a perfect tariff;

ideal tariffs are an impossibility under the method of tariff legislation we have employed. I signed it because it was the best I could secure under the circumstances; because it represented a considerable downward revision from the Dingley tariff; and because, all things considered, I did not believe myself justified in holding up the business of the country for months longer by vetoing this bill, on the chance of getting a better one.[24]

The President's public retreat, however, had come too late, for he had already convinced the country that he was satisfied with the tariff.[25] In December 1911 he was again interviewed and asked whether, if he had another chance, he would repeat his Winona address. "In phraseology no; in effect yes," was his reply. "Had I known as much then as I do now, I should have realized that there are some things one cannot leave to be taken for granted." Taft blamed the imprudent use of "best" in the speech upon the hasty circumstances under which it had been written. "The comparative would have been a better description than the superlative," he concluded.[26]

Critics might have found less to attack in the address had "better" been substituted for "best." Roosevelt could defend the Tariff in the *Outlook*—"I think that the present tariff is better than the last, and considerably better than the one before the last."[27]—without adverse political effects. Taft, however, did not possess the reservoir of public confidence and good will of a Roosevelt and would have encountered trouble whatever his explanation. Roosevelt probably could have delivered the Winona address with a minimum of personal damage because he was trusted by the people and the press while Taft was not.

As previously noted, Taft had ruined his public image by his open identification with the standpat leadership in Congress. Although attacked by progressives for merely trying to trust Cannon and Aldrich, Taft continued to defend his associates and even inaugurated an annual dinner for Cannon as an official state function. Roosevelt had honored Cannon with similar unofficial dinners given in a "half-surreptitious way," but Taft, grateful for Cannon's cooperation, was unconcerned about the public reaction to the inception of such a formal affair.[28] Thus, many of Taft's problems were of his own making, for he deliberately continued to show favoritism toward the standpatters without corresponding gestures of goodwill to the progressives. He displayed little skill at straddling political fences. He acknowledged candidly to critic Lucius B. Swift, "I am not so constituted that I can run with the hare and hunt with the hounds, and when a man has stood by me as Aldrich has, I propose to stand by him; and I do not care what happens in regard to the matter, ultimately history will show the wrong that has been done him. . . . In respect to Mr. Cannon, the same thing is true in a less degree."[29]

Taft compounded these early mistakes by challenging the postal subsidies of the weekly magazines and newspapers. A more politically minded president might have shunned further conflict with the news media, but not Taft. In his December State of the Union message to Congress, much to the amazement of the publishers, he labeled the postal deficit an "enormous subsidy" to the weekly magazines and recommended that Congress "consider whether radical steps should not be taken to reduce the deficit in the post office department" from second class mail.[30] When protests from the publishers began to flood the White House, Taft displayed no awareness of the political implications of his actions. As he explained to Fred Lockley, manager of the *Pacific Monthly*, "the reduction of the second class rates on periodicals was not a matter of politics, but "a mere matter of evidence and business sense." He continued, "Nothing but proper sense of duty would be likely to induce the Executive to bring this matter to the attention of the public, involving as it does the necessary hostility of a very influential element in forming public opinion."[31] The President's sense of duty, however, had been affected by his anger over his bad press. He could see little reason for continuing to subsidize his critics, especially when they were attacking subsidies for everyone else. As he explained to Otto Bannard, he was determined to do "justice" to his muckrakers.

The truth is that the present magazines are getting about fifty millions of dollars out of the Government that they are not entitled to, and I am going to fight that thing through. I do not care anything about them. They have shown themselves just exactly as selfish as the interests which they have attacked, and I propose to have justice done. If we wish to contribute a subsidy of fifty millions to the education of the country, I can find a good deal of better method of doing it than by the circulation of Collier's Weekly and Everybody's Magazine.[32]

The President's vindictiveness further alienated an already critical press eager to expose his deficiencies.

The publishers fought back with an organized lobbying campaign against the postal rate hike. The proposal earned Taft virtually the unanimous condemnation of the Publishers' Association as well as increased criticism of his administration. According to John A. Sleicher of *Leslie's Weekly*, there was no doubt in the minds of the publishers that "they were being discriminated against for the purpose of punishing them."[33] Taft was angered by and appalled at the effectiveness of the publishers' campaign. He complained to Senator Frank Flint of the Post Office Committee:

I never in all my knowledge of lobbies and of organized efforts to influence legislation have seen such flagrant mis-representation and such bold defiant attempts by the payment of the heaviest advertisement bills to arouse the press of the country against the proposed legislation.[34]

However, at the lame duck session of the Sixty-first Congress, an increasingly sophisticated President admitted to Senator Boies Penrose of the same committee that it would be "a great mistake" if some settlement were not reached with the magazine publishers on the postal rates.[35] Taft finally compromised with the publishers and agreed to the formation of a judicial commission to study the merits of the whole issue. The commission ultimately appointed by the President was composed of Supreme Court Justice Charles Evans Hughes, President A. Lawrence Lowell of Harvard, and Harry A. Wheeler, president of the Chicago Association of Commerce.

Although the final report of the commission recommended an increase in second class rates, the President decided not to press the issue. In a message to Congress in 1912, he concluded, "The business enterprises of the publishers of periodicals . . . have been built up on the basis of the present second class rate, and therefore it would be manifestly unfair to put into immediate effect a large increase in postage."[36] The President had been soundly beaten. Congress proved equally reluctant to alter the second class rates in an election year and decided to continue investigating the matter. For the duration of the administration, the issue remained safely under study.

The President's proposed increase in second class rates had recklessly entangled him in a battle with the magazines at a time when he needed all the positive coverage he could get. By the time he had realized his tactical mistake, his public image had been damaged almost beyond repair. It was only after the din of the 1912 election had faded that he philosophically concluded, "It was not necessary for me to run amuck among the magazines and attempt to curtail the profit they made in the transportation of their products at an unconscionable low rate."[37] But contrition had again come too late.

III

Media criticism of the President and his reaction to it cannot be fully appreciated without some understanding of the press of the period. The progressive movement had injected a spirit of reform and sensationalism into many of the popular magazines and newspapers, making it difficult for public officials to approach the question of economic and political reform in a responsible manner. Theodore Roosevelt had appropriately labeled much of the press as "muckrakers." That there was much "muck" to be raked up neither Taft nor Roosevelt would have denied, but it was a matter of perspective. Taft, like all presidents, was required to consider every issue from a national point of view. The responsibility of office made instant solutions to complex problems a luxury which a democratic leader could not afford. It was Taft's misfortune to have been elected in a period in which muckraking was at its height.[38] The inexperienced President made an easy target for the sensationalists.

Perhaps Speaker Cannon captured the essence of the problem as well as any of his contemporaries when he noted that the "Politics of Propaganda" had replaced the parties as the initiators of public policy. He saw the new politics threatening the basis of party government, for the "propagandists care little for party conventions or party platforms." Major legislation originated more and more, according to Cannon, not in party platforms or election campaigns, but in the concerted efforts of propagandists who self-righteously proclaimed their aims as the will of the American people. Elected officials found it more and more difficult to withstand the unselfish appeals of the reformers, and party government was disintegrating. Congress, Cannon believed, had "accepted the voice of Propaganda as the voice of God."[39]

The President shared Cannon's view of the state of American politics and the muckraking press, for of course he too was at a disadvantage in combating opponents who asserted rather dogmatically that moral right was on their side and all evil on the side of their opponents. As criticism of his administration rose in late 1909 and early 1910, Taft concluded that much of it resulted from a condition of mass hysteria and hypocrisy "in which anything asserted with sufficient emphasis, without proof, will be believed about any man, no matter how disinterested or high his character."[40]

When Guy W. Mallon of Cincinnati complained to Taft of the growing disillusionment with the President in the West, Taft attributed his problem to hypocrisy:

The truth is, we are passing through a period of supreme hypocrisy, in which the man who makes the loudest protestation of hatred of monopoly and political corruption and bossism has the great advantage. The only person who is at a disadvantage is the one upon whom falls the necessity for affirmative action and the enactment of beneficial legislation.[41]

In April 1910, Taft described the temper of the public mind to Ambassador Whitelaw Reid in London. "The people are restless," he noted. "They have a yearning for something startling and radical that we are not likely to furnish them, and they have a degree of suspicion of public men, promoted by muckraking newspapers and magazines, that it will take some time for the country to recover from."[42] The self-interest of the press only aggravated the condition of the public mind. As Taft wrote to H. H. Kohlsaat, owner of the *Chicago Record-Herald*,

I have not been familiar myself with any situation politically where there has been so much hypocrisy, so much hysteria, so much misrepresentation by the press growing out of their own personal interest in legislation as within the last year, and this affects not only the newspapers but also the periodicals.[43]

When the Republican party suffered serious setbacks in the 1910 elections, the President's election analyst attributed much of the slippage to the "pathology of hysteria."[44] It was the worst of times for a president unversed in the arts of public persuasion.

True, the public mood made governing more difficult, but Taft's response to it was politically self-destructive. At first he sought a scapegoat. When he returned to Washington in October 1909 from his nationwide tour, he found his cabinet and close friends "full of despair and predicting all sorts of evil" for the administration. Taft could not understand what he might have done to produce such gloom. "I have done nothing that I would not do over again," he confessed to Major Butt, "and therefore I must feel that their troubles are either imaginary or else someone else is to blame."[45] As criticism of the administration increased, he began to attribute most of it to a conspiracy among the progressives and the press against his administration. He agreed with Lafayette Young of Iowa "that there is a cooperative-knockers association against my administration, and that their chief stock in trade is in misrepresenting what I have said."[46]

Within a few months, the President had become dangerously reconciled to a bad press and had assumed a devil-may-care attitude toward his public image and political fortunes. He admitted to his brother Charles that no elected official "has the right to violate any of the prejudices of the people; but for any effect it would have on my own fortunes, I do not think I care."[47] Taft appeared resigned to his unpopularity, which had hardened and prepared him "to carry on government without regard to these waves of popular clamor that find their impetus in muckraking magazines and newspapers affected by the smallest monetary considerations with reference to that tariff."⁴⁸

The more his public image deteriorated, the more the President ignored the abuse of the press. His attitude toward public opinion slowly hardened. "If I live I will have three years to do what I 'dern' choose," he wrote in January 1910, "and to follow what I believe to be right and to regard threats of popular ill will as of no moment whatever if their expressions are directed against what I know to be right or in favor of what I know to be wrong."⁴⁹ By mid-March, he had nothing but utter contempt for the press in general. When H. H. Kohlsaat informed him of Republican apathy toward his administration, Taft replied:

> You describe the feeling among the Republicans as a "don't care a damn" feeling. I have that myself. It is exactly that feeling that I have with reference to the views of the press and of those people who think that they are going to have a better government by defeating the Republican party, or are going to accomplish anything by doing so.⁵⁰

Unable to neutralize unfounded criticism, the President had abandoned any immediate hope of changing a poor public image.

The complacency of the President can also be attributed to two other factors—his strong desire to be himself and his simplistic belief that his accomplishments would speak for themselves. After only two weeks in office, Taft had recognized that he was no Roosevelt and could never become one. Amid the mounting criticism of his first year, he plodded on in his own unspectacular but solid way, unwilling to change radically the methods of operation so rooted in his personality. "There is no use trying to be William Howard Taft with

Roosevelt's ways," he remarked to Major Butt. Taft's strategy was to be "straightforward and natural":

I am going to be honest with myself, whatever else I do. I cannot be spectacular, and I will not be insincere with those I deal with. If I did as many of my friends want me to do, and play the role as Roosevelt played it, I would be accused in the first place of imitation and then denounced as a hypocrite, and both would be true.[51]

When he was chided for not using the presidency as a "bully pulpit" like Roosevelt, Taft pleaded guilty and blamed his judicial training:

I could never feel exactly easy or at home in discussion of subjects that did not seem relevant in some way to the duties of my office, and I could not but feel that where I invaded topics that were really under the control of the states my expressed opinion was, as lawyers would say, subject to a plea of jurisdiction. The fact that there were precedents to the contrary did not alter my feeling.[52]

Taft was painfully aware of the handicap under which he labored, especially from what he called the "little coterie of persons engaged in holding over me the club of so-called Rooseveltism." Nevertheless, he was determined to stick to his own personal style and policies and "after a while to obtain from a reasonable number of my constituents support because of myself and not because I happened to have adopted anybody else's policies."[53]

The President's public image also suffered grievously from his incredibly naive strategy of letting his accomplishments speak for themselves. Unlike Roosevelt, Taft believed that what he *did* as president would be more important than what he *was* as president. When William Allen White had complained of the President's poor public image, Taft affirmed his desire to accomplish reforms rather than talk about them: "I have confidence in the second judgment of the people based on what is done rather than what is proclaimed or what is suspected from appearances."[54] Taft retained a stubborn confidence in his strategy of accomplishment throughout his first two years in office. He interpreted progressive uneasiness toward his administration as a mere lack of faith:

The trouble is that they don't believe me when I say a thing once. . . . I think the next Congress will show my sincerity. I can't reiterate and reiterate, for when I have said a thing once I see no reason to repeat it; and what's more, I will not repeat my position.[55]

In December 1909 he confided to Judge C. W. Dustin of Ohio, "I am hopeful that a consistent, steady, quiet course, trying to do what I think is right, will ultimately convince people that the Administration is worthy of their respect."[56] When the editor of *Everybody's Magazine* suggested that Taft improve his publicity techniques, Taft replied:

I am going to do what I think is best for the country, within my jurisdiction and power, and then let the rest take care of itself. I am not looking for a second term, and I am not going to subject myself to the worry involved in establishing a publicity bureau, or attempting to set myself right before the people in any different way from that which is involved in the ordinary publication of what is done. The misrepresentations which are made by the muckraking correspondents I cannot neutralize, and I don't intend to.[57]

When the critical editor of the *Weekly Clintonian* also urged Taft to alter his publicity techniques, Taft replied, "I am anxious to point to things done, not to exploit with egotistic trumpet what I propose to do."[58] Taft reiterated this approach in an interview published in June 1910 in *McClure's Magazine:* "What I hope for my administration is the accomplishment of definite results, which will be self-explanatory."⁵⁹ As Taft explained to R. L. O'Brien of the *Boston Evening Transcript,* "I have had an abiding faith that if I could get things done the credit would take care of itself ultimately."⁶⁰ Such faith may have been adequate for a federal judge—for the judiciary is expected to appeal to the sober second thought of the nation—but it was inadequate for a president without life tenure.

IV

Despite serious problems with the press, Taft moved very slowly to change his public relations policy. True, he did venture across country on a month-long tour in the fall of 1909, but the tour only tarnished his image further. The President, moreover, refused to assume any responsibility for press reports about his administration and adopted a policy of silent indifference. In April 1910, Oscar King Davis of the *New York Times* found Taft still operating according to the outmoded style of his first few months. Davis came away from a White House visit convinced that Taft had learned nothing about the management of news. "Only this afternoon," he angrily remarked to Major Butt, "he killed four good stories."⁶¹ It is hard to imagine Theodore Roosevelt doing the same. Taft's attitude toward news-making remained one of frustrated helplessness. "I am not responsible for reports of those who would aid me by friendly comment," he explained to the editor of *Everybody's Magazine,* "any more than I can restrict those who would wish to injure me by unfounded criticism and scandal."⁶²

Charles Taft, Wickersham, and Hitchcock were more alarmed at the shabby public image the President was generating than Taft himself. As a result of their pressure, Taft eventually replaced his original personal secretary Fred Carpenter with businessman Charles D. Norton. The President's relations with the press were improved by Norton's willingness to help newsmen obtain stories, but there was no substitute for the President's own sense of public relations. Norton tried to reorganize the President's relations with Cannon and Aldrich, but he merely succeeded in substituting Senator Crane, another loyal member of the Republican establishment, for Aldrich as the President's chief adviser on legislative strategy.[63] Norton also succeeded in having Ballinger ousted from the cabinet, but his constant scheming eventually led to his dismissal in September 1911.

Although unconcerned about his personal image, Taft did worry about public misunderstanding of his policies. His first major attempt to dispel such misunderstanding, his fall tour, had only succeeded in beclouding the tariff issue. He began to foresee a Republican defeat in November 1910. "If so," he explained to Judge David Pugh of Ohio, "it will be due to a misunderstanding by the people of what the Republicans have done." The President, of course, blamed the "lying by newspapers and magazines" for his predicament. The ultimate solution to such misrepresentation lay in a long-term campaign of education. "[T]he people can not be fooled all the time," he explained, "and I hope that within the coming two years the facts may be known to the people by campaigns of education, and when they are made known I do not think the Republican party will appear to a just people to have been undeserving of their support."[64]

It did appear for a moment that spring that Taft might well emerge from the shadow of his predecessor and establish a respectable independent image of his own. During a private meeting in New York with a group of editors and educators late in March, Taft impressed his hosts favorably by his grasp of issues and congenial personality. Hearst editor Arthur Brisbane placed his finger upon the major burden of the President at the meeting when he remarked:

The fact of the matter is, none of us has ever given the President a fair show as yet. We have all been judging him by the standards of his predecessor, and we have yielded to the public clamor for him to use the attacking methods of Roosevelt. We are beginning to see him rightly, and I think he will win out if this Roosevelt homecoming does not upset all plans and purposes of thoughtful men.[65]

However, just as the President's unpopular legislative strategy began to bear fruit in June and the press began to change its tune toward Taft, Theodore Roosevelt triumphantly returned from Europe on June 19. The press was filled with reports of the President's legislative successes, but they were buried by the more sensational news of Roosevelt's impending return, his glorious reception in New York, and a running account of his activities, including his unwillingness to endorse the Taft record wholeheartedly. Roosevelt had stolen the thunder from Taft in his moment of glory as a legislative leader.

Taft continued to hope that the upturn in his popular fortunes might help the party in November. "[W]e ought to win this fall," he wrote to Francis B. Loomis. "We have the arguments with us, if they can only be properly put before the people."[66] The President's thinking was further reflected in his public letter to Congressman William B. McKinley, chairman of the Republican Congressional Campaign Committee, in which he argued that "it is of the utmost importance to make this a campaign of education as to facts and to clear away the clouds of misrepresentation that have obscured the real issues."[67] Taft failed to realize that election campaigns are seldom campaigns of education, but of propaganda and rhetoric designed to persuade men to vote, not necessarily to think. There was no time for genuine education, and the Republicans suffered a stunning defeat that fall. Taft discovered that a good record or the best arguments were not enough. The ability to appeal to popular wants and emotions was essential for electoral success. Chastened by the election returns, he began to reconsider his relationship with the press.

V

The first major change in the President's attitude toward the press came at the lame duck session of the Sixty-first Congress on the issue of Canadian reciprocity. In order to neutralize the anger of the nation's publishers over the Payne-Aldrich Act and the proposed increase in second class postage, Taft decided to push for lower tariffs on print paper and wood pulp. His decision was undoubtedly influenced by the American Newspaper Publishers' Association, which had continued to press for lower rates up to the final signing of the reciprocity agreement with Canada in January 1911.[68] The negotiations with Canada produced a conditional agreement whereby Canadian print paper and wood pulp not restricted by Canadian export charges or regulations would be admitted duty free into the United States.[69] The free entry of these items from practically all private timber lands in Canada was thereby guaranteed. Moreover, this section of the agreement was separated from the remainder of the reciprocity act in Congress and would go into effect regardless of Canadian action on the agreement.[70] This section amounted to a revision of the Payne-Aldrich tariff, and it gave the publishers what they had demanded in 1909, and then some. Immediately after the President submitted the agreement to Congress on January 26, the American Newspaper Publishers' Association began to distribute favorable materials on the agreement to the press across the country. In contrast to their position on the Payne-Aldrich Act, the publishers became Taft's staunchest ally in his drive for reciprocity.[71] It was a pleasant, though unusual alliance.

The President's public indiscretions contributed to the ultimate defeat of the agreement in Canada. When he submitted the agreement to Congress, he described the situation with Canada in words which later came back to haunt him—"They [Canada] are coming to the parting of the ways."[72] Taft felt that if Canada did not seize the opportunity to lower her trade barriers with the United States at this moment, she would become further enmeshed in the British imperial customs system, and that all hopes for a North American free-trade area would disappear. After Champ Clark, Democratic House leader, endorsed the agreement "because I hope to see the day when the American flag will float over every square foot of the British North American possession clear to the North Pole,"[73] no statement by the President or other public officials, however, innocuous, could escape the scrutiny of the Canadian foes of reciprocity. As Taft attempted to sell the agreement at home, he inevitably made verbal slips which were harmful to the Canadian sponsors of the agreement. His words—"Canada is at the parting of the ways."[74]—he repeated again, only to add fresh ammunition to the Canadian opponents. Moreover, on April 27, in an address to the Associated Press and the American Publishers' Association, he warned against the British drive for a worldwide preferential tariff system that would include Canada and exclude the United States.

I have said that this was a critical time in the solution of the question of reciprocity. It is critical, because, unless it is now decided favorably to reciprocity, it is exceedingly probable that no such opportunity will ever again come to the United States. The forces which are at work in England and in Canada to separate her by a Chinese wall from the United States and to make her part of an imperial commercial band, reaching from England around the world to England again, by a system of preferential tariffs, will derive an impetus from the rejection of this treaty, and if we would have reciprocity with all the advantages that I have described, and that I earnestly and sincerely believe will follow its adoption, we must take it now or give it up forever.[75]

The speech only provided Canadian opponents with another club with which to beat the Liberal government. When Congress finally passed the agreement on July 22, Taft jubilently congratulated William Randolph Hearst for "the energetic work of the seven Hearst papers and of your staff for their earnest and useful effort to spread the gospel of reciprocity."[76] Such public praise for Hearst would not have been so damaging had the Hearst chain of papers not been a notorious advocate of the annexation of Canada. Although Taft was silent on the matter for two months, the Liberal Government went down to defeat on September 21 over the issue.

A week after the Liberal defeat, the Canadian Minister for Financial Affairs M. S. Fielding explained the defeat of reciprocity in a candid letter to Secretary Knox. Although the minister recognized the domestic difficulties of the President, he admitted, "I must say that some utterances of the President were made to do much work against us." In particular, Fielding thought the oft-used expression—"We have come to the parting of the ways"—and the President's April 27 address were Taft's two most damaging acts.[77] Unlike Roosevelt, Taft never developed a talent for choosing his public words carefully, and his verbal slips added to his burdens. No wonder his biographer concluded that "at least one unfortunate phrase seems to have been inevitable in every major campaign conducted by Taft."[78]

VI

That the Republican defeat of 1910 had sobered the President became more evident in the fall of 1911 when he embarked upon an extensive western tour to publicize his policy objectives. "I go into it from a sense of duty," he wrote to Henry Taft. "I feel as if I had a gambler's chance for re-election, and that I should be cowardly if I did not take that chance and improve it as much as I can."⁷⁹ Taft hoped that his western tour would overcome the "constant persistent misrepresentation" of his views by at least guaranteeing him headlines wherever he went.⁸⁰ But his heart was not in the fight. "I don't expect that speeches are going to do much or any good," he wrote to Bannard. "But I must go through the motions. . . . I just grit my teeth and go through it."⁸¹

The President was still a poor campaigner. Although his ease in handling large audiences had improved since 1909, his oratory remained soporific. According to Major Butt, the President's speeches were still "dry and full of statistics, and we cannot get him away from figures. . . . He gives too much detail and not enough general principles." Butt also lamented that when a congressman would advise the President to shy away from some controversial issue, "it is the very subject he does touch on—not only touching on it but pounding it in." Nowhere in enemy territory did Butt see the President flinch from expounding his views forthrightly.⁸²

Taft's fearless style originated in his desire to educate the public on the issues of the day. As he explained to his brother Horace, "I wished to state my case to the people of the United States on the veto messages, on peace, and on the trusts, in such a way that they would know the reasons for my action, and then weigh as they chose."⁸³ Taft refused to appeal to popular emotions and prejudices. "He has told his audiences not what he thought they wanted to hear, stated the *Out-*

look, "but what he thought they ought to hear. . . . It has been distinctly a political campaign," the editorial continued, "but a campaign for national policies, not for personal advancement."[84] Although the President had learned the necessity of fighting for his policies, he remained unable and unwilling to dramatize himself or temper his speeches to the desires of his audiences.

Strangely enough, the western tour did not increase Taft's appreciation of the public mood. Despite the rising fury of western progressives against him, warm public receptions again lulled the President into a false sense of security. He returned to Washington confident that the progressive fever throughout the West had been overrated. As his own party disintegrated around him, he remained naively optimistic about the effects of his tour, describing it to his brother Horace as "a great success."[85] He also explained the trip to Archie Butt as "the greatest thing I have ever done from a political standpoint."

That trip, if it did not dispel and break up the whole insurgent movement which was aimed at me, at least demonstrated to the country how weak it was and that there was no substance for any of the claims which the leaders of it were making. It was a great success, and we will hear more of it within the next four months than we did even while we were on the road.[86]

Taft again had mistaken the natural warmth of the crowds for popular confidence in his policies and had discounted the skepticism of the trailing newsmen about the efficacy of the tour.

William Allen White had a much keener appreciation of the public mood in the West and Middle West and thought that the President had failed to instill any confidence in the people. Walter Fisher, however, believed that all was not lost for the administration. He thought that "the next Presiden-

tial campaign is going to depend upon the developments of
the next six months, and that the present state of public opinion is a receptive one." White acknowledged the fluid state
of public opinion and hoped against hope that Taft would
wake up to the real sentiments of the people:

There is to my mind a strong abiding hope in the minds, even
of those who have been forced to make disagreement of the President that someone will tell him the truth, that someone will show
him how the people feel, that some frank, kind, candid friend
will come to his rescue before it is too late.[87]

The President, of course, was not completely blind to criticism of his administration, but, because of his thin political
skin, he chose to ignore as much of it as he could. "It was
not true that the unfavorable view of others did not reach
the president," he later remarked after leaving office. "I had
candid friends and there were also those who were not friends,
but who were candid."[88] The fact remains, however, that the
President's aversion to criticism and dissenting views was a
marked characteristic of his personality. Among the President's candid friends, for example, was his brother Horace.
One day in August 1911, Taft turned on him and called him
a "theoretical pedant" because of his free tariff views. After
that episode, Horace was careful not to antagonize his brother
and, according to Butt, "has not expressed his real views to
him again."[89]

Taft dealt with much of the criticism of the press by simply
refusing to read his bitterest foes. In 1914 he explained how
solicitous he had been in reading the newspapers for constructive criticism:

I never picked up a newspaper, I never glanced at the headlines,
that I was not concerned lest the indiscriminate, though often
sincere, criticism of the unfriendly to which I had become hard-

ened might not have discovered some real ground for serious consideration.[90]

But memories blur, and this was only partly true. The truth is that Taft tended to read only those papers favorable to his administration. Mrs. Taft admitted as much in her *Recollections* when she wrote, "I think we both avoided much perturbation after we became convinced of the unfairness and injustice of much that was said by hostile newspapers, by not reading it."[91]

This view of the President's reading habits is substantiated in a number of instances. After Taft returned from his tour in 1909, for example, he upbraided his personal secretary Fred Carpenter for furnishing him with clippings from the *New York Times* which opposed the Payne-Aldrich Tariff:

I observe that you are constantly sending me clippings from the New York Times, which is in a state of free trade fury. I only read the headlines and the first sentence or two, and then I omit the further consumption of time. Possibly the wiser course, therefore, is not to send me those articles. They are prompted by such wild misconceptions and such a boyish desire to point the finger of scorn, that I don't think their reading will do me any particular good, and would only be provocative of that sort of anger and contemptuous feeling that does not do anybody any good.[92]

When the *Times* continued its criticism of the administration, Taft stopped taking the paper. When the paper's editorial policy changed in 1911, Taft began to read it again regularly. The President had also been reading the *Washington Times*, but stopped when it became too critical of the administration.[93] When former Senator Chester I. Long of Kansas sent him some editorials to read of sentiment back home, Taft curtly replied, "I am not reading editorials from the Kansas City *Times* and *Star*, either for pleasure or instruction."[94]

In his third year in office, the President's reading habits had not changed appreciably. "He will not read newspapers which differ from him," Major Butt noted, "and his clippings are chiefly culled from papers which support his policy." Butt began to worry about the President's reliance upon the *New York Sun* as his prime newspaper source. "I wish the President would not read the *Sun* so much," he noted. "He always wants to see it first thing." The *Sun* was Taft's favorite paper because it was one of Roosevelt's bitterest satirists. By January 1912, Taft was reading the *New York Tribune* and the *New York Times,* but the *Sun* admittedly remained his favorite.[95]

An incident during the special session of the Sixty-second Congress in 1911 illuminates Taft's reading habits. When Taft vetoed a wool tariff bill passed by the Democratic-Insurgent coalition, a number of papers, including the Hearst chain, reversed their policy of support for the President. One evening soon thereafter, when his wife handed him the *New York World* (a Pulitzer paper) to read, Taft replied, "I don't want the *World.* I have stopped reading it. It only makes me angry." "But you used to like it very much," said Mrs. Taft. "That was when it agreed with me," he answered, "but it abuses me now, and so I don't want it." "You will never know what the other side is doing if you only read the *Sun* and the *Tribune,*" she replied.

"I don't care what the other side is doing," he retorted.[96]

That was Taft in a nutshell. Once he was convinced of the maliciousness or error of his critics, he preferred to ignore them. He displayed little desire to remain up to date on their views or to neutralize them by a sustained public relations effort. Like most human beings, he preferred to think and read the best about himself. He did not fully appreciate his critics and enemies for the harsh truths they could reveal which his friends would not. Taft himself was consequently responsible for curtailing the flow of information to the White

House essential to the decisions of any democratic leader. The result of Taft's folly was his deepening estrangement from public opinion and the progressive wing of his party.

VII

One important footnote must be added here about Taft's difficulties in projecting a favorable public image. Taft had not been oblivious to the importance of protecting the reputation of the judiciary when he had served on the bench, but he unfortunately carried over to the presidency his judicial perspective and habits. It is difficult to conceive of a president who was more concerned with defending the judiciary than himself, but this was clearly true of Taft. Since the presidency was not under attack during his term, he felt no need to defend the prerogatives of his own office. The judiciary, however, needed protection against the attacks of irresponsible progressives, including Roosevelt, and Taft was willing to provide it, even if it diminished his popularity as president.

Henry Pringle and Alpheus T. Mason have amply documented Taft's desire to serve on the Supreme Court, especially as chief justice. Having been associated with the judicial system as judge or prosecutor for seventeen years, Taft understood the role of the courts better than that of any other branch of government. Although he entered the presidency deficient in his understanding of the importance of image-making, he was aware of the value of a judge's public reputation, the creation of which required techniques and talents different from those of an elected official. Two years before he became president he had written:

> A most important principle in the success of a judicial system and procedure is that the administration of justice should seem to the public and the litigants to be impartial and righteous, as well as that it should actually be so. Continued lack of public confidence in the courts will sap their foundation.[97]

Had he brought a similar concern for his public image to the presidency, he might have spared himself and his party much grief. Shortly after his election he wrote to a friend, "If I were presiding in the Supreme Court of the United States as Chief Justice, I should feel entirely at home, but . . . I feel just a bit like a fish out of water."[98] The revealing nature of the President's remark became more evident as Taft chose to neglect his own immediate interests as chief executive to protect the judicial system.

When Insurgent Republicans sponsored an income tax bill despite the Supreme Court's decision in *Pollock* v. *Farmers' Loan & Trust Co.* (1895) outlawing the income tax, Taft finessed the move, as we have seen earlier, by supporting a constitutional amendment to reverse the decision. Insurgents were bewildered and angered by Taft's move, for it denied them an immediate tax on income for a more problematical, though constitutional one. The President, however, was not worried about his reputation among Insurgent Republicans—he was more interested in protecting the reputation of the Supreme Court. Taft questioned the wisdom of the *Pollock* decision privately, but not its finality. In his special message of June 16, 1909, proposing the Sixteenth Amendment, he explained:

This course is much to be preferred to the one proposed of re-enacting a law once judicially declared to be unconstitutional. For the Congress to assume that the court will reverse itself, and to enact legislation on such an assumption, will not strengthen popular confidence in the stability of judicial construction of the Constitution. It is much wiser policy to accept the decision and remedy the defect by amendment in due and regular course.[99]

Preserving popular respect for the Court was more important to Taft than maintaining his popularity among progressives.

Taft's legalistic approach to conservation also injured his

political reputation in the Ballinger-Pinchot row, where his respect for law overruled his desire for popularity. Taft was not against conservation; he merely favored a policy based on valid statutes. He could not accept the proposition that it is legitimate for reformers to violate the laws in order to achieve their objectives, even on the grounds of high moral principle.[100]

Although other factors were undoubtedly involved, Taft's bitter opposition to Roosevelt was heightened by Roosevelt's increasingly radical rhetoric against the courts and the Constitution. When Roosevelt stumped for Republicans in the fall of 1910, Taft became worried about Roosevelt's vehement attacks upon the judiciary. Taft agreed with his predecessor that the Court had erred in the *U.S. v. E. C. Knight Co.* (1895) and *Lochner v. New York* (1905) cases, but he objected to the inflammatory tone of Roosevelt's remarks about the court and its power of judicial review—in his estimation, the foundation of the American political system.[101]

The President seized the Arizona and New Mexico Statehood Bill in August 1911 as an opportunity to express his views on the nature of the Constitution. The state constitutions contained the rather novel but increasingly popular principle of judicial recall, which permitted the people, six months after an election, to seek the ouster of a judge by petition and election. According to Taft, the recall provisions were "so destructive of independence in the judiciary, so likely to subject the rights of the individual to the possible tyranny of a popular majority, and, therefore, to be so injurious to the cause of free government, that I must disapprove a constitution containing it." The majority, he felt, could only rule wisely after its views had been refined through deliberation and discussion required by various constitutional procedures, judicial review included. Because the courts were the "cornerstone" of individual liberty, our constitutional system required nothing less than "an independent and untrammeled judiciary."[102] A few months later, Taft went even further and qualified an old Jeffersonian maxim:

I fully and freely admit and assert that when the American people have had time to learn all the facts and have had time to consider their bearing, their deliberate judgment is a wiser and better guide to be followed by the State than the judgment of the most experienced statesman, the most learned jurist, the most profound student of history. In this proper sense the voice of the people is nearer to the voice of God than any other human decision.[103]

By "their deliberate judgment," Taft was referring to those decisions taken only after they had been filtered through the constitutional procedures, including judicial review, required by the Constitution.

Once Roosevelt became an active candidate for the Republican nomination, Taft fought all the harder for those principles which he felt were threatened. Because of Roosevelt's increasing progressivism, Taft's campaign took on the air of a crusade for constitutionalism. He was willing to suffer defeat for his constitutional beliefs rather than compromise with the foes of the judicial system.

When Roosevelt organized the Bull Moose party to continue his quest for the presidency, Taft again perceived the issue between the parties as "whether we shall retain, on a sound and permanent basis, our popular constitutional representative form of government, with the independence of the judiciary as necessary to the preservation of those liberties that are the inheritance of centuries." This was the "supreme issue" of the campaign.[104] He felt that progressives had gone to an extreme in advocating a greater role for the people through devices such as the initiative, referendum, and recall. He was determined "to stamp out the pernicious theory that the method of reforming the defects in a representative government is to impose more numerous and more burdensome political duties upon the people when their inability properly to discharge their present duties is the cause of every ground of complaint."[105]

Had Taft been as determined to fight for himself and his reputation as he was for the judiciary and the Constitution, it is likely that his record would have been marked with far greater political success.

VIII

This is not to say that Taft learned nothing about the necessity of protecting his own reputation as president. As a number of presidential moves clearly indicate, his appreciation of the importance of publicity grew steadily, especially after the 1910 election. In addition to appointing more publicity-conscious personal secretaries, Taft permitted two long interviews to be published in the weekly magazines in 1910 and 1911. In March 1911, when revolution in Mexico threatened the lives of many Americans and troops were mobilized along the Mexican border, Taft sent detailed letters explaining his decision to major newspaper editors of the country.[106] The letters had the intended effect of bringing public discussion of the move down to the level of fact and reason, and indicated that the President had begun to learn some lessons about the art of securing a favorable press. By retreating in his demand for a hike in postal rates on weekly magazines, the President showed his increased awareness of the importance of the magazines to his public image. In March 1912, he encouraged his wealthy brother and newspaperman Charles P. Taft to seize an opportunity to become a part owner in the *Washington Post*. "I can conceive that the paper properly managed would be a tremendous instrument for the formation of public opinion the country over," he explained.[107]

In addition, he increased the use of special messages to Congress in order to focus more public attention upon his proposals. In response to his critics who thought his messages "too long and too judicial and prosaic," he also began in 1911 to read presidential messages aloud to his cabinet to enliven them with what Butt described as "telling epigrams."[108] In September 1912, he had Hilles instruct every department to prepare their daily news items by noon in order to reach the afternoon papers, a reform long overdue.[109] Finally, as his term drew to a close, he admitted his mistakes with the press over the tariff and postal rates.[110] But after his first two years of appalling indifference, it was too little and too late.

Shortly after his defeat in 1912, Taft delivered an introspective address at the Lotos Club of New York about the effects of muckraking upon himself:

I don't know that this evil [muckraking] has been any greater in this administration than in a previous administration. All I know is that it was my first experience and that it seemed to me as if I had been more greatly tried than most Presidents by such methods. The result in some respects is unfortunate in that after one or two efforts to meet the unfounded accusations, despair in the matter leads to indifference and perhaps to an indifference towards both just and unjust criticism. This condition helps the comfort of the patient, but I doubt if it makes him a better President.[111]

One year after his retirement as president, Taft again conceded his failure as his own publicity agent. In an unpublished article entitled "Personal Aspects of the Presidency," he revealed a more sophisticated awareness of the value of public relations to the presidency. "The question of publicity," he maintained, was "a most important one" for a president to consider. Taft now recognized that the President "should devote close attention to the proper methods of getting to as wise a circle of readers as possible the facts and reasons sustaining his policies and official acts. . . . I must confess," he continued, "that I was lacking in attention to matters of this kind and was derelict." He attributed his deficiencies primarily to his "judicial training," which had accustomed him to making decisions under different circumstances:

When the judgment of the court was announced and the opinion was filed it was supposed that all parties in interest would inform themselves as to the reasons for the action taken. Newspaper men and other publishers and writers for the public know, however, that the people do not learn the facts and arguments on any subject by one announcement, and that it needs a constant effort of iteration and reiteration to send the matter home to the people whom it is wished to reach.

Many newsmen had been more than willing to help Taft explain his policies, "But they properly complained that I did not help them to help me."[112]

Had Taft reached the presidency through an elective rather than appointive route, his whole attitude toward the press and image-making undoubtedly would have been more sophisticated. Certainly he would not have believed so naively that the accomplishments of his administration would somehow be "self-explanatory." Through trial and mostly error, he had discovered that public confidence in the chief executive is as important to his success as substantive accomplishments themselves—indeed, it is a substantive accomplishment itself! Although the public cannot understand the complexities of a president's programs, they can know and trust him as a person, or at least they think they can. Without such trust, there can be little effective public support for his objectives. Four years of the presidency and one year of philosophical reflection had taught Taft the hard way what Theodore Roosevelt had once tried to teach him—that "it is not only necessary to do exactly what is right, but to do it so that the knaves can not mislead the fools into believing it to be wrong."[113]

7. "Shirt Sleeves Diplomacy"

The assumption by the press that I contemplate intervention on Mexican soil to protect American lives or property is of course gratuitous, because I seriously doubt whether I have such authority under any circumstances, and if I had, I would not exercise it without express Congressional approval.

William Howard Taft to
General Leonard Wood,
March 12, 1911[1]

Taft brought to the presidency a remarkably modern view of America's expanding role in the world and a knowledge of foreign affairs unrivaled by any other candidate for the presidency. Two factors are important in the assessment of Taft's role as chief diplomat—his administrative style and his ambitious goals of commercial expansion and peace. The constant tension between these means and ends accounts for his mixed record in foreign policy, for he was forced to reconcile his ideals with the realities of responsibility. What emerges from a brief and selective look at Taft's foreign policy is a picture of a president who could rise to the occasion of leadership if his spirit was willing.

I

In 1908, Taft, as secretary of war, had identified himself with the McKinley-Roosevelt policies at every opportunity. He had outspokenly termed the traditional American policy of "nonentanglement" as outdated in the modern world, supported Roosevelt's big navy policy, endorsed the Monroe Doctrine, praised the idea of the Panama Canal as a boon to the navy and American trade, and generally approved of the Republican record in foreign affairs.[2] Roosevelt had little to fear that any of his basic foreign policies would change with the election of his lieutenant.

In spite of basic agreements, there were inevitable differences. The Taft administration began to promote foreign trade more vigorously—a change in emphasis that originated in the different temperaments and experiences of the two presidents. Roosevelt the intellectual, hunter, sportsman, and soldier—the proponent of the "strenuous life"—found it difficult to respect the businessman who valued profits more than virtue or glory. Preoccupied with consolidating American control over the nation's newly won possessions, Roosevelt never became as concerned about foreign trade problems as his successor. "I think, if the truth be known," Speaker Cannon once astutely observed, "Mr. Roosevelt rather despised trade and failed to understand that without commerce there could have been no civilization."[3]

Taft's experiences as governor-general of the Philippines and secretary of war, on the other hand, had imbued him with a penchant for working with the details of organization and foreign trade statistics. Taft was interested in reemphasizing the great aim of the McKinley administration—American commercial supremacy in the markets of the world. By 1908, Taft had concluded that the intense big-power economic rivalry which he had witnessed in the Far East required more positive diplomatic action to secure Amercian markets.

Taft's desire for trade expansion had been evident in his speech of April 4, 1908, before the Commercial Club of Chicago. Outlining his views on the state of American commerce, Taft foresaw the tremendous expansion of American foreign trade required by the nation's growing industrial strength.

"The opportunity for vast expansion in the sale of our manufactures lies not in the direction of the countries of Europe," he predicted, "but in the Orient, in Japan, China and the Philippines, and even as far as India." The real issue before the nation was whether America could grasp the new opportunities open to her:

The question is whether we of the United States are going to take advantage of the various circumstances favoring us in competition for all this trade, with an intelligent purpose of conserving and increasing that trade, or shall we pursue the happy-go-lucky policy of getting as much of it as the other nations will permit us to have, and when we might by proper effort have a great deal more?[4]

Taft was speaking not as a political opportunist, but as an economic statesman interested in world trade patterns fifty years hence.[5]

II

The President set out to strengthen the instruments of his new commercial diplomacy—the diplomatic and consular service, the navy, and the merchant marine. His first task was to reorganize the State Department. Unlike the vast majority of his countrymen, Taft realized that American foreign policy could only be as good as the eyes, ears, and voice of the nation abroad.[6] Philander C. Knox, as we have seen, was appointed secretary of state and given the broad mandate of overhauling the State Department.

To carry out the President's wishes, Knox selected Huntington Wilson as his first assistant secretary and then proceeded to implement Wilson's ideas for the organization of the department. Upon strong recommendation from Taft and Knox, Congress quickly appropriated $100,000 for the reorganization. Wilson's plans for geographical-political divisions for the Far East, Near East, Latin America, and Western Europe were accepted by Congress. The department was encouraged to bring in regional experts from the foreign service to staff the new divisions. The Bureau of Trade Relations was expanded, and a new Division of Information was added to keep American embassies posted on all aspects of American foreign policy. The only innovation Knox made in Wilson's plans was to create the office of Counselor to accommodate his former associate in the Justice Department Henry M. Hoyt. Another significant feature of the reorganization was the adoption of a "chief of staff" system in which the first assistant secretary functioned as the principal adviser, administrative assistant, and channel of business and information to the secretary.[7] The office was hand-tailored by Wilson for the close relationship that had developed between the secretary and himself. Taft also issued an important executive order on November 26, 1909, instituting a merit system for the foreign service extending up to the grade of minister.[8] The President himself, however, could derive little political mileage out of the new efficiency of the department, for administrative reform was not a subject of burning interest to most Americans at the time.

Neither was a revitalized merchant marine. Taft continued to push for Roosevelt's merchant marine policy, which had died in Congress. With the Panama Canal soon to open, Taft felt that a strong merchant marine was more imperative than ever for American commercial expansion into Latin America and the Orient. During his fall tour of 1909, he admitted that his unabashed aim was to see "the American commercial flag to be made to wave upon the seas as it did before the Civil War."[9] In his first annual message to Congress, he proposed a ship subsidy bill to encourage the establishment of steamship lines along routes beneficial to American trade. Taft's preoccupation with other high priority bills and the subsequent election of a Democratic House killed all chances for the bill, which smacked of just another subsidy to business to many congressmen.[10]

What Taft failed to achieve directly he sought to accomplish indirectly in the Panama Canal Act of 1912. On December 21, 1911, he recommended the enactment of legislation providing for the operation of the canal and giving the President discretionary authority to fix canal tolls. Taft maintained that since the United States had the power to subsidize American shipping by law, "a subsidy equal to the tolls, and equivalent remission of the tolls, can not be held to be a discrimination in the use of the canal." Congress agreed to the President's recommendation by exempting American coastal shipping from tolls and by delegating authority to the President to regulate the tolls of American ships engaged in coastal and international trade.[11] Although the exemption allegedly violated the Hay-Pauncefote Treaty of 1900 with Great Britain, the President signed the act.[12] Supported by the prominent lawyers in his cabinet (Knox, Wickersham, and Stimson), the President maintained that the issue of exempting American coastal traffic from tolls was not a question of legal right prohibited by the treaty, but merely a question of national policy. "I believe that we have the right at least to exempt our coast-wide trade from tolls," he wrote to Theodore Marburg. "The act leaves me the discretion to discriminate in favor of American vessels in international trade. I shall never do so."[13] Since the United States had built the canal, the President thought that the United States should be able to enjoy the fruits of ownership as long as it did not discriminate among nations in charging tolls.[14]

Although the President refused to budge from his position in the face of stiff British protests, he was willing to submit the matter to arbitration if necessary.[15] But he refused to back down on the tolls issue. Undoubtedly his personal involvement in the construction of the canal, his desire to provide competition to the transcontinental railroads, and his goal of subsidizing the American merchant marine strengthened his nationalist position on the question. Moreover, he had secured from Congress discretionary authority to provide even larger subsidies to American shipping engaged in both coastal and international trade, an authority which could be invoked when the political climate for subsidies became more friendly. By exploiting the anti-British, nationalistic feeling of Congress and capitalizing upon the antirailroad sentiment of progressives, the President had obtained by indirection what he had lost in open confrontation with Congress—a ship subsidy bill. The deterioration in American-British relations, however, was a high price to pay. Woodrow Wilson subsequently refused to pay it and successfully sponsored congressional repeal of the tolls exemption in June 1914.[16]

Considering his precarious position within the Republican party and Democratic control of the House during his last two years in office, Taft could not expect to rebuild completely the instruments of his diplomacy. The Democratic party objected to a large navy and ship subsidies on principle and would have stymied any other Republican president, as they had Roosevelt. Fortunately Taft did succeed in reorganizing the State Department and in fending off attacks upon its structure from the Democratic House. Many of the reforms in the department contributed to the permanent improvement of American diplomacy. The public, however, remained indifferent to the President's policy of promoting foreign trade and, understandably, could not be roused to the support of subsidies to private shipping companies, no matter how necessary or profitable the cause. The President was aware of America's growing strength as a world power, but the public was not yet concerned with America's new role.

III

Despite limited successes, Taft remained firmly committed to American commercial expansion. More than any previous president, he entered the White House "deeply interested" in the Far East and immediately made China the focal point of his diplomacy.[17] Because of his wide experience and travels in the Roosevelt administration, Taft was well aware of Japanese and Russian policies, particularly their mutual commercial treaty of July 1907 pledging joint cooperation in protecting their interests in Manchuria against outside interests, an agreement which threatened to undermine America's Open Door policy in the region.[18]

Roosevelt had been concerned about the precarious status of the Open Door but realized that the American public would never countenance the use of force to maintain the policy against an imperialistic Japan or Russia. He had also recognized that mere threats of military action could not prevent Japan and Russia from dividing the spoils of Manchuria. Roosevelt consequently had sought to promote a balance of power in the area in the hope that competition among the major powers would allow the United States some remaining commercial opportunities. He refrained from bluffs or threats of force which he could not back up.[19]

Taft was willing to go farther than Roosevelt in promoting American interests in China, at least rhetorically. He had supported Roosevelt's balance of power policy, but he also recognized that the Russians and Japanese presented a growing threat to its success. In October 1907, Taft, then heir apparent to Roosevelt, told a group of American businessmen in Shanghai "that the American Chinese trade is sufficiently great to require the government of the United States to take every legitimate means to protect it against diminution or injury by the political preference of any of its competitors." Although

the American government had been apathetic toward trade
with China, Taft assured the businessmen "that in the future
there will be no reason to complain of seeming government
indifference to it."[20] After the secretary of war conferred
later in December with Willard Straight, American counsul
at Mukden, China, Straight came away from the meeting with
the belief that the presidential candidate would return to the
United States and advise the government "to regard Manchuria as a fair field and not as one that must be approached
either with aquiescence, or with the special regard for the
sensibilities, of the Japanese."[21] Straight had reconfirmed Taft's
fears that the Open Door in China was slowly closing.

The Shanghai speech reflected Taft's real views and inten-
tions toward China. On April 4, 1908, before the Commercial
Club of Chicago, he bluntly stated the basic issue facing
America in the Far East:

The question is whether by an announced foreign policy for the
preservation of our Oriental trade, we mean business or we do
not. If we mean business, then it is of the highest importance that
the hands of the State Department at Washington should be held
up by the courageous public opinion of the merchants and business men of the country, and that in the assertion of their claim
to equal opportunity and just share of the Oriental trade, determined only by legitimate methods of business competition, they
should approve and insist upon a firm stand by the Government,
whatever befall. I have no idea that the result of such a policy
will lead to international breaches if it be understood that we
are not afraid of them in seeking to maintain our rights; but if
the impression gets abroad that we are merely bluffing, that we
do not think that the advantage that we seek to maintain is worth
great effort or fortitudes, we shall be at once at a disadvantage.[22]

Taft again focused attention on China in his Inaugural Address, in which he reiterated his determination to make the

244 William Howard Taft

Open Door a reality. The United States would never be able to uphold her rights and interests in the Orient, he maintained, "if it is understood that she never intends to back up her assertion of right and her defense of her interest by anything but mere verbal protest and diplomatic note." The President's remarks were coupled with a call for an army and navy "suitable" to the foreign policy goals of the nation.[23] There is little doubt that the President hoped to make the Open Door more than a pious platitude. How far he was really willing to go remained to be seen.

The President tried to raise the American legation at Peking to the full status of an embassy and to find the right man to head it. Hoping to secure a "position of advantage" with the Chinese government, Taft worked unsuccessfully during the lame duck Congress of 1908–1909 for the necessary legislation. Rival claims of Chile and Spain for similar status and Secretary of State Root's sensitivity toward Latin American opinion left the matter unresolved. Taft was sure that legislative inaction would make it more difficult to attract an able man for the Chinese legation.[24]

Despite his setback, the President set out to replace William W. Rockhill, American minister at Peking, with a more forceful personality. Taft considered the scholarly minister a "dilletante" who had "not the slightest interest in American trade or in promoting it." As the President explained to Rollo Ogden of the *New York Evening Post*, "He is pessimistic and not optimistic in his views of what can be done, and he is not a man of strength and force of action such as we need at Pekin." Taft was determined to find someone who shared his perspective:

Now, I regard the position at Pekin as the most important diplomatic position that I have to fill, and it is necessary to send there a man of business force and perception and ability to withstand the aggressions of the Japanese, the English and the Russians.

China is very friendly to us, and they are anxious to encourage American trade and the American investment of capital, because she does not distrust our motives. The opportunities it seems to me, therefore, for the development of the Oriental trade are great if we can only have a man on the ground who realizes the necessity and has the force and pluck and experience to take advantage of the opportunity.[25]

Departing from his usual procedure of letting Knox find suitable candidates for diplomatic appointments, Taft discovered Charles R. Crane, a Chicago businessman and world traveler, who had been recommended to him by the President's business friends. "I think we have really made a great find in him," the President wrote to his wife. "What I am especially anxious to secure in China is the investment of American capital. American capital is looking in that direction, and is much more likely to go into investments with a Minister of the standing of Crane, than with one who does not understand anything about it."[26] Unfortunately Crane proved to be an embarrassing choice because of his inability to curb his tongue in public and his headstrong desire to shape rather than execute policy. After a number of public indiscretions about his instructions and open defiance of the State Department over the proper role of a minister, Knox, with the approval of a disappointed President, recalled Crane before he could leave for China.[27]

IV

To promote American commerce in China, Taft tried to guarantee American participation in the construction of Chinese railroads and in the reform of the Chinese currency. He felt that the State Department, rather than being a passive agent for American foreign enterprise, should actively promote capital investment in China. China in 1908 was on the verge of a huge railroad expansion, which had attracted the attention and capital of all the major Far Eastern powers—England, France, Germany, Japan, and Russia. In order to float extensive foreign loans to build her railroads, China intended to reform her whole currency system, a step which would also require substantial foreign loans. Since such loans were frequently backed by Chinese customs revenues or internal trade taxes which affected foreign trade directly, Taft felt that United States participation was absolutely necessary. He realized that such participation would give the United States enough economic and political leverage in internal Chinese affairs to guarantee American access to Chinese markets and would also prevent China from being dismembered into spheres of influence. The President hoped that the creation of American economic interests in China would in turn help generate greater public support for stronger diplomatic and military policies in the Far East.[28]

When the new President learned of the impending flotation of a foreign loan to China for the construction of a railway line from Canton to Szechwan—the Hukuang Loan, as it was called—he immediately sought American participation. On the initiative of the State Department, an American syndicate of prominent bankers was organized to provide the necessary capital for the American part of the loan. The American Group, as the syndicate was called, was composed of four of the strongest American banking houses—J. P. Morgan & Co., Kuhn, Loeb, and Co., the First National Bank, and the National City Bank. With the exception of the First National Bank, all had displayed some previous interest in Chinese financial schemes.[29]

Assured of the support of the most powerful bankers, Secretary of State Knox attempted throughout the summer of 1909 to force American entry into the Hukuang Loan. State Department records indicate that the President kept a close watch on developments and continually prodded the department to indicate to the Chinese the "paramount importance" which he attached to American involvement in the loan.[30] Taft let it be known that if China refused American participation he would consider it a "breach of faith" on the part of the Chinese and would discontinue the remission of the Chinese indemnity from the Boxer Rebellion.[31] Although the European bankers from Great Britain, France, and Germany had already concluded their negotiations for the loan, the department, under constant presidential pressure, continued to push flimsy American legal claims for inclusion.[32] When the Chinese foreign minister proved too stubborn on the issue, Taft took matters into his own hands and personally wired the Prince Regent of China to seek his intervention:

I am disturbed at the reports that there is certain prejudiced opposition to your Government's arranging for equal participation by American capital in the present railway loan. To your wise judgment it will of course be clear that the wishes of the United States are based not only upon China's promises of nineteen hundred three and nineteen hundred four, confirmed last month, but also upon broad national and impersonal principles of equity and good policy in which a regard for the best interests of your country has a prominent part. I send this message not doubting that your reflection upon the broad phases of this subject will at once have results satisfactory to both countries. I have caused the Legation to give your Minister for Foreign Affairs the fullest information on this subject. I have resorted to this somewhat unusually direct communication with your Imperial Highness because of the high importance that I attach to the successful result of our present negotiations. I have an intense personal interest in making the use of American capital in the development of China an instrument for the promotion of the welfare of China, and an increase in her material prosperity without entanglements or creating embarrassments affecting the growth of her independent political power and the preservation of her territorial integrity.[33]

The message broke the deadlock and helped secure American participation in the Hukuang Loan. A number of political and economic factors lay behind the President's bold diplomatic move. First, American participation in the loan implied full Chinese recognition of the equality of American interests in China with those of Great Britain, France, and Germany. Second, the final agreement, signed in November 1910, established the principle of joint American participation in all future loans negotiated by European bankers. According to the State Department, this would aid in preserving a balance of power in China. The administration hoped that diplomatic cooperation with the European powers would help to restrain the imperial ambitions of Japan and Russia and forestall any embarrassing military confrontations over the Open Door.[34] Furthermore, because the loan was tied closely to the Chinese likin (internal taxes essential to the Chinese administrative and financial system), American participation, according to Knox, would enable the United States "to support China in urgent and desirable fiscal administrative reforms, such as the abolition of the likin, the revision of the custom tariffs, and general fiscal and monetary rehabilitation."[35] American supervision of these reforms would help guarantee American access to Chinese markets. According to Assistant Secretary of State William Phillips, the United States had sought increased influence in China "so that when the commercial interests and exporters of the United States turn their attention more vigorously toward securing the markets of the Orient, they will find those of China open to their products and the Chinese public favorably disposed toward American enterprise."[36] Finally, immediate financial gain prompted American concern with the loan. The State Department was acutely aware of the potentially vast market for railway equipment and locomotives which Chinese railroad construction would create. Knox saw "almost boundless commercial possibilities" in such development. "There is no doubt that the construction of railways to any considerable extent will be attended by enormous internal development," he wrote to the Senate Appropriations Committee, "and that the further introduction into the Far East of the methods and improvements of western civilization will present countless commercial opportunities to American manufacturers and capitalists."[37] As Taft had indicated previously, he was interested in shaping world trade patterns fifty years in the future.

The Hukuang Loan episode represents one of the few instances of what we might term "personal diplomacy" by the President and contrasts with his usual mode of operation involving the extensive delegation of power to Knox and the State Department. American participation in the Loan was the key to Far Eastern policy and was simply too important to Taft to be left to the diplomats. Fortunately the Chinese Emperor acceded to the President's plea and secured American participation in the loan agreement.

The President's successful intervention marked a major victory for what the press dubbed "shirt sleeves diplomacy."[38] "I think it quite a diplomatic victory," Taft confided to Major Butt.[39] Great Britain, Germany, and France had been dealt a serious defeat and had lost "face" before the Chinese. According to the State Department:

As a result of this victory the United States becomes a greater power in the East than it has ever been before, for the significance of America's participation in this Chinese loan lies not alone in the fact that American money is to be invested in China, but of more importance is the fact that our request for recognition was opposed by the great nations of Europe who have always held a monopoly of such financial plums and that in spite of this opposition the United States has won and thereby secured a political prestige in China which is virtually paramount.[40]

For Willard Straight, Taft's success represented a triumph of "big stick" diplomacy.[41] The only question remaining was whether "big stick" diplomacy could long succeed in a remote region where Americans were unwilling to fight.

v

The President had set the course of Far Eastern policy. Now it was up to his State Department to maintain and extend it. Secretary Knox, Wilson, and E. T. Williams and Ransford S. Miller of the Far Eastern Division shared the view that the United States should take positive steps to promote the Open Door in China and Manchuria.[42] Wilson, in particular, appears to have been a strong advocate of American expansion in Manchuria.[43] This strong consensus in the department served to reinforce the President's disposition to reinvigorate the Open Door. As the protege of Theodore Roosevelt, Taft should have known better than to have challenged Japan and Russia in their own back yard, but his "experts" in the department did not discourage him.

American participation in the Hukuang Loan secured, the State Department shifted its attention to efforts of the American Group to build a railroad from Chin-Chow to Aigun in Manchuria (the Chin-Ai Railway Project). The department and the group worked closely together to secure the support of the Chinese Emperor and the British government for the contract. Formally allied with Japan in the Far East, Britain was wary of Japanese objections to the project, which would compete directly with the South Manchurian Railroad operated by Japan. Trying to avoid the hostility of the various powers interested in Manchuria, Knox proposed a plan to Great Britain on November 6, 1909, calling for the neutral-

ization of all Manchurian railroads, including the proposed
Chin-Ai. The plan would have combined all the Manchurian
railroads into one unified system, owned by the Chinese themselves, but financed and operated for the term of the necessary
loans by an international consortium of powers committed to
the principles of the Open Door. Aware of Japanese and Russian hostility to a plan directly challenging their interests,
Knox suggested further that the ultimate purpose of his plan
could be realized if applied to the future financing and construction of Manchurian railways. According to E. T. Williams, Knox was responsible for the plan, which was patterned
after railroad magnate E. H. Harriman's earlier scheme for
control of the Chinese Eastern and South Manchurian Railways.[44] Taft acquiesced in his secretary's plan.

After submitting the neutralization plan to Britain, Knox
broached the subject to all of the other Far Eastern powers.
Although Britain accepted it in principle, opposition from
Japan and Russia quickly cooled her enthusiasm for the idea.
Perhaps Knox had been too candid about the advantages of
the proposal to the United States. "Such a policy," he admitted to the press, "would effect complete commercial neutralization of Manchuria, and in so doing make a large contribution to the peace of the world by converting the provinces
of Manchuria into an immense commercial neutral zone."[45]
Why he thought Japan and Russia would be willing to give
up their privileged positions in the region remains a good
question.

The Knox plan produced one disastrous, unintended effect
—it drove Japan and Russia closer together in defense of their
vested interests in Manchuria. On July 4, 1910, the two powers signed a surprise agreement pledging their mutual consultation in defense of the status quo in Manchuria, agreeing on
a common policy for the development of the Manchurian
railroads, and delineating spheres of interest in Manchuria and

Mongolia. The neutralization proposal had backfired. Roosevelt's old fears of a Russian-Japanese rapproachment were realized, the direct result of his successor's policy. Japanese-Russian attitudes on Manchuria had been slowly crystallizing since the Russo-Japanese War of 1905, but, according to the influential Russian newspaper *Novoye Vremya*, the neutralization proposal accelerated the process of cooperation "with a rapidity which could only be dreamed of beforehand."[46]

Brave rhetoric about making the Open Door a reality for all of China was not enough. Japan and Russia had called the American bluff in Manchuria and had dealt American prestige a severe blow. "It is not presumed that the United States would ever resort to war," reflected R. S. Miller of the Far Eastern Division, "either alone or in combination with other powers, to insure the integrity of China's territory, nor does it seem probable that our commercial interests would warrant or require a resort to war for their protection."[47] When special Chinese envoy Liang Tun-yen arrived in Washington in December 1910, to seek American assistance against Japan and Russia, Knox promised everything except military support.[48] The Chinese had to face the wrath of Russia and Japan alone. Although Willard Straight felt that the United States could have called Russia's bluff and unilaterally promoted the Chin-Ai agreement without war, he also realized that the administration's unwillingness to go it alone doomed the United States as a force in Manchuria.[49]

When the Chinese central government, threatened by Russia, abandoned the Chin-Ai project, the United States was left diplomatically isolated. When the American Group considered abandoning the project, the Far Eastern Division became frightened. "It is respectfully suggested," Williams wrote Knox, "that any retreat, orderly, or disorderly, upon the part of the American group, unless forced by the refusal of the Chinese Government to sanction the contract, will be disastrous to American commercial interests in China." He recognized that the neutralization proposal had failed miserably. "Our policy in Manchuria has won us the ill will of Russia, irritated Japan, and failed of support in France and Great Britain; should we now turn back, we shall have to count on the enmity of China also, and reckon with a decided loss of prestige throughout the Far East."[50]

When the President learned that the American Group was seriously considering abandoning the project, he urged Knox to prevent it. "I know your interest in this whole matter," he wired the secretary, "and I beg of you that you go to New York at once and invite the members of the syndicate to confer with you before they shall take the final step which will defeat entirely our international purpose. . . . I greatly fear a severe blow to our prestige unless we made (*sic*) much more decided effort to secure recognition of our right to have this railway built by American capital in Chinese territory when China is desirous that it be done."[51] But the group withdrew anyway.

When the Chin-Ai project collapsed, the department turned its attention toward the negotiation of a comprehensive currency loan to China. The President's role in the negotiations appears to have been strongly supportive of State Department efforts to gain a dominant position vis à vis the Europeans. When the Chinese requested State Department aid in securing a major loan for currency reform in September 1910, they at first appeared willing to promise the unpledged customs and likin of China as security for the loan, to employ an American financial adviser, and to give preferential treatment to American bankers in negotiating a conversion of all the outstanding small loans of China. Knox referred the request to the American Group, which agreed to negotiate on condition that an American financial adviser be appointed by China.[52]

The appointment of an adviser was a major stumbling block

in the complicated negotiations. Knox was insistent on an American adviser, and the President also stubbornly supported the idea throughout the negotiations, despite second thoughts by the Chinese. In November 1910, when Taft learned that the European powers interested in the currency loan would insist upon naming the financial adviser jointly or else not participate, he wired Knox to hold out for an American adviser:

The New York people leave the matter to the State Department with assurance that they are able to raise the whole loan themselves. Subject to your concurrence I have directed Norton to notify them that if they will carry the whole loan we shall insist on naming the advisers; that the loan was American and was intended to be so by the borrower and the lender and we do not propose to give up the advantage inherent under that circumstance.[53]

Although the European powers would be allowed to share in the proposed loan, Taft was acutely interested in securing the added power and prestige an American adviser would give the United States. The President's policy appeared nationalistic and opportunistic to the Europeans, who a year earlier had been forced to accept American participation in the Hukuang Loan, but the President was willing to risk their anger for a preferred position. He favored an Open Door policy only when the United States was on the outside. Secretary Knox subsequently instructed the American legation in Peking to settle the question of an American adviser "before other Powers press for a voice in this matter."[54]

The President pushed his desire for an American adviser when special Chinese envoy Liang Tun-yen met with him to discuss Chinese-American relations that December. Since China had offered to appoint an American originally, the President thought it only proper for the Chinese to keep their promise. The United States did not desire control over internal Chinese politics, the President explained, only a genuine currency reform which would strengthen China. "If you want us to help you Mr. Liang," Taft argued, "you must trust us."[55] But the Chinese trusted no one, and conversations with Liang failed to settle the thorny issue. The meeting did, however, indicate the President's personal interest in breaking the diplomatic log jam over the issue.

Willard Straight, who became involved in the currency loan negotiations for the American Group, feared that the State Department had been too rigid in demanding an American, especially since the department sought to give him extensive power to supervise the expenditure of loan funds. The Chinese rightly feared that such a powerful adviser would place control of their finances in the hands of the consortium of foreign bankers involved and would guarantee continued foreign meddling in their internal affairs.

It was not until Taft and Knox dropped their demand for an American adviser that the loan agreement was finally signed on April 15, 1911. Chinese fears of foreign domination, Japanese and Russian intrigues against the loan, and the outbreak of revolution in 1911 in China destroyed the administration's hopes for a major role in Chinese currency reform. Taft's attempt to consolidate an American financial presence in China had failed again.[56]

Taft also became involved in the sensitive issue of diplomatic recognition of the new Chinese government. Upon the outbreak of rebellion against the Manchu dynasty, the United States reached a "firm understanding" with Japan, Russia, England, France, and Germany to act jointly in extending diplomatic recognition to any new government that emerged.[57] On February 12, 1912, the Chinese emperor abdicated and a new provisional government was set up in Peking. At that time no one knew whether the rebellious factions throughout the country would accept the provisional government as legitimate. Aware of the President's intense desire to strengthen American prestige in China, Wilson suggested to him that the administration secretly sponsor a congressional resolution of support for the provisional government. Such an expression of support, Wilson explained, would "reap all the benefits of the policy of concerted action and of that of advanced recognition" at the same time.[58] The separation of powers could be used to give the United States two attitudes toward the provisional government and hopefully gain the United States a preferred position with the new Chinese government. Taft apparently approved of Wilson's suggestion, for three days later a joint resolution was passed by the House sympathizing with the provisional government at Peking. After changing the joint resolution to a concurrent resolution so that the President would not be embarrassed by having to sign or veto it, the Senate passed it on April 17, 1912.[59] Wilson then dispatched a copy to Peking for circulation. "The text should be circulated among the American consulates in China to be discreetly given such publicity as will be conducive to the interests of the United States," he advised the legation. "It may be regarded as an expression of the sympathy of the American people, through their representatives, with the new order of things in China."[60] The ruse permitted the United States to remain formally committed to a policy of joint action with other powers while simultaneously exploiting American sympathy toward the provisional government.

Taft's intense interest in the Far East failed to secure the Open Door in Manchuria or establish a strong American economic or political presence in China despite the extraordinary amount of energy expended by the administration. The President had correctly remarked to Chinese envoy Liang that "in all the history of the United States there had never been any administration that had taken so much interest in China as the present."[61] The State Department, of course, had borne the brunt of the work. Wilson later maintained that the Department's correspondence on China was "incredibly complicated and far exceeded in volume that on any other matter."[62] According to Knox, it was a "common saying . . . that China took all the time of the Department, the rest of the world received what was left."[63] But interest or workload could not compensate for the inadequacies of basic policy.

Taft was certainly to blame for believing a policy of bluff could be successful, but the State Department, and more specifically the Division of Far Eastern Affairs, were equally at fault. Certainly Willard Straight and William J. Calhoun, American minister to China, thought the blame rested with the department. Straight credited the failure of American policy to the generally poor system of communication between Peking and Washington, the inexperience of State in diplomacy of this nature, and the inability of responsible officials in Washington to appreciate the situation in far-off China. Straight credited Wilson with influencing the course of diplomacy, particularly toward Manchuria, but he also attributed some of the "egregious errors" to Wilson's lack of tact and knowledge of men.[64] Elihu Root shared a similar opinion of Wilson, for he thought Knox's mistakes resulted from delegating too much responsibility to Wilson.[65]

Regardless of the deficiencies of Knox, Wilson, the Far Eastern Division, or American representatives on the scene, final responsibility for policy rested with the President. By relying heavily upon the State Department, Taft became the prisoner of its misconceptions, as well as of his own. In delegating so much responsibility to Knox, the President was forced to rely upon the inexperienced diplomatic judgments of his secretary, who, in turn, was unduly influenced by his first assistant secretary and the Division of Far Eastern Affairs, both committed to American commercial and political expansion in the Far East. Even if Taft had occasionally bypassed Knox to seek advice from others in the department, it is unlikely he would have discovered any dissenters on his policies. Career men like Alvey A. Adee, third assistant secretary, who may have had reservations about dollar diplomacy in China, were more interested in maintaining their positions in the department or too busy in other areas to play the devil's advocate. Even if Taft had taken greater interest in the day-to-day affairs of State—a step that would have jeopardized his relations with Knox—his decisions on China policy would have been substantially the same. A diversity of opinion on China among top policy-makers might have saved the President from his more serious mistakes.

VI

In his diplomacy with Latin America, Taft maintained a similar relationship with the State Department. As with China, he set the broad course of policy and left Knox and the department to apply the principles to concrete situations. Taft wished to continue the Root-Roosevelt policies toward Latin America, particularly those intended to guarantee the peace and stability of the banana republics located near the Panama Canal. "I expect to continue the same policy toward Latin America, thus so happily entered on by Mr. Root and Mr. Roosevelt," he explained to John Barrett, director of the Internal Bureau of American Republics, "and shall count my administration fortunate if further steps can be taken and new measures adopted to secure a closer and mutually more beneficial commercial association, and to awaken a greater international sympathy, than even now obtain."[66] Taft and Knox decided to promote financial stability and economic development of the area with American capital, rather than by force. Their ultimate aim was to eliminate political instability and thereby make the Panama Canal secure for the United States.

Knox and the State Department were to give concrete form to the President's hopes.

The new administration faced an immediate problem of revolutionary turmoil in Nicaragua and Guatemala. The Washington Conference of 1907 among the Central American states had failed to establish a lasting peace, and the United States needed a more effective Central American policy to avoid future military intervention.[67] When Mexico refused to join the United States in guaranteeing the political neutrality and financial integrity of strategically important Honduras, the State Department felt free to encourage American bankers to begin negotiations with Honduras for the rehabilitation of her finances.[68] By January 1911, the negotiations were completed and awaited approval by the Senate.

The administration hoped that the financial convention with Honduras, and later Nicaragua, approved and guaranteed by the American government by treaty, would help build peace and prosperity in Central America. The treaties committed the United States to approving and guaranteeing the conditions of private American loans to these countries. The policy was not original; it was patterned after Roosevelt's Dominican Agreement of 1905, in which the United States had agreed to staff and supervise the customs houses of the island to prevent revolution. According to Taft, if the customs houses of Honduras and Nicaragua could also be placed under American supervision, revolution could be forestalled, peace would reign, commerce would flourish, and American hegemony in Central America would remain unchallenged by European powers. The policy was logical, but based upon the faulty assumption that the major cause of revolution was the prospect of booty from customs houses.[69]

The Honduran convention represented a test case for Taft's Central American policy. Hopefully it would promote the financial and political stability of a strategically important country and guarantee the security of the Panama Canal. Second, it would save Honduras from international loan sharks by permitting the State Department to scrutinize American loans to her. Third, it would give the United States a legal right to intervene in Honduran affairs when necessary. Fourth, it would supposedly decrease the need for armed American intervention. Fifth, the loan would help build railways in Honduras to tap the wealth of the interior and make it "available for shipment by the Caribbean Sea to Gulf ports of the United States." Finally, the treaty would become a model for other Central American countries. If it failed in the Senate, American policy in Central America would suffer a severe setback.[70]

Although the loan negotiations were complicated, the import of the agreement was not. Under the Honduran convention, Honduras would select a collector of general revenues from a list presented by American bankers and approved by the President of the United States. The convention authorized the United States to provide "additional protection" to the collector general if it became necessary in the future.[71] In short, the State Department guaranteed the wisdom of the loan and the American government would guarantee the security of the customs houses, by force if necessary.

On January 26, 1911, the President submitted the convention to the Senate for its approval. "If the arrangement made proves, upon closer scrutiny, to be just and equitable," the President wrote, "then this Government will be prepared, with the consent of the Senate if a treaty is desirable, to give it such sanction as shall afford the bankers legitimate security for their investment."[72] There was no threat in the President's message to use an executive agreement to bypass the Senate if it refused to act. The alternative which Roosevelt had employed in his Dominican Agreement in 1905 was never seriously considered by the President. Knox had advised Taft "that the Senate should assume its full share of the responsibility" and was undoubtedly instrumental in striking any thought of bypassing the Senate from the President's mind.[73] The two lawyers preferred to pursue their policy in a conventional, constitutional, and, as it turned out, unsuccessful manner.

Both the Honduran and Nicaraguan conventions failed in the Senate. Stalling by Insurgents and Democrats led to the withdrawal of the J. P. Morgan Company from the Honduran loan contract in June 1911. The Senate returned the treaty to the Foreign Relations Committee, where it languished for the duration of the Congress. Taft lobbied extensively for the Nicaraguan treaty, but it too died. According to Fred M. Dearing of the Latin American Division, Taft "had spoken about the matter to all the Senators and other people concerned" and "had done his utmost in everything possible to secure favorable action" but "was convinced that nothing was to be accomplished."[74] Although Taft made one last appeal to the senators on behalf of the convention, it proved futile in the face of determined Insurgent and Democratic opposition.[75] Disapproval of the administration's close cooperation with Wall Street and isolationist sentiment prevented any immediate action on the convention. When violence erupted in the Dominican Republic in 1912, all chances of treaty passage were destroyed. The disturbance was, according to Wilson, " a very severe blow to American diplomacy."[76] If the model for the Honduran and Nicaraguan loan conventions would not work, who could blame the Senate for refusing to approve the treaties?

The administration's preoccupation with trade expansion and its close cooperation with the giants of Wall Street had antagonized many progressives and Democrats. When critics labeled the President's foreign policies as "Dollar Diplomacy," Taft was unable to neutralize the politically damaging connotations of the phrase. He did try to explain and justify his policies, but to no avail. On May 2, 1910, for example, he defined his policy as one of "active intervention to secure for our merchandise and our capitalists opportunity for profitable investment which shall inure to the benefit of both countries concerned."[77] Like its European counterparts, the State Department had simply become the active promoter of national commercial interests throughout the world. The President realized that to "call a particular piece of statecraft 'dollar diplomacy' is to invoke the condemnation of muckraking journals, whose chief capital is in the use of phrases of a lurid character."[78] Knox and Wilson, however, contributed to the popular misunderstanding of their policies by eventually accepting the phrase as a backhanded compliment to their foreign policies.[79] By December 1912, the President himself had become a prisoner of the epithet when he described his policies as merely one of "substituting dollars for bullets."[80] By trying to explain his policies within the derogatory emotional framework of "Dollar Diplomacy," Taft could never shake the popular notion that his administration was in cahoots with the malevolent octopus of Wall Street.

The truth is, of course, that Taft cooperated closely with the large banking houses interested in foreign investment opportunities. What incensed many of the administration's critics the most, however, was not the cooperation between government and Wall Street, but the discrimination of the State Department against small banks in favor of a few big ones. When Taft once asked Knox about an alleged discrimination against a banker interested in Latin American loans, Knox admitted to the President what the department had refused to admit publicly—that it had the right "to choose whatever bankers it please as its instrumentalities."[81] The department, of course, had chosen the J. P. Morgan Company, Kuhn, Loeb, and Company, National City Bank, and the First National

Bank, all of which were already involved in the Far East. When critics continued to object to the close relationship between the Department and the big bankers, Knox tartly replied to the press, "When you want to borrow ten millions you don't go ask the grocer for it or the bootblack; you go to the man that has it."[82] Although the bankers were obviously interested in profit, they did go out of their way, particularly in the Far East, to cooperate with the administration's diplomatic objectives. "I am quite sure that those gentlemen," Wilson later observed, "accustomed to making money pretty easily by underwriting American issues, had never before taken so much trouble and spent so extravagantly with such modest prospects of profit."[83] In any case, Taft saw nothing wrong with using Wall Street as an instrument of his diplomacy.

VII

The ill-fated loan conventions with Honduras and Nicaragua represented only a small part of the administration's efforts to promote American trade in Latin America. The President also actively encouraged the sale of American battleships to Argentina in the hope of winning a larger share in the expanding world market of armaments.[84] Taft was so eager to have American companies secure the battleship contracts that he actually offered the latest American naval secrets on gun, turret, and sighting designs to Argentina as "a special act of friendship" and upon the understanding that such secrets would be "considered confidential."[85] The State Department successfully encouraged American bankers to provide Argentina with a $10 million loan to make the battleship contracts possible. Finally, Taft himself fought for lower tariff duties on hides in the conference on the Payne-Aldrich tariff to woo the battleship contracts from the Argentine government. The President, of course, was interested in promoting

American trade, but he also desired to minimize European influence in South America if possible. Since Argentina was determined to have the battleships, he felt that American rather than European construction would be the lesser of two evils. As a result of his generosity with American naval secrets and tariff rates, Argentina negotiated American contracts worth $23 million for two battleships and ordnance materials.[86]

When a suspicious Senate, upon the initiative of Senator La Follette, passed resolutions calling upon the secretaries of state and navy to furnish them with all communications regarding the battleship contracts, Knox refused to comply.[87] Wilson, who wrote the first draft of Knox's reply, had been willing to acknowledge the transfer of naval secrets to private industry:

This Department was glad to be able to advise the Argentine Government that the Navy Department had found it proper under certain conditions to allow the use of Government designs of ordnance material by the only American Company interested in this work, provided a contract between the Argentine Government and this firm for the armor and armaments was signed, and provided further, that the two battleships were constructed in this country.[88]

But Knox wisely eliminated this language from his final message to the Senate on the basis that disclosure would be incompatible with the public interest.[89] The administration was unwilling to jeopardize the agreements by confessing that a private American company had been allowed to use naval secrets to win the contracts. The administration considered them a major diplomatic victory for the United States, which had previously been frozen out of the naval armaments market in South America.

The State Department also promoted private American loans to Guatemala and Haiti, although with very limited success. The department, however, was successful in securing American contracts for submarines from Chile and Peru, and small warships from Brazil. American contracts worth $1,670,-271 for railway equipment in Argentina and a paper contract for *La Prensa* worth $200,000 annually filled out the notable accomplishments of "dollar diplomacy" in South America. Through direct official efforts alone, Taft boasted of having brought American industry $50 million in new business.⁹⁰

VIII

A president can often allow his secretary of state to handle the routine problems of diplomacy as long as no serious crisis emerges, but when momentous questions of war and peace arise, no president can avoid the ultimate burden of responsibility. No foreign crisis tested Taft's patience, statesmanship, or deep commitment to peace more than the outbreak of revolution in Mexico. The President's deferential relationship toward the State Department temporarily broke down as events forced him to move energetically to keep the peace with Mexico. Taft's policy toward Mexico deserves recognition as a great act of presidential statesmanship and self-restraint in the use of national power.

When Taft entered office, he clearly sympathized with the authoritarian regime of the aging Porfirio Diaz of Mexico. Taft believed that Diaz had immeasurably aided the economic development of his country by attracting billions of dollars of foreign capital, much of it American. In October 1909, Taft consented to a personal meeting with the old President to help prop up his tottering regime. As he explained, "we have two billions of American capital in Mexico that will be greatly endangered if Diaz were to die and his government go to pieces." Taft was aware of the brewing storm in Mexico and confided to his wife at the time, "I can only hope and pray that his demise does not come until after I am out of office."⁹¹

Neither hope nor prayer sufficed. In 1910 disturbances, sometimes violently anti-American, grew more widespread and severe against the Diaz regime. Knox and the State Department, however, remained naively complacent about the depth of the turmoil reported by the United States Ambassador Henry Lane Wilson. When an anxious President inquired about anti-American riots in Mexico City in November 1910, for example, Knox minimized the significance of the incident. "It is so far a cause for deep regret for what has happened rather than anxiety for the future," he replied.[92] Despite continuing disorders in Mexico in January and February of 1911, Knox was not alarmed enough to postpone a March vacation to Florida.

During Knox's absence, Ambassador Henry Lane Wilson returned briefly to the United States and, on March 6, was granted a personal interview with the President to discuss the Mexican situation. Taft was shocked at the developments described by Wilson, the significance of which had apparently escaped the secretary and his department. Taft immediately got in touch with Secretary of War Dickinson, Secretary of Navy Meyer, Army Chief of Staff General Leonard Wood, and Admiral Richard Wainright and ordered the immediate mobilization of twenty thousand American troops along the Mexican border and precautionary naval maneuvers in the Gulf of Mexico. The President made his decision without consulting Knox or the cabinet, a highly irregular procedure for him, but he sped an explanation of his decision to the vacationing Knox along with appropriate apologies for the swiftness of his decision. Although rumor reached the President that the secretary was angered by the mobilization order and was seriously considering resigning from the cabinet, Knox reluctantly endorsed Taft's decision by letter. The secretary realized that Taft could do little else given the various pressures operating upon him, particularly, as he wrote, "with

Wilson throwing fits about the iminence (*sic*) of Diaz going up in an explosion."[93] But Ambassador Wilson and the President were soon vindicated by events in Mexico, for President Diaz was overthrown in May 1911.

All of Taft's reasons for mobilization could not be made public immediately, but he did set some of them down for the record in a letter to General Wood. The letter was circulated among other military figures, prominent newspaper editors, and eventually published in the President's State of the Union address of December 7, 1911. The Wood letter, written six days after the President's order to mobilize, was designed for a wide audience that had become apprehensive at the prospect of the President plunging the country into a bloody war with Mexico. In explaining his decision, Taft expressed the hope that the show of military force along the border would have a "healthy moral effect" upon Mexico and prod her into giving more protection to American lives and property. The President was well aware of press criticism of the sudden mobilization and tried to assure his critics, in language as temperate as he could employ, that he would not abuse his powers as commander-in-chief of the armed forces:

The assumption by the press that I contemplate intervention on Mexican soil to protect American lives or property is of course gratuitous, because I seriously doubt whether I have such authority under any circumstances, and if I had, I would not exercise it without express Congressional approval.

According to the Wood letter, the President felt his duty as commander-in-chief was to mobilize troops so that "if Congress shall direct that they enter Mexico to save American lives and property, an effective movement may be promptly made."[94]

Although Taft's deference toward Congress, repeated in

private correspondence to some congressmen and personal friends, would appear to prove the President's genuine devotion to a "literalist" view of presidential power, policy considerations dictated the President's expressions. For example, Taft's explanation of his decision to Knox differed somewhat from that provided General Wood the following day. No doubt Taft believed that he would wait for congressional consent before intervening in Mexico, but he was referring to a hypothetical situation and addressing himself to an audience alarmed at the prospect of war through unilateral presidential action. Whereas he minimized the possibility of intervention in the Wood letter—indeed, he hoped that mobilization would make it unnecessary—he admitted to Knox that the stationing of troops along the border would make it easier for him to protect the thousands of Americans in Mexico if law and order disintegrated completely. Taft had decided to prepare for any eventuality. His letter to Knox did not mention the need to consult Congress before sending troops into Mexico.[95] This letter was not intended for widespread distribution or publication, and he felt no need to reassure the secretary of his sanity or limited objectives. Taft's commitment to consult Congress was primarily a tranquilizer for an edgy public.

Another indication of how the nature of the audience affected the content of the President's assurances can be gleaned from a comparison of responses given to a militant congressman and to a close personal friend. In responding to Congressman James L. Slayden of Texas, who desired bolder presidential action against Mexico for disturbances along the border, Taft informed him, "I shall not intervene in Mexico until no other course is possible, and then only by authority of Congress."[96] But in a letter to a personal friend the day before, the President had explained:

Confidential. I am not going to intervene in Mexico until no other course is possible, but I must protect our people in Mexico as far as possible, and their property by having the Gov't understand there is a God of Israel and he is on duty. Otherwise they will utterly ignore our many great complaints and give no attention to needed protection which they can give.[97]

Taft did not mention presidential consultation with Congress because no reassurance was needed.

As events in Mexico became more turbulent, Taft found that his commitment to consult Congress, originally made for the benefit of progressives and Democrats across the country, became valuable in fending off the interventionist pleas of regular Republicans. This commitment tended to blunt attacks against him and left him free to pursue a policy of preparedness without intervention. Taft chose a policy of restraint toward Mexico, not out of constitutional scruples, but because it was the best way of guaranteeing the safety of American residents in Mexico. Although he assured the public that he would not intervene without consulting Congress, it is difficult to believe that he would have waited for Congress to debate the issue if many American lives were seriously threatened. Ambassador Henry Lane Wilson's assessment of Taft's position is probably the most accurate one available. "My understanding of the Taft policy," he later wrote, "was that if intervention for the protection of our own people or other foreigners became a matter of solemn and sacred duty, *there would be no hesitation* [italics mine], but that intervention for other reasons would not be justified by public opinion either in this country or elsewhere."[98] A President who had dispatched troops to Honduras (twice), Nicaragua, China, Panama, Cuba, and Turkey to protect American citizens and interests during his administration without any constitutional qualms would probably have done the same in Mexico under similar circumstances. Had a difficult situation arisen, perhaps

Taft would have had time to consult Congress or the legislative leadership before sending American troops into Mexico. Perhaps he would have sought retroactive approval for such an action. Perhaps public opinion would have made the issue academic and ratified any presidential decision. The only problem Taft might have encountered would have been that of explaining away his repeated assertions of deference toward Congress. Although issued partially to disarm his critics, those assertions might well have limited his freedom to respond swiftly to a crisis. Taft appeared willing to run the risk because he felt the risk was negligible.

Once the President ordered a show of military force along the Mexican border, he encountered many difficulties in keeping his objectives limited. To his shock and dismay, he found it necessary to reprimand an overly aggressive Navy Department for dispatching, without his knowledge or consent, American warships into Mexican ports to show the flag.[99] Moreover, when Knox failed to respond to Taft's suggestion that Latin American nations be informed of the limited nature and purpose of American mobilization, Taft personally informed a number of Latin American envoys of the situation and then suggested that the department confidentially do the same for the remaining ministers.[100] Determined not to be caught off guard again, Taft also ordered Ambassador Wilson to keep the State Department informed of any new developments and requested Knox to maintain closer contacts with American consuls in Mexico. In the midst of the March crisis over mobilization, Taft remained in personal touch with Ambassador Wilson, and also kept close watch over affairs in Mexico for the duration of his term.[101]

Public criticism and misunderstanding of the mobilization order sorely disturbed the President, who could not reveal all his reasons for acting without compromising his policy. He explained to Roosevelt at the time that he had no alternative but to take a "pounding" from his critics:

> It would be embarrassing to me . . . to give out exactly the facts upon which I had to act. Wilson could no longer remain as Ambassador in Mexico after having told me these circumstances, and the publication of his views . . . could not but acquire an official character and might produce the greatest embarrassment with a friendly government.[102]

Insurgent and Democratic congressmen attributed sinister motives to the President, claiming that he was preparing to invade Mexico to protect American investments there. To neutralize some of the criticism, Taft discreetly chose to circulate his March 12 letter to General Wood to prominent editors across the country. If the press were to take him to task for mobilization, at least, Taft thought, the editors should have their basic facts straight. Only when he was threatened with a congressional investigation into his mobilization order did he provide the foreign affairs committees of both Houses with enough information to forestall any investigation.

As revolutionary disturbances in Mexico grew more violent in April 1911, Taft resolutely maintained his policy of nonintervention. On April 13, fighting between Mexican government and rebel forces near Douglas, Arizona, resulted in the loss of two American lives and the wounding of eleven more, the third such incident along the border.[103] Although Taft protested to the Mexican government, he refused to be goaded in any aggressive action that might jeopardize the lives of American residents in Mexico. He informed Governor Richard E. Sloan of Arizona of his policy of forebearance:

> I can not . . . order the troops at Douglas to cross the border but I must ask you and the local authorities in case the same danger recurs to direct the people of Douglas to place themselves

where bullets can not reach them and thus avoid casualty. I am loath to endanger Americans in Mexico where they are necessarily exposed by taking a radical step to prevent injury to Americans on our side of the border who can avoid it by a temporary inconvenience.[104]

Forty thousand American lives were more important to the President than a few American casualties along the border. Domestic pressures for stronger presidential action, however, began to mount. A few weeks after the Douglas incident, when a worried Mrs. Taft inquired whether there would be war with Mexico, the President replied, "I don't know Nellie. I only know that I am going to do everything in my power to prevent one."[105]

Taft had become alarmed at the growing militancy of regular Republicans, who were encouraging Taft to intervene in Mexico to help the party's chances in 1912. The President refused to give in to the pressures and, indeed, found some comfort in his position that he could not send troops into Mexico without consulting Congress. With Congress sharply split on the question, Taft could continue his policy of restraint, assured that the legislature would take no action. Pressure for stronger measures against Mexico, however, mounted. In July 1912, Texas congressman W. B. Howard encouraged the President to deliver a strong ultimatum to the Mexican government demanding protection for American citizens—"a splendid political move," he called it—and possibly take more "drastic action" against Mexico. "Prompt action on this line will also draw the western people to you," Howard argued, "and they will to a great extent drop the third party talk."[106] An alarmed Harry W. Daugherty of Ohio also reported a "systematic plan" by American residents of Mexico to encourage the election of the more bellicose Roosevelt in 1912.[107] Despite pressures to take a more popular stand for stronger military action, Taft refused, election year or no election year. He could not follow his party on Mexico.

Theodore Roosevelt did not make Taft's plight any easier. In March 1911, Roosevelt asked Taft for permission to raise a division of cavalry if war with Mexico should come. This Taft cleverly agreed to do, subject, of course, to congressional approval. The President realized that such approval was impossible. Moreover, Roosevelt's subtle suggestion that he personally go to Mexico to reconcile the political differences between warring factions was politely ignored by Taft.[108] The President's cool response to Roosevelt's requests further contributed to the eventual break between the two. What nettled Roosevelt most was Taft's adamant pacifism and his commitment to consult Congress before taking any military action against Mexico. "Imagine Washington, or Lincoln, or Andrew Jackson taking such a position," he exclaimed to James Garfield. "The first duty of a leader is to lead."[109] When the two men finally split, Roosevelt did take the more popular position that the United States should stand up more firmly in defense of American citizens along the Mexican border and within Mexico itself.

Roosevelt had condemned Taft for not leading, but Taft was leading in his own responsible way. His objective, unlike Roosevelt's, was to keep the United States out of the Mexican revolution and to save as many American lives as possible. Had Taft loved war, had his ego thrived on public adulation, had he been a clever party candidate concerned with reelection, he might have ordered a military response against Mexico to mollify his critics, but he was determined to pursue a statesmanlike course regardless of personal or party fortunes. Even while President Diaz was being overthrown by Francisco Madero in May 1911, and Madero in turn by General Victoriano Huerta in February 1913, Taft persisted in his policy of nonintervention.

The President's policy of restraint was undoubtedly strengthened by the position of the State Department, reflected in two important memoranda drawn up by Solicitor J. Reuben Clark, Jr. In his memorandum of February 26, 1912, to Taft, Clark warned that if the President ordered armed intervention or shooting across the boundary, outraged Mexicans would massacre a "considerable number" of the forty thousand American residents. He recommended what Taft had already requested in the skirmishes along the border —that Americans inconvenience themselves if necessary to avoid the occasional hostilities on the Mexican side. "This seems to be the unanimous opinion of all American representatives in Mexico," Clark argued.[110] Taft could not ignore the "unanimous opinion" of the experts, especially when that opinion reinforced his own basic instincts. In a subsequent memorandum prepared for the department, Clark concluded that "the time to intervene will be when we can save more American lives by going into Mexico than by staying out of Mexico."[111] That remained the guiding principle of Taft's policy until he left office.

When Huerta overthrew Madero in February 1913, the lame duck administration had to decide whether to recognize the new Huerta government. The State Department appeared eager to extend recognition as soon as Huerta could establish effective control throughout most of Mexico. Clark again prepared a memo for the Department in which he recommended the recognition of the Huerta regime and continued nonintervention, regardless of the destruction of American property: "American blood is worth more than American dollars."[112] In principle, both Taft and Knox were willing to recognize Huerta, but wanted American property claims against the Mexican government settled first. Since Taft's term of office would soon expire, he was reluctant to bind his successor by recognizing Huerta, although he later deeply regretted his decision. He did not foresee that Woodrow Wilson would transform the question of recognition into a moral issue, refuse recognition, and eventually intervene militarily. Taft became increasingly disillusioned with President Wilson's Mexican policy of nonrecognition and later concluded bitterly that "while dealing with a country like Mexico one can not allow ethical considerations to influence one in respect of a state policy when the time has been reached making the only thing worthy of consideration to be the capacity of the man at the head of things to introduce law and order." The former President believed that Wilson was "playing to the gallery."[113] There was no greater expression of opprobrium in Taft's vocabulary.

The Mexican crisis of 1911–1913 vividly illustrated Taft's firm commitment to peace and his magnanimous self-restraint in the use of American power. In mobilizing troops, Taft proved that he could act decisively when necessary, and yet with restraint. His commitment to consult Congress before armed intervention, however, must be viewed as the *result*, not the *cause* of his policy toward Mexico. Because of his legal background, the improbability of intervention, and the alarmed audiences he was trying to soothe, Taft's public deference toward Congress must not be confused with his private views, nor with his possible reaction to an imminent slaughter of Americans in Mexico. As a former lawyer and judge, he was naturally inclined to phrase his policies in constitutional terms, but he was hardly the feckless chief executive his legalistic rhetoric would indicate. His self-deprecating statements issued during the crisis must be read in connection with his firmly held policy of maintaining peace with Mexico.

IX

In contrast to his behavior toward Congress during the Mexican crisis, Taft directly challenged the prerogatives of

the Senate by pushing for comprehensive arbitration treaties
with Britain and France. Taft's advocacy of the treaties reflected his broad view of his role as world peacemaker and
indicated that his attitude toward Congress depended upon
policy considerations, not constitutional scruples.

Arbitration treaties were nothing new to the Roosevelt-
Taft generation. Secretaries of State John Hay and Elihu
Root had attempted to negotiate such agreements with the
major foreign powers with rather disappointing results. Before his death in 1905, for example, Secretary Hay had negotiated nine arbitration treaties only to see them scuttled by a
jealous Senate. The treaties had called for the use of executive
agreements to implement the arbitral procedures, but had been
amended by the Senate, which demanded "special treaties"
to initiate the procedures in each particular dispute. An in-
furiated Roosevelt had recalled the treaties and let the issue
rest until 1908, when Secretary Root capitulated to the Senate. Root negotiated twenty-four agreements covering all issues except those involving "the honor, independence, and
vital interests" of the United States. The arbitration procedures would become operative in a dispute only if two-thirds
of the Senate approved of a special treaty to cover that case.[114]
In other words, the Senate was not prepared to compromise
the sovereignty and freedom of the United States, or its own
prerogatives, through such comprehensive agreements. Taft
and Woodrow Wilson were to learn this fact the hard way.
When Taft entered office, however, he had no plans for alter-
ing agreements already accepted by the Senate or for pushing
the cause of arbitration. He had carefully observed the fate of
previous treaties and had been too preoccupied with domestic
issues in 1909 to expend much energy on the matter.

Taft had great faith in the efficacy of international law to
promote a more peaceful world. "There is no other single
way in which the cause of peace and disarmament can be so

effectively promoted as by the firm establishment of a permanent international court of justice," he wrote to Theodore Marburg, organizer of the American Society for the Judicial Settlement of International Disputes.[115] Despite his aversion to resurrecting the Root treaties, Taft accidentally initiated what was to become, in his mind at least, one of the most important policies of his administration. On March 22, 1910, he startled the American Arbitration and Peace League meeting in New York by attacking the exception contained in the Root treaties on the question of national honor:

Personally, I don't see any more reason why matters of national honor should not be referred to a court of arbitration any more than matters of property or national proprietorship. . . . I don't see why questions of honor may not be submitted to a tribunal supposed to be composed of men of honor who understand questions of national honor, to abide by their decision, as well as any other question of difference arising between nations.[116]

Soon the President was caught up in his own rhetoric.

Taft had not intended a major departure in his foreign policy. "I had no definite policy in view," he later confessed to Major Butt. "I was inclined . . . merely to offset the antagonism to the four battleships for which I was then fighting, and I threw that suggestion out merely to draw the sting of Old Carnegie and other peace cranks."[117] What began as a tactical maneuver to neutralize criticism of his naval program was soon transformed into a major objective of the whole administration. A surprised President was buoyed by the favorable reactions of commercial, religious, and peace groups to his speech. Press editorials were generally favorable. "Never in my experience," he later admitted, "was there such a unanimous expression of earnest interest in carrying out the proposal, and such fervent hope expressed for a successful issue in the matter."[118] When the President repeated his views in

December 1910 before the American Society for the Judicial Settlement of International Disputes, only England and France responded favorably. The President hoped that he had discovered a popular rallying point for his faltering administration.[119]

The task of drafting and negotiating the arbitration treaties with Britain and France fell to Knox. Taft's personal intervention in the process came only at the last moment when he inserted his own version of Article III into the treaties. Article III pledged the parties to a controversy to submit matter that had been declared "justiciable" by a joint high commission to arbitration without any independent judgment by the Senate as called for previously in the Root agreements. The final draft of the treaty came as an unpleasant surprise to the Senate Foreign Relations Committee, which had not been apprised of its contents. Supporters of the treaty later charged that Knox had bungled by not consulting with the committee about the details. Although Knox denied the allegation, arguing that the treaty had received much general publicity in the press, Taft did acknowledge the validity of the criticism. "It did not seem wise," he admitted, "to submit the matter to the Senate until after we had found that the other countries were willing to join us in such treaties."[120] Perhaps Taft and Knox knew that no meaningful treaty could have been drafted with Senate knowledge or participation and hoped to present the upper house with a popular fait accompli. Whatever the reasons, the tactic bore a remarkable similarity to that used by Woodrow Wilson eight years later in the ill-fated fight over the League of Nations.

The arbitration treaties with Britain and France were finally signed on August 3, 1911, and submitted to the Senate for approval. Unlike the Root treaties, the agreements called for the arbitration of all issues "justiciable in their nature" by the application of "the principles of law or equity" by the Permanent Court of Arbitration at The Hague, or by a tribunal created by special executive agreement. Article II provided for the creation of a Joint High Commission of Inquiry, composed of three Americans and three nationals from the other country, which would determine the "justiciability" of an issue when disagreement arose. The American commissioners would be appointed by the President. Five out of six votes on the commission would be necessary to render an issue "justiciable." Thus, if two American commissioners opposed arbitration, the dispute could not be arbitrated. However, even such traditional questions involving "national honor" or "national interest" could be arbitrated if they were found to be "justiciable."[121] The President was correct when he described the treaties as "broader in their terms than any that body [Senate] has heretofore ratified, and broader than any that now exist between nations."[122]

The agreements marked a potentially radical departure from the traditional nationalism of American diplomacy and were so interpreted by the Senate. Members of the Senate Foreign Relations Committee, already piqued at Knox and Taft for having been slighted, soon were busy drafting reservations to the agreements. Henry Cabot Lodge, among others, was convinced that questions involving the Monroe Doctrine, immigration laws, and territorial claims should not be arbitrated. Lodge argued, furthermore, that the Joint High Commission's power to bind both parties to arbitrate a "justiciable" issue would usurp the Senate's power over foreign policy. When the committee report was issued on August 11, it was clear that a majority believed the treaties would undermine the constitutional powers of the Senate. Even the three signers of the minority report, Republicans Cullom, Burton, and Root, desired a reservation which would have withdrawn from the treaties all issues involving the "traditional attitudes of the United States concerning American questions or other purely governmental policy." Though he had not intended to, Taft had challenged the prerogatives of the Senate. When the treaties faltered before the Senate, Taft successfully appealed for a postponement of action until the following December.[123]

Taft had done little to sell his ideas to the public, and the delay gave him an opportunity to mobilize public opinion. His restrained approach had been evident, for example, at a banquet of the American Society of International Law in April 1911, where he mentioned the treaties only very "casually." He had explained to Major Butt at the time:

I am not hunting this bird with a brass band. I realize that if it goes through it will be the great jewel of my administration. But just as it will be the greatest act during these four years, it will also be the greatest failure if I do not get it ratified, so for that reason I do not want to stir up too much hostility toward it by appearing to be too eager for it. I would rather the country should get aroused for it without my leadership, if this can be done. There are men in the Senate . . . who would try to kill it just because I advocate it.[124]

When the President's casual approach failed to move a jealous Senate, Taft was faced with the disagreeable prospect of taking his case to the people. Despite his distaste for this, he was determined not to let the treaties be killed "without a whisper."[125] On his October tour across the country, Taft probably spent more time discussing his arbitration treaties than any other issue. Unfortunately, the further West he traveled, the more indifference he encountered.

For a President remembered today for his conservatism and Whiggish views, Taft's speeches contained some rather novel, even radical ideas. Expanding upon his belief that war had always brought more sorrow than benefit to the world, Taft denounced the necessity of previous American wars:

We had the War of 1812, in which our neighbor, England, asserted rights that she would not now think of pressing. I think that war might have been settled without a fight and ought to have been. So with the Mexican War. So I think with the Spanish War.

To frequent objections that the United States could not arbitrate a question of national honor, Taft's simple reply was, "Well why can you not?"[126] He also attacked the notion that the agreements would deprive the Senate of its constitutional powers in the area of foreign relations. If the Senate could bind the United States to arbitrate a single question, he argued, it could bind the United States to arbitrate all questions. The real issue was not that of presidential versus senatorial power, but of national power.

[I]f the Senate can not now bind us to abide the judgment of an arbitral court as to whether a question is justiciable, it can never bind us, and if the Senate can not bind us, the nation can not bind us, and this peace-loving people is forever incapable of taking a step along the great path which all the world wishes to tread, and along which all the world thinks America best fitted to lead.[127]

In San Francisco, Taft championed a broad constructionist view of the Constitution:

We ought to give a liberal construction to the Constitution if the Constitution really forms any obstacle to the power of the Senate to make such a treaty. The obstacles cannot be found in the Constitution; it has to be construed into it.[128]

Because he believed his treaties were wise, Taft saw no reason why constitutional scruples should stand in the way of their acceptance.

Unfortunately the President also used his western speaking tour to bolster his chances for renomination and election. By making his treaties prime legislative goals before an election, he made it difficult for the Democrats to view his proposals with much objectivity. Taft realized his predicament and tried to woo William Jennings Bryan to his side in the struggle. At Los Angeles, he admitted that Bryan had made recommendations which had been incorporated into the treaties, thereby associating the former presidential candidate with the agreements.[129] "What I am most anxious to avoid is that the issue over them should be given a political flavor," he wrote to Bryan, "and I am hopeful that your attitude in respect to them may make such a result impossible."[130] Bryan's support was not enough. Democratic senators not only had serious doubts about the treaties, but they longed to see their party in power again.

Nothing could budge the Senate, which ultimately won out. First, in the face of a hostile majority on the Senate Foreign Relations Committee, Taft and Knox were forced to make substantial crippling concessions. Knox and Lodge worked out a compromise proposal which called for Senate approval of the presidential nominees to the Joint High Commission. The amendment also guaranteed the Senate a veto over any matters deemed "justiciable" by the High Commission by requiring the negotiation of a special agreement, subject to Senate consent, defining the powers of the arbitrators and the questions to be arbitrated. Thus modified, they resembled the Root treaties approved in 1908. Meanwhile, opponents of the treaties unearthed a number of presidential speeches to indicate that Taft really took a more comprehensive view of the binding nature of the agreements than did Knox. The Senate consequently amended the treaties, including in the process a reservation, opposed by Lodge and Root, which eliminated questions concerning the Monroe Doctrine, territorial disputes, immigration laws, and state debts from arbitration. The treaties were so emasculated that Taft refused to submit them to Britain and France for ratification. He believed that his only hope lay in incorporating his ideas into the Republican platform of 1912 and then trying again if reelected.[131]

The President's vigorous efforts on behalf of arbitration indicate that in the pursuit of his own policies Taft could be a broad constructionist, even challenging the prerogatives of the Senate if necessary. His advocacy of the treaties was not so much a struggle for increased executive power as for national power. Even though he hoped that the treaties would increase the popularity of his administration, he was primarily motivated by a deep commitment to the universal rule of law. The fate of previous agreements and the League Covenant in 1919–1920 would indicate, however, that the passage of arbitration treaties was impossible without surrendering their substance to a jealous, nationalistic Senate.

X

Although Taft revealed his deep pacifist inclinations by his Mexican and arbitration policies, Theodore Roosevelt had won more acclaim as an international peacemaker because of his successful mediation of the Russo-Japanese War (1905) and the Moroccan crisis (1906). Taft had assisted Roosevelt in those two disputes and tried to follow his predecessor's footsteps in the Turco-Italian War of 1911–1912. His unsuccessful attempt to mediate this conflict casts significant light upon his relationship with the State Department, his conception of office, and his view of America's role in the world.

The outbreak of war between Turkey and Italy in the fall of 1911 did not cause a great stir in the United States. For the vast majority of Americans, citizens and public officials alike, the conflict was a purely European question. Although an American syndicate called the Ottoman-American Development Company had been negotiating with Turkey for railway concessions, the war did not threaten any vital national interests. On September 29, 1911, however, former Ambassador to Turkey Oscar S. Straus publicly urged the President to try to mediate the dispute under The Hague agreements, which had recently established a World Court. The Turkish ambassador to the United States, Zia Pasha, responded with interest: "For the President of the United States to act as mediator in the dispute between Turkey and Italy would be to fill a magnificent role and prove a great practical step in international peace-making." Since the war was not expected to last long, however, the ambassador thought no mediation would be necessary.[132]

Taft was interested in the Straus proposal and solicited the advice of Knox. Alvey A. Adee, acting secretary of state in the absence of both Knox and Wilson from Washington, replied that the "general sentiment" of the department regarded mediation as "inexpedient." The next day, Knox reaffirmed Adee's view and informed the President that mediation attempts at the present time would "lead to embarrassment if not mortification. . . . Our hands are full in maintaining peace upon this Hemisphere, and we would probably resent European interference in any disturbance here." When Adee informed Knox the next day of evidence that Turkey might ask the United States to mediate, Knox agreed with Adee to discourage such a request. Adee then wired the American Embassy at Constantinople: "It would be desirable to avert any formal request for the mediation of the United States."[133] The State Department was obviously averse to any American involvement in European affairs which might jeopardize American hegemony in the Western Hemisphere.

The department could not shelve the issue so easily. Two months later, in December 1911, Taft was again urged by Lyman Abbott, editor of the *Outlook,* and Mrs. Mary P. Eddy, an American physician living in Turkey, to offer his services as mediator to Italy and Turkey. When the President solicited Knox's opinion again, the secretary discouraged him.

Knox saw no basis for peace acceptable to both sides. "Moreover, if intervention were possible," he replied, "it might properly be considered the province of others than us to initiate such steps."[134] Taft again dropped the idea.

In the fall of 1912, while Knox was attending the funeral of the Japanese Emperor in Tokyo, Taft received additional appeals urging him to mediate the conflict. Obviously eager to do whatever he could, Taft, for the third time, requested the opinion of the State Department on the subject, only to be met with the standard response that the war was a European question to be avoided if possible. With Knox absent from Washington, however, the President was not put off so easily. On October 1, he again broached the issue with the State Department by sending Samuel R. Bertron, a New York banker and personal friend of the Italian and Turkish prime ministers, to talk to Wilson about the possibility of mediation. "This is a matter of momentous importance," Taft informed Wilson, "and it would gratify me very much if through our agency peace could be brought about between Turkey and Tripoli." Since it was "too long to wait" for Knox's return in five days, the President directed Wilson to act immediately upon Bertron's information.[135]

Samuel Bertron apparently had gained the confidence of both the Italian and Turkish prime ministers and had discovered that neither looked unfavorably upon a mediation effort by the President. Although he was interested in negotiating a major loan with Turkey himself, Bertron was able to persuade Taft to make a serious effort at peacemaking. A successful effort on Taft's part would, of course, have smoothed Bertron's way to the Turkish loan. Wilson informed the banker that although the President desired to act as mediator, the initiative would have to come from Italy and Turkey. With Bertron's consent, Wilson wired a private message from the banker to Vincenzo Giolitte, the Italian prime minister, informing him of the President's willingness to mediate. "I am able to assure you positively," the note stated, "that it would be most gratifying to him [Taft] as a friend of both countries and as a friend of peace to act as mediator in case he should be invited by both Governments to do so." A similar wire was sent by Wilson to Bertron's business associate in Constantinople with access to the Turkish prime minister. As Taft and the department waited, Wilson explained to Taft, "I think that the steps taken will bring about an invitation to mediate if there is any chance of accomplishing this."[136] Then, on October 9, word reached Washington that both nations had reached a peaceful settlement of their dispute and that the need for mediation had passed.[137] Taft's dream of emulating Roosevelt as a peacemaker had been foiled.

Immediately afterward, when war erupted between Turkey and the Balkan states of Serbia, Montenegro, Greece, and Bulgaria, presidential mediation became a possibility again. Although Taft maintained that he was doing "all that is possible" to mediate between Turkey and the Balkan states, events again conspired to deprive him of any role in resolving the war.[138] By mid-October, Knox had returned to Washington to discourage further peacemaking attempts by the President. As he explained to Taft, America's "absolute political disinterestedness" in the Near East precluded any effective attempt to mediate the new dispute.[139] Also, the President lacked the services of a special intermediary like Bertron on intimate terms with the parties at war. Consequently, his term of office ended with the Balkan War still raging and his hopes of emulating Roosevelt shattered again.

These faltering attempts at mediation illustrate certain facets of Taft's presidency. First, Taft's deferential attitude toward Knox and the State Department placed a damper upon his enthusiasm to mediate. A stronger president would have found a way to bypass the department earlier. Had Taft been

more determined or less deferential toward Knox, he might
have been more successful. Second, Taft's lack of personal
contact with foreign personalities made it more difficult for
him to bypass the normal channels of diplomatic communication, perhaps through the use of a special envoy, or to be
invited to mediate. Taft's friendships were more parochial
than Roosevelt's and limited his potentiality as an international peacemaker. Third, the President's peacemaking efforts
highlighted his broad vision of America's role as an emerging
world power. He did not pursue this role with as much energy and expertise as his predecessor, but his view of his responsibilities was remarkably similar to Roosevelt's. Finally,
although the President was interested in maintaining the balance of power in Europe, his primary motives for seeking to
mediate these two conflicts originated in his profound dedication to peace, his desire to match Roosevelt's record, and,
perhaps, his need to bolster his sagging popularity at home.
In any case, mediation was primarily a question of prudence
and policy, not constitutional theory.

XI

Taft is historically identified as a Whig or "constitutional"
President, but the real test of his conception of office lies in
his actions rather than words. Taft's record of deference toward Congress in foreign affairs is a mixed one. His constitutional scruples led him to refuse to use executive agreements
with Honduras and Nicaragua to supervise their customs
houses in the absence of Senate approval. His decision contrasts with Roosevelt's precedent-setting action in the Dominican Republic in 1905 and seemingly casts Taft as a confirmed Whig. On the other hand, Taft challenged Congress
on several occasions: he attacked the prerogatives of the Senate by promoting comprehensive arbitration treaties and bypassed Congress in using naval secrets to win battleship con-

tracts from Argentina. Even his handling of the Mexican crisis, which has been used to portray him as a feeble president, shows Taft to have been a much stronger executive than his rhetoric would indicate. The President's stated deference toward Congress in the crisis stemmed primarily from policy considerations and only secondarily from constitutional theory. On the whole, Taft appears to be neither a dogmatic Whig nor a confirmed disciple of Roosevelt, but a president who judiciously employed both conceptions of office in his actions when it suited his purposes. As chief diplomat, Taft combined Roosevelt's vision of America's growing responsibility as a world power with William McKinley's aim of American commercial expansion. He was not always successful in realizing those aims because of his inability to combine a rigid administrative style with activist foreign policy objectives, some of which were unattainable, and also because of his deficient understanding of the relationsship between public opinion, national power, and diplomacy. Perhaps Willard Straight had been right in January 1911 when he had lamented over the ashes of American policy in the Far East that the United States was not "yet well enough equipped or sufficiently experienced to deal in a masterful manner with the problems which confront the country now embarking on its career as a world power."[140]

8. "Our Chief Magistrate and His Powers"

The Constitution does give the President wide discretion and great power, and it ought to do so. It calls from him activity and energy to see that within his proper sphere he does what his great responsibilities and opportunities require. He is no figurehead, and it is entirely proper that an energetic and active clear-sighted people, who, when they have work to do, wish it done well, should be willing to rely upon their judgment in selecting their Chief Agent, and having selected him, should entrust to him all the power needed to carry out their governmental purpose, great as it may be.

William Howard Taft,
Our Chief Magistrate and His Powers[1]

The inexorable growth of presidential power in the twentieth century has increasingly thrown into relief the divergent theories and traditions of the American presidency. The classic views of the office expressed by Taft in *Our Chief Magistrate and His Powers* and by Roosevelt in his *Autobiography* still provide the basic categories around which contemporary discussions of presidential power revolve. Because Taft's "constitutional" view of presidential power is a reaction to the excessive claims of power contained in Roosevelt's *Autobiography*, both theories must be considered together if either of them is to be understood. In the excessive rhetoric of Roosevelt's "stewardship" theory can be found the origins of Taft's stringent constitutionalism, and that, perhaps, is why both theories should be read skeptically.

I

Immediately after his predictable defeat in November 1912, Theodore Roosevelt began a series of articles in the *Outlook* which formed the basis for his famous *Autobiography*. While defending the record of his administration, Roosevelt sketched in bold strokes his classic "stewardship" theory of the presidency:

The most important factor in getting the right spirit in my Administration, next to the insistence upon courage, honesty, and a genuine democracy of desire to serve the plain people, was my insistence upon the theory that the executive power was limited only by specific restrictions and prohibitions appearing in the Constitution or imposed by the Congress under its Constitutional powers. My view was that every executive officer in high position, was a steward of the people bound actively and affirmatively to do all he could for the people, and not to content himself with the negative merit of keeping his talents undamaged in a napkin. I declined to adopt that view that what was imperatively necessary for the Nation could not be done by the President unless he could find some specific authorization to do it. My belief was that it was not only his right but his duty to do anything that the needs of the nation demanded unless such action was forbidden by the Constitution or by the laws.

Roosevelt condemned the "Buchanan-Taft" types of presidents who "conscientiously believe that the President should solve every doubt in favor of inaction as against action, that he should construe strictly and narrowly the Constitutional grant of powers both to the National Government, and to the President within the National Government." Although distinguishing between proponents of the theory who were "highminded and wrong-headed or merely infirm of purpose," Roosevelt argued that the consequence of their views was a "cramping precedent" for the president who viewed himself as a steward of the people.[2]

While lecturing at Columbia University in 1915, Taft responded to Roosevelt's deft but devastating caricature of his own presidency with his classic "constitutional" or "literalist" view of office:

The true view of the Executive function is, as I conceive it, that the President can exercise no power which cannot be fairly and reasonably traced to some specific grant of power or justly be implied and included within such express grant as proper and necessary to its exercise. Such specific grant must be either in the Federal Constitution or in an act of Congress passed in pursuance thereof. There is no undefined residuum of power which he can exercise because it seems to him to be in the public interest. . . . The grants of Executive power are necessarily in general terms in order not to embarrass the Executive within the field of action plainly marked for him, but his jurisdiction must be justified and vindicated by affirmative constitutional or statutory provision, or it does not exist.[3]

Taft's lectures were quickly published under the title of *Our Chief Magistrate and His Powers*. No two views of the presidency have been so frequently quoted and contrasted by political scientists and historians. Yet the similarities between the two conceptions are actually greater than the apparent differences. Both theories obscure the simple truth that all American presidents have been firmly committed to the concepts of limited government. Although it has been useful to contrast the views of these two presidents, neither man measured up to his own conception of office completely. If we accept these conflicting views as accurate descriptions of their years in office, then we deal with a fanciful history in which mere assertion of fact by the historical participants makes it so. Furthermore, conceptions of the presidency are complex phenomena which change, along with the circumstances under which they are uttered or acted out. A closer look at William

Howard Taft's ideas reveals the changing nature of such views.

In pursuing Taft's conception of the presidency we can discern three basic stages—prepresidential, presidential or operational, and postpresidential—through which his views evolved. Even these categories, however, are misleading. By delineating rigid boundaries, they obscure the consistent though constantly evolving nature of his views and the circumstances under which they were made. Perhaps it would be more fruitful to say simply: What a candidate says he will do as president, what he does, and what he says he did will rarely coincide.

Taft's prepresidential conception of office is a far cry from his views in *Our Chief Magistrate*. It would seem impossible for a man of Taft's acknowledged integrity to serve a president whose views were essentially alien to the Constitution. Since Taft was not outraged by Roosevelt, it seems logical to assume that the differences between the two men were not accurately described in Roosevelt's *Autobiography* or Taft's *Our Chief Magistrate*. In fact, their views were far more similar than stated. Roosevelt was not quite so bold as he said he was; Taft was not so deferential to the Constitution as he alleged. Taft agreed essentially with Roosevelt's presidency, but not with his postpresidential rhetoric.

A glance at Taft's preelection statements on the presidency indicates the essential congruity between his and Roosevelt's ideas. As secretary of war, Taft was second to none in defending the President's power to govern the new colonies and possessions in the Pacific and Caribbean. "The contention that we are not a nation with power to govern a conquered or purchased territory," he argued in 1908, "robs us of a faculty most important for the good to every sovereignty." If Jefferson could use his powers as commander-in-chief to govern

Louisiana, Taft maintained, so too could the President exercise such power in the Philippines, Puerto Rico, Cuba, and the Panama Canal.[4] Taft had no scruples in negotiating an executive agreement for Roosevelt delineating American areas of government in the Panama Canal Zone, and he was even roundly attacked by the Senate for usurping the treaty-making power.[5]

Personal involvement in the Philippines led Taft to argue that nothing, not even the Constitution, ought to stand in the way of American interests in the islands:

It is said that there is nothing in the Constitution of the United States that authorized national altruism of that sort. Well, of course there is not; but *there is nothing in the Constitution of the United States that forbids it* [emphasis added]. What there is in the Constitution of the United States is a breathing spirit that we are a nation with all the responsibilities that any nation ever had, and therefore when it became the Christian duty of a nation to assist another nation, the Constitution authorizes it because it is a part of national well-being.[6]

In reviewing the extensive powers which Roosevelt was exercising over American possessions, Taft argued:

I don't think there has been any variation in the constitutional limitations upon executive power but rather a change of conditions, which has made necessary the exercise of unusual, perhaps, dormant powers in the executive for the purpose of maintaining the government of the United States and preserving the property which belongs to it in these dependencies.[7]

Taft also defended Roosevelt against charges that he was usurping congressional power. As previously indicated in Chapter IV, Taft felt that it was natural for a president to use his popularity and position as party leader to influence Congress—he had no choice. "He is visited by the people with more responsibility in respect to the legislative course of his administration than the Constitution vests him with," he argued. Executive leadership of Congress "is never likely to be dangerous to the body politic or subversive of the liberties of a people."⁸

Although no man could have served Roosevelt for five years without having second thoughts about some of the President's actions, Taft supported him wholeheartedly. Roosevelt's willingness to listen to the advice of conservatively minded men like Taft assured their continuing support. As Taft later acknowledged, "Mr. Roosevelt in office was properly amenable to the earnest advice of those whom he trusted."⁹ Of course, Roosevelt had no real opportunity to judge how Taft would use the powers of elective office, but he thought that Taft would perpetuate his policies. So both men believed that their conceptions of the presidency were essentially the same, not realizing, until events proved them wrong, that the style or manner in which those views were applied would determine their real differences as presidents.

II

In assessing Taft's actual conduct of office (his operational conception), it is evident that he tried to become a far stronger executive than the role suggested either in *Our Chief Magistrate* or Roosevelt's *Autobiography*. Taft desired to become a vigorous, effective president in his own right just as Roosevelt had been, but his attitudes, values, style of operation, and expectations of the public precluded achieving the political success of his predecessor.

Taft basically was a Hamiltonian in his view of office. He believed in a strong, energetic president, but one operating within the confines of the separation of powers. He desired neither executive supremacy over Congress and the courts nor congressional supremacy over the executive. Whereas Roosevelt had actively sought to dominate the other two branches,

Taft sought to maintain the balance of power between them. In this respect, he shared George Washington's desire "neither to stretch nor relax" executive power "in any instance whatever, unless imperious circumstances should render the measure indispensable."[10] Taft respected the Constitution too much to see its underlying genius upset by the deliberate expansion of executive power. He felt, however, that Roosevelt had done little to actually change the balance between the executive and the legislature. That is why Taft had been able to work so easily with him.

It should be emphasized that Taft was never more deferential to Congress than the Constitution, as he broadly interpreted it, required him to be. Moderation in speech or manner should not be mistaken for his acquiescence in congressional supremacy. His constitutional views permitted him to be as big and as strong as a Roosevelt or a Lincoln, if and when he chose to be. Taft believed in a dynamic, aggressive, persuasive president, a steward of the people, but he simply lacked the energy, imagination, and political skill to fill the role. In conception he was relatively strong, in execution weak. William Allen White perceptively noted near the end of the Taft presidency, "I am inclined to believe that in the main the President has been doing the right thing in the wrong way."[11]

III

Circumstances and personalities affect the form in which executives express their notions of power and duty, and Taft's and Roosevelt's conceptions of the presidency must also be assessed from these perspectives.

Differences in temperament and experience certainly influenced the manner in which the two presidents stated their views of office. Roosevelt was an aggressive moralist who perceived the world, especially when performing for it, in terms of the "good guys" and the "bad guys." Thomas B. Reed,

Cannon's predecessor, once wryly discerned, "What I like about you, Theodore, is your original discovery of the Ten Commandments."[12] Roosevelt's public statements are heavily laden with the moralistic words and phrases of a preacher. His *Autobiography*, published for mass consumption, glorifies the chief executive's role as the moral leader and, in biblical terms, "steward" of the people. Not only was Roosevelt inclined to cloak his ideas in such self-righteous rhetoric, but he also possessed an uncanny instinct for gaining maximum publicity for himself and his ideas. When he declared that he belonged to the "Jackson-Lincoln" class of presidents and Taft to the "Buchanan" class, he was merely dramatizing his own virtues while destroying a straw man. Roosevelt, the aggressive activist, moralist, and consummate showman, eulogized himself with his "stewardship" theory. It is a theory which emphasizes action, the public good, and the opportunities, not the limitations, of power.

Taft, on the other hand, was preeminently a man of the law and the Constitution. His presidential speeches and his treatise on the presidency bear the tedious stamp of the legal profession. Valuing precedent and continuity, a respect for form over content, and still oblivious to the requirements of rhetoric, Taft was inclined to express his views in the technical language of the law, which emphasized the limitations rather than the opportunities of power. Taft's legalistic view was inevitably overshadowed by one of the most dramatic presidential sermons in the history of the presidency. Roosevelt had captured the spirit of the office; Taft the form.

The circumstances surrounding the publication of Roosevelt's *Autobiography* and Taft's response go far to explain their more memorable differences on the presidency. The writing of the two men, though enlightening and informative, should not be interpreted literally. Presidents who produce memoirs or autobiographies of their administrations are usually interested in justifying their actions and are naturally inclined to gloss over their deficiencies and failures. Roosevelt's bitter defeat may have been the catalyst for his remarkable apologia, the *Autobiography*. What he could not win by ballot he sought to salvage by pen, and an explanation for his party-shattering conflict with Taft must have seemed necessary to him. Both his bitterness and his self-justification are evident from the fact that he does not make any positive references (not one!) to Taft in the *Autobiography*. Such treatment of opponents and former friends, of course, is not uncommon in politics. When Roosevelt could no longer remain silent about Taft, he caricatured himself as a Jackson-Lincoln-type president in contrast to the Buchanan-Taft type to justify splitting the party. Roosevelt found it easy to create a straw man and then blow him down with vigor, style, self-righteousness, and apparent good sense. He had been doing it all his political life.

Because he was not a Buchanan-type president, Taft fought back, and the views he expressed must be evaluated in that context. In a series of lectures in 1915 (although he had been saying the same thing in numerous speeches for two years), Taft, then Kent Professor of constitutional law at Yale, replied to Roosevelt's extravagant claims and charges in the only language he had ever mastered—that of a constitutional lawyer. Roosevelt's theory—"[I]t was not only the [President's] right but his duty to do anything that the needs of the nation demanded unless such action was forbidden by the Constitution or the law"[13]—challenged the legal underpinnings of the American political system. Taft rejected the theory:

My judgment is that the view . . . of Mr. Roosevelt, ascribing an undefined residuum of power to the President is an unsafe doctrine and that it might lead under emergencies to results of an arbitrary character, doing irremedial injustice to private right.[14]

Roosevelt, concerned with the growing burdens of the presidency, emphasized the opportunity and need for moral leadership, while Taft, conscious of the legal basis of power, emphasized the limitations within which a president must operate in a truly constitutional system. Roosevelt recognized the growing responsibilities of the chief executive; Taft was acutely aware of the gap between constitutional power and responsibility. Roosevelt was wiser politically, Taft more correct legally.

The major misunderstanding between the two men and their theories centers about the use of the word *power*. Roosevelt claimed that the president should have the "power" to do whatever was necessary for the common good, but Taft would not accept such a notion if the "power" could not be traced to any specific provision of the Constitution. From a legal point of view, Taft was certainly right, and Roosevelt wrong. Although Taft felt that the president had no undefined power to act as a "universal Providence," he did recognize that, in fact, a president could exercise a great deal of "influence" through force of personality or party leadership. "Influence," however, was quite different from "power" in the lexicon of a constitutional lawyer. Because Taft was reacting to Roosevelt's extravagant claims, his views are expressed in defensive terms which make him appear to reject the notion that the president ought to do all he can to promote the public welfare.

We know, of course, that Taft's prepresidential views recognized the importance of "influence" on presidential leadership. Taft had seen no danger in the president's use of "influence" to achieve his political objectives. His postpresidential views likewise recognized the distinction between "power" and "influence." In an address at Pottstown, Pennsylvania, in November 1913, for example, Taft noted that, in addition to the legal powers of the office, the president possessed powers "that naturally come to him through our political system, and because he is the head of his party."

He can thus actually exercise very considerable influence, sometimes a controlling influence in the securing of legislation by his personal intervention with members of his party who are in control in each House. *I think he ought to have very great influence,* [emphasis added] because he is made responsible to the people for what the party does, and if the party is wise, it will bend to his leadership as long as it is tolerable, and especially where it is in performance of promises that the party has made in its platform and on the faith of which it must be assumed to have obtained its power. But such power as he exercises in this way is not within the letter of the law.[15]

Taft was hardly hostile to the exercise of presidential "influence," but "influence" was not legal power.

But Roosevelt was not a constitutional lawyer. When he expressed his "stewardship theory" and claimed that it would have justified his seizure of the coal mines in the anthracite strike of 1902, Taft rebelled at the constitutional implications of the argument. He did not condemn Roosevelt's efforts to settle the private dispute:

What was actually done was the result of his [Roosevelt's] activity, his power to influence public opinion and the effect of the prestige of his great office in bringing the parties to the controversy, the mine owners and the strikers, to a legal settlement by arbitration. *No one has a higher admiration for the value of what he did there than I have* [emphasis added].[16]

But he did take issue with the president's alleged power to seize private property without due process of law. He had severe reservations over the invocation of some "undefined

residuum" of power in such a case. Actually Taft felt that
Roosevelt's assertion that he would have seized the coal mines
if there had been no settlement was a mere boast and that
Roosevelt would never have resorted to such an act after consulting his cabinet.[17]

Roosevelt based his justification of extraordinary executive
power on Lincoln's actions during the Civil War. He argued
that his own action in the 1902 strike

illustrated as well as anything that I did the theory which I have
called the Jackson-Lincoln theory of the Presidency; that is, that
occasionally great national crises arise which call for immediate
and vigorous executive action, and that in such cases it is the duty
of the President to act upon the theory that he is the steward of
the people, and that the proper attitude for him to take is that
he is bound to assume that he has the legal right to do whatever
the needs of the people demand, unless the Constitution or the
laws explicitly forbid him to do it.[18]

Roosevelt was undoubtedly thinking of Lincoln's extraordinary actions taken at the outbreak of the Civil War before
Congress had convened and perhaps of Lincoln's oft-quoted
defense of the suspension of the writ of habeas corpus ("Are
all the laws *but one* to go unexecuted, and the Government
itself go to pieces lest that one be violated?"). Taft, however,
argued that "Lincoln always pointed out the sources of authority which in his opinion justified his acts, and there was
always a strong ground for maintaining the view which he
took." What may surprise some is that Taft believed that
Lincoln's claim of power to suspend the writ of habeas corpus
was "well founded." Lincoln's Emancipation Proclamation
was likewise constitutional because, in Taft's view, it was "an
act of the Commander-in-Chief justified by military necessity
to weaken the enemies of the Nation and suppress their rebellion." Although Lincoln may have exercised extraordinary

power, Taft argued that "Lincoln never claimed that whatever authority in government was not expressly denied to him he could exercise."[19] If Taft and Roosevelt could agree with Lincoln's actions and views, where then is the conflict between the two? Taft and Roosevelt really did not disagree. The differences between the two lie in the rancor of 1912 and in Taft's concern for constitutional continuity. Roosevelt claimed that a president could use broad undefined powers without attaching them to any specific clause of the Constitution. But Taft feared that no one would know where such power was to be found except the president, and nothing would prevent him from taking extraordinary measures which invaded the constitutional rights of citizens. All Taft really asked was that a president specify which clause of the Constitution justified his action, unusual though it might seem. Lincoln acted constitutionally not because he found emergency power somewhere in the interstices of the Constitution, but because he found them implied in the grants of power (vague though they might be) in the "Commander-in-Chief," "shall take care," and "executive power" clauses of Article II. Lincoln expanded those powers under unusual conditions, but he did not create a new source of power as Roosevelt seemed anxious to do.

Our Chief Magistrate and Taft's opinion in *Myers v. U.S.* (1926)[20] as chief justice shed further light on his real view of presidential power. In his lectures, Taft defended the president's absolute power to hire and fire subordinates:

The framers of our Constitution had one essential feature of efficient government clearly in mind. They gave to the Executive officer charged in law with the responsibility and actually charged the people with the responsibility of carrying on the Executive department of the government, the power and means of meeting that responsibility. They vested in him complete power to appoint all the officers of the government who were subordinate to him, and upon whose political capacity and governmental discretion would depend the wise carrying out of his policies. They gave him the power of absolute removal, and they placed in his hands the control of the action of all those who took part in the discharge of the political duties of the executive department.[21]

Later, in the *Myers* opinion, Taft argued that the president has virtually unlimited discretion to dismiss subordinate executive officials—in this case, a postmaster of the first class. The Lincolnian claim of executive power in the opinion forced vigorous dissents from Justices Louis D. Brandeis, James Mc-Reynolds, and Oliver Wendell Holmes, who defended the prerogatives of Congress against the president. The Taft opinion actually encouraged presidential usurpation of congressional power over the federal bureaucracy, a radical position which seemed totally out of character for a Whig who emphasized the limited nature of government in his 1915 lectures. The contradiction, however, is illusory, for Taft believed in limited government *and* broad executive power over administration.

In upholding the power of the president to dismiss a postmaster whose term of office had not yet expired, the Court invalidated an 1876 law which required Senate approval of such removals. Taft argued that the "executive power" and "take care" clauses of the Constitution gave the president the power to execute the laws. Enforcement of the laws requires subordinates. The president must be able to appoint and remove them to fulfill his constitutional responsibilities. Taft's interpretation of the "executive power" clause was breathtaking in scope:

The executive power was given in general terms, strengthened by specific terms where emphasis was regarded as appropriate, and was limited by direct expressions where limitation was needed, and the fact that no express limit was placed on the power of removal by the Executive was convincing indication that none was intended.[22]

Alexander Hamilton, Abraham Lincoln, or Teddy Roosevelt could have subscribed to this. What the Constitution does not specifically prohibit to the president, it grants to him through that vague "executive power" clause! Since the Constitution does not contain specific limitations on the president's removal power, there are none. The power of removal, Taft continued, is exclusive:

The power of removal is incident to the power of appointment, not to the power of advising and consenting to appointment, and when the grant of the executive power is enforced by the express mandate to take care that the laws be faithfully executed, it emphasizes the necessity for including within the executive power as conferred the exclusive power of removal.[23]

In short, if the president can appoint, he can fire. Only if Congress vested appointment in other officials or in itself could it place any restrictions on removal.

Taft recognized that the Congress could vest the president's appointed subordinates with special duties and powers, but that, finally, it could not prevent a president from exercising his duty to "take care that the laws be faithfully exercised."

The ability and judgment manifested by the official thus empowered, as well as his energy and stimulation of his subordinates, are subjects which the President must consider and supervise in his administrative control. Finding such officers to be negligent and inefficient, the President should have the power to remove them.[24]

This meant that the president could fire appointees exercising quasijudicial powers, a member of the Interstate Commerce

Commission, for example. Even though the president might not be able to influence the decision of such an official,

he may consider the decision after its rendition as a reason for removing the officer, on the ground that the discretion regularly entrusted to that officer by statute has not been on the whole intelligently or wisely exercised. Otherwise he does not discharge his own constitutional duty of seeing that the laws be faithfully executed.[25]

The fact that Congress may have stipulated the reasons for removal did not negate the fact that the "power of removal inhered in the power to appoint." Such laws, Taft argued, "are to be reconciled to the unrestricted power of the President to remove, if he chooses to exercise his power."[26]

The major difference between the *Myers* opinion and Roosevelt's "stewardship" theory is that Taft justified his extraordinary claim of power on the "executive power" and "take care" clauses of the Constitution while Roosevelt tended to invoke the higher laws of justice and morality for his positions. *Myers* is not an aberration but a logical expression of Taft's philosophy formed during his long career in government. When Taft, for example, had been solicitor general in the Harrison administration in 1891, he was asked for an opinion by the assistant secretary of the treasury about the secretary's power to remove an assistant appraiser in the Customs Service and replied:

All I can say is that if I were Secretary of the Treasury, in charge of the duty of administering that great department, I should not wish to have as one of my subordinates a man who allows himself to manifest so much sympathy, and render so much substantial aid to persons whose interests are entirely opposed to those of the Government.[27]

As governor-general of the Philippines, secretary of war, and president, Taft had developed a further appreciation for strong executive authority over organizations. His firm defense of presidential prerogative to draft and submit a budget to Congress, for example, indicates that his *Myers* opinion was not a fluke but a reasoned defense of views long held but little publicized. Taft was as jealous of his executive powers as any president and, though the occasions were rare, resisted congressional encroachments on them.

V

Taft's preoccupation with constitutional continuity and his almost religious commitment to the rule of law contributed to his major disagreements with Theodore Roosevelt over the conduct of the presidency. Had Roosevelt shown greater deference toward the Constitution in explaining his conception of office, Taft could probably have accepted the view. But Roosevelt was too preoccupied with justice, too aggressively result-oriented, too much the innovator and moralist ever to bind his rhetoric with the legalistic phrases of the Constitution. Taft, on the other hand, believed that, even when the Constitution had to be changed to accommodate reform, appearances of continuity had to be preserved to maintain popular respect for our institutions. If the judiciary lost its reputation for impartially interpreting and applying the grand clauses of the Constitution, the legitimacy of all government would be diminished. Substituting the rule of men for the rule of law would ultimately produce a state of lawlessness in which no genuine reform would be possible. Taft's legal philosophy was not easily comprehended by or communicable to the public. According to the *Outlook*, the public consequently lost confidence in Taft, "not because of personal unpopularity or personal distrust, but because the people have come to believe not that human rights must be made to fit the Constitution, but that the Constitution must be made to fit human rights."[28]

In restrospect, the conflict between Taft and Roosevelt represented a phase of a long, continuing struggle in American history between those forces pushing for change and reform without regard to constitutional procedures and those demanding conformity to legal procedures even at the cost of immediate justice. The conflict seems destined to continue as long as our constitutional democracy can survive. It is out of this dialectical conflict between form and content, between legality and justice, between constitutional government and majority rule that our government has been able to adapt itself to the needs of each new generation without discarding the wisdom embodied in our fundamental institutions. As long as that healthy tension remains, neither the demands for immediate justice nor the requirements of constitutional government will, in the long run, undermine our national commitment to "Equal Justice under Law."

Notes

Knox Corr.	The Correspondence of Philander Chase Knox, in the Papers of Philander Chase Knox, Manuscript Division, Library of Congress, Washington, D.C.
Num. Case	U.S. Department of State, Numerical Cases, National Archives, Washington, D.C. The Decimal file will be referred to by file numbers alone.
Root Gen. Corr.	General Correspondence, in the Papers of Elihu Root, Manuscript Division, Library of Congress, Washington, D.C.
Root Spec. Corr.	Special Correspondence, Root Papers.
SPF	Secretary's Private Files, 10,692, in the Walter L. Fisher Papers, Manuscript Division, Library of Congress, Washington, D.C.
Straight Misc.	Miscellaneous Correspondence, in the Papers of Willard D. Straight, Collection of Regional History and University Archives, Olin Library, Cornell University, Ithaca, New York.
Taft Adrs.	Addresses and Articles of William H. Taft, in the Papers of William Howard Taft, Manuscript Division, Library of Congress, Washington, D.C.
Taft-TR	Correspondence with Theodore Roosevelt, Series 4, Taft Papers.
TL	Letterbook, Series 8 [Secretary of War, Presidential, & Yale], Taft Papers.
TPS 2	Presidential Series 2, Taft Papers.
TPS 3	Presidential Series 3, Taft Papers.
TRL	*The Letters of Theodore Roosevelt*, ed. Elting E.

Morison and John M. Blum (8 vols.; Cambridge: Harvard University Press, 1951–1954).

TR-Lodge   Henry Cabot Lodge, *Selections from the Correspondence of Theodore Roosevelt and Henry Cabot Lodge, 1884–1918* (2 vols.; New York: Charles Scribner's, 1925).

Introduction

1. Russel B. Nye, *Midwestern Progressive Politics* (New York: Harper Torchbooks, 1965), 183.

Chapter 1

1. Quoted in Henry F. Pringle, *The Life and Times of William Howard Taft* (New York: Farrar & Rinehart, 1938), I, 290.

2. For a detailed account of Alphonso Taft's political career, see Ishbel Ross, *An American Family: The Tafts—1678 to 1964* (Cleveland: World, 1964), 3–81.

3. For Taft's family and political background, see Pringle, *Taft*, I, 3–153; and also Ross, *American Family*, 82–125.

4. *Ibid.*

5. Herbert S. Duffy, *William Howard Taft* (New York: Minton, Balch, 1930), 72.

6. As quoted by Taft, Address before the New York County Lawyer's Association of New York, March 13, 1915, Addresses and Articles of William Howard Taft, XXXIV, 189, in the Papers of William Howard Taft, Manuscript Division, Library of Congress, Washington, D.C.; cited hereafter as Taft Adrs.

7. Address before the National Geographic Society, Washington, D.C., Nov. 14, 1913, Taft Adrs., XXXI, 329.

8. Pringle, *Taft*, I, 161; see also Taft to Elihu Root, Feb. 2, 1900, Special Correspondence, Box 164, in the Papers of Elihu Root, Manuscript Division, Library of Congress, Washington, D.C.; cited hereafter as Root Spec. Corr.

9. Taft to Theodore Roosevelt, May 12, 1901, Correspondence with Theodore Roosevelt, Series 4, Taft Papers; hereafter cited as Taft-TR.

10. Roosevelt to Paul Morton, Nov. 11, 1905, and to Taft, April 22, 1903, *The Letters of Theodore Roosevelt*, ed. Elting E. Morison and John M. Blum (Cambridge: Harvard University Press, 1951–1954), V, 74, III, 464; cited hereafter as *TRL*.

11. Roosevelt, as quoted in Oscar King Davis, *William Howard Taft: The Man of the Hour* (Philadelphia: P. W. Ziegler, 1908), 13,

12. Pringle, *Taft*, I, 165.

13. Roosevelt to H. K. Love, June 6, 1900, *TRL*, II, 1325.

14. Roosevelt to Taft, July 15, 1901, Feb. 7, 1900, *TRL*, III, 121, II, 1175.

15. Roosevelt to Love, Nov. 24, 1900, *TRL*, II, 1141.

16. Roosevelt to Taft, Oct. 25, 1902, *TRL*, III, 368.

17. Taft to Roosevelt and Elihu Root, Oct. 27, 1902, Taft-TR.

18. Alpheus Thomas Mason, *William Howard Taft: Chief Justice* (New York: Simon and Schuster, 1964), 23.

19. Jan. 25, 1903, Root Spec. Corr.

20. Helen Herron Taft, *Recollections of Full Years* (New York: Dodd, Mead, 1914), 263.

21. Roosevelt to Taft, April 22, 1903, *TRL*, III, 464.

22. Roosevelt to Taft, Feb. 14, 1903, *TRL*, III, 426.

23. Taft to Roosevelt, April 3, 1903, Taft-TR.

24. Quoted in Pringle, *Taft*, I, 252.

25. Roosevelt to Gen. Leonard Wood, June 4, 1904, *TRL*, IV, 820.

26. Archie Butt, *Taft and Roosevelt: The Intimate Letters of Archie Butt, Military Aide* (Garden City: Doubleday, Doran, 1930), I, 386.

27. Quoted in Archie Butt, *The Letters of Archie Butt* (Garden City: Doubleday, Page, 1924), 310–11.

28. R. & W. Jenkinson Co. to Boies Penrose, Sept. 26, 1904, in Taft-TR.

29. Roosevelt to Taft, Oct. 11, 1904, *TRL*, IV, 980.

30. Roosevelt to John Hay, March 30, 1905, *TRL*, IV, 1150.

31. Roosevelt to Taft, April 20, 27, 1905, *TRL*, IV, 1162, 1161.

32. Roosevelt to Lodge, July 11, 1905, *TRL*, IV, 1271, 1272; and July 2, in Henry Cabot Lodge, ed., *Selection from the Correspondence of Theodore Roosevelt and Henry Cabot Lodge, 1884–1918* (New York: Scribner's, 1925), II, 161; hereafter cited as *TR-Lodge*.

33. Roosevelt to Taft, March 15, 1906, *TRL*, V, 183, 184.

34. Taft to Roosevelt, July 30, 1906, Taft-TR.

35. See Mason, *Taft*, Chap. I, for a detailed account of Taft's ambition to become Chief Justice of the Supreme Court.

36. Quoted in Butt, *Letters*, 244.

37. Taft to Roosevelt, July 6, 1905, Taft-TR.

38. Roosevelt to Taft, July 31, 1906, Taft-TR.

39. Helen Taft, *Recollections*, 291.

40. As quoted by Henry F. Pringle, *Theodore Roosevelt* (New York: Harcourt, Brace & World, 1956), 233.

41. Roosevelt to Taft, Sept. 17, 1906, *TRL*, V, 414–15.

42. See Taft to Roosevelt, Sept. 20, 22, 1906, Taft-TR.

43. Roosevelt to Taft, Sept. 28, 30, *TRL*, V, 432, 435.

44. Philip Jessup, *Elihu Root* (New York: Dodd, Mead, 1938), II, 156.

45. Pringle, *Taft*, I, 272.

46. See Dana G. Munro, *Intervention and Dollar Diplomacy in the Caribbean, 1900–1921* (Princeton: Princeton University Press, 1964), 94–111, for a full account of the event.

47. Roosevelt to John Hay, March 30, 1905, *TRL*, IV, 1150.

48. Butt, *Taft and Roosevelt*, I, 345.

49. See Chapter 7, p. 259 below, regarding Central American Loan Conventions.

50. Jessup, *Root*, II, 4–5.

51. Taft to Roosevelt, ca. July 29, 1905, Taft-TR; Roosevelt to Taft, July 31, 1905, *TRL*, IV, 1293.

52. See Howard K. Beale, *Theodore Roosevelt and the Rise of America to World Power* (New York: Collier Books, 1962), 210–11, for a discussion of Taft's Japanese visit.

53. Quoted in Pringle, *Taft*, I, 304; see also Jessup, *Root*, II, 26.

54. See Chapter 7, pp. 242–43.

55. Straight to G. Casenave, Dec. 4, 1907, Miscellaneous Correspondence, Box 3, File 116D, in the Papers of Williard D. Straight, Collection of Regional History and University Archives, Olin Library, Cornell University, Ithaca, New York; cited hereafter as Straight Misc.

56. Katsura to Taft, Aug. 7, 1909, Presidential Series 3, File 462, Taft Papers; hereafter cited as TPS 3.

57. Address before the National Geographic Society, Washington, D.C., Nov. 14, 1913, Taft Adrs., XXXI, 238.

58. Roosevelt to Taft, July 26, 1907, *TRL*, V, 727.

59. Pringle, *Taft*, I, 276.

60. Quoted in Francis E. Leupp, "President Taft's Own View," *Outlook*, XCIX (Dec. 2, 1911), 811.

61. Quoted in Pringle, *Taft*, I, 290.

Chapter 2

1. Roosevelt to Kermit Roosevelt, Jan. 27, 1908, *TRL*, VI, 916.

2. As quoted in Malcom Moos, *The Republicans* (New York: Random House, 1956), 250.

3. Roosevelt to George Otto Trevelyan, June 19, 1908, *TRL*, VI, 1087.

4. Roosevelt to Whitelaw Reid, June 13, 1908, *TRL*, VI, 1073.

5. Roosevelt to Trevelyan, June 19, 1908, *TRL*, VI, 1089.

6. Quoted in Jessup, *Root*, II, 125.

7. Quoted in M. A. deWolfe Howe, *George von Lengerke Meyer* (New York: Dodd, Mead, 1920), 373–74.

8. Taft to Roosevelt, Aug. 5, 1906, Taft-TR.

9. Quoted in Jessup, *Root*, II, 125.

10. Roosevelt to Kermit Roosevelt, Jan. 27, 1908, and to Taft, Nov. 5, 1906, *TRL*, VI, 916; V, 486.

11. Roosevelt to William Allen White, July 30, 1907, *TRL*, VI, 735–36.

12. Quoted in Howe, *Meyer*, 365.

13. Roosevelt to White, July 30, 1907, *TRL*, VI, 735–36.

14. Roosevelt to Taft, Sept. 3, 19, 1907, *TRL*, V, 780–81, 796.

15. Roosevelt to White, July 30, 1907, *TRL*, V, 734.

16. Roosevelt to Taft, Sept. 3, 1907, Taft-TR.

17. William Rea Gwinn, *Uncle Joe Cannon: Archfoe of Insurgency* (Bookman Associates, 1957), 92–94.

18. Butt, *Taft and Roosevelt*, I, 303–4.

19. Roosevelt to Kermit Roosevelt, Jan. 27, 1908, *TRL*, VI, 916.

20. Roosevelt to Butler, Sept. 14, 1907, *TRL*, VI, 807.

21. Roosevelt to Lee, Dec. 26, 1907, *TRL*, VI, 875.

22. Helen Taft, *Recollections*, 304. (See also Mason, *Taft*, 26–27.)

23. *Ibid.*, 304–5.

24. Taft to Roosevelt, Oct. 31, 1906, Taft-TR.

25. *Ibid.*

26. Helen Taft, *Recollections*, 304.

27. Roosevelt to Taft, Sept. 3, 1907, *TRL*, V, 781.

28. Quoted in Moos, *Republicans*, 259.

29. *New York Times*, June 19, 1908, 1. For an account of the convention, see Pringle, *Taft*, I, 353; and Moos, *Republicans*, 258–59.

30. Roosevelt to Benjamin Ide Wheeler, June 17, 1908, *TRL*, VI, 1082.

31. Joseph Cannon, as quoted in the *New York Times*, June 10, 1908, 1; see also George E. Mowry, *The Era of Roosevelt* (New York: Harper, 1958), 228–29; and *TRL*, VI, 1077, for convention proceedings.

32. Roosevelt to White, July 30, 1907, *TRL*, V, 735.

33. The letter read as follows: "I have been informed that certain officeholders in your Department are proposing to go to the national convention as delegates in favor of renominating me for the Presidency, or are proposing to procure my endorsement for such renomination by State conventions. This must not be. I wish to inform such officers as you may find it advisable or necessary to inform in order to carry out the spirit of this instruction, that such advocacy of my

renomination, or acceptance of an election as delegate for that purpose, will be regarded as a serious violation of official propriety, and will be dealt with accordingly." Roosevelt to William D. Foulke, Feb. 7, 1908, *TRL*, VI, 932–33.

34. Quoted in Pringle, *Taft*, I, 321.

35. Kirk H. Porter and Donald B. Johnson, eds., *National Party Platforms*, 1840–1956 (Urbana, Ill.: University of Illinois Press, 1956), 145.

36. Roosevelt to Richard Watson Gilder, Nov. 16, 1908, *TRL*, VI, 1357–58.

37. Taft to Roosevelt, Nov. 7, 1908, Letterbook, Series 8 [Secretary of War, Presidential, & Yale], Taft Papers; cited hereafter as TL.

38. *New York Times*, June 18, 1908, 8.

39. Roosevelt to Taft, Nov. 5, 1906, Sept. 19, 1907, *TRL*, V, 486, 796.

40. Roosevelt to Lodge, June 8, 1908, *TR-Lodge*, II, 302.

41. Oscar S. Straus, *Under Four Administrations* (Boston: Houghton Mifflin, 1922), 253–54.

42. Quoted in Roosevelt to William Jennings Bryan, Sept. 23, 1908, *TRL*, VI, 1252.

43. Roosevelt to Taft, Sept. 19, 1908, *TRL*, VI, 1244; Pringle, *Taft*, I, 370–72.

44. Roosevelt to Abbott, Sept. 23, 1908, *TRL*, VI, 1248–49.

45. Taft to Roosevelt, July 12, 1908, TL, and Roosevelt to Taft, July 10, 1908, *TRL*, VI, 1117.

46. Taft to Roosevelt, July 9, 1908, TL.

47. Taft to Cromwell, Aug. 6, 1908, TL.

48. Roosevelt to Taft, Aug. 7, 1908, *TRL*, VI, 1157.

49. Taft to Roosevelt, July 4, 1908, TL; and Roosevelt to Taft, July 7, *TRL*, VII, 1113.

50. Taft to Roosevelt, July 31, 1908, Taft-TR; and Roosevelt to Taft, Aug. 3, 1908, *TRL*, VI, 1149.

51. Taft to Cromwell, Aug. 6, 1908, TL.

52. Taft to Roosevelt, Aug. 10, 1908, Taft-TR; and Roosevelt to Taft, Sept. 5, *TRL*, VI, 1209–10.

53. Roosevelt to Taft, Sept. 21, 1908, and to Hitchcock, Sept. 23, *TRL*, VI, 1247, 1249; see also Moos, *Republicans*, 260.

54. Taft to Roosevelt, Aug. 10, 1908, Taft-TR.

55. Taft to Charles P. Taft, Sept. 9, 1908, TL.

56. Taft to Lodge, Sept. 12, 1908, TL.

57. Roosevelt to Taft, July 17, 21, Aug. 29, Sept. 1, 1908, *TRL*, VI, 1132, 1139–40, 1202, 1204.

58. Elihu Root to Roosevelt, Sept. 5, 1908, Root Spec. Corr.

59. Taft to E. N. Huggins, Aug. 11, 1908, TL.

60. Francis Bacon, "Of Boldness," in *Selected Writings of Francis Bacon* (New York: Modern Library, 1955), 32–33.

61. See in particular Taft Adrs. at Hartford, Conn., Feb. 15, 1908, VIII, 233–234; before the McKinley Club, Omaha, Neb., April 6, X, 10–12; to the Commercial Club of Chicago, April 4, IX, 243–52, for indications of Taft's foreign policy views.

62. Quoted in Pringle, *Taft*, I, 340; see also Taft to Roosevelt, Nov. 9, 1902, Taft-TR, for Taft's views.

63. See Taft to Roosevelt, Nov. 9, Taft-TR; Pringle, *Taft*, I, 342, 523; II, 654–57; *New York Times*, June 8, 1908, 6.

64. Roosevelt to Taft, Sept. 4, 1906, Taft-TR; see also Roosevelt's final State of the Union message to Congress in James D. Richardson, ed., *A Compilation of the Messages and Papers of the Presidents* (New York: Bureau of National Literature, 1897–1914), XVII, 7578–7618; hereafter cited as *Messages*.

65. Roosevelt to Conrad Kohrs, Sept. 9, 1908, *TRL*, VI, 1218.

66. Speech delivered at Milwaukee, Wis., Sept. 24, 1908, Taft Adrs., XII, 11–12.

67. "The Essence of Taftism," *Journal of the Knights of Labor*, Feb. 1908, in the Correspondence of Philander Chase Knox, IV, Papers of Philander Chase Knox, Manuscript Division, Library of Congress, Washington, D.C.; hereafter cited as Knox Corr.; see also Mowry, *Era of Roosevelt*, 235.

68. Quoted in *TRL*, VI, 1321.

69. Porter and Johnson, *Party Platforms*, 160.

70. See Paolo E. Coletta, *William Jennings Bryan: Political Evangelist, 1860–1908* (Lincoln, Neb.: University of Nebraska Press, 1964), 431, 411–29.

71. Taft to Roosevelt, May 9, 1903, Taft-TR.

72. Taft to Roosevelt, July 16, 1907, Taft-TR.

73. Taft to Roosevelt, July 12, 1908, TL.

74. Porter and Johnson, *Party Platforms*, 145.

75. Taft to Col. W. R. Nelson, Aug. 25, 1908, TL.

76. Taft to Dr. D. D. Thompson, ca. Aug. 28, 1908, TL.

77. Porter and Johnson, *Party Platforms*, 150.

78. Roosevelt to Goethals, Dec. 13, 1908, *TRL*, VI, 1421; and to Root, June 7, 1904, Root Spec. Corr.

79. Porter and Johnson, *Party Platforms*, 148.

80. *Ibid.*, 150; see also Roosevelt to Taft, July 13, 1908, *TRL*, VI, 1127.

81. Address at Hartford, Conn., Feb. 15, 1908, Taft Adrs., VIII, 233.

82. Figures cited from Joseph Nathan Kane, *Facts about the Pres-*

idents (New York: Pocket Books, 1964), 279, 289–90; see also Mowry, *Era of Roosevelt*, 231.

83. Roosevelt to Taft, Nov. 10, 1908, *TRL*, VI, 1340.

84. Jessup, *Root*, II, 132.

85. Quoted in Butt, *Letters*, 158–59.

86. Helen Taft, *Recollections*, 392.

Chapter 3

1. Taft to William Kent, June 29, 1909, TL.

2. Speech of Acceptance, July 28, 1908, Presidential Series 2, File 563, Taft Papers; hereafter cited as TPS 2.

3. Max Weber, *From Max Weber*, ed. H. H. Gerth and C. Wright Mills (New York: Oxford University Press, 1958), 52–55.

4. Taft to James Rudolph Garfield, Jan. 22, 1909, TL. Similar letters were sent to all cabinet members.

5. Roosevelt to Charles Spencer Francis, March 18, 1909, in General Correspondence, Box 81 (1911), Root Papers, hereafter cited as Root Gen. Corr.; see also Roosevelt to Whitelaw Reid, Jan. 31, 1909, and to Taft, Jan. 4, 1909, *TRL*, VI, 1499, 1458.

6. Butt, *Letters*, 307.

7. See Roosevelt to Taft, Jan. 27, 1909, *TRL*, VI, 1487.

8. Butt, *Letters*, 314, 307–8.

9. Irwin Hood Hoover, *Forty-Two Years in the White House* (Boston: Houghton Mifflin, 1934), 38–39.

10. See Taft to Sen. P. C. Knox, Dec. 22, 23, 1908, Feb. 1, 20, 1909, TL.

11. Taft to Roosevelt, Jan. 8, 1909, Taft-TR.

12. Taft to Horace Taft, Feb. 1, 1910, TL.

13. Butt, *Taft and Roosevelt*, II, 718.

14. Mowry, *Era of Roosevelt*, 237–38.

15. Quoted in Butt, *Taft and Roosevelt*, I, 196–97.

16. Taft to W. H. Phipps, July 1, 1909, TL.

17. Allan Nevins, *Henry White: Thirty Years of American Diplomacy* (New York: Harper, 1930), 297–98.

18. Root to Whitelaw Reid, May 29, 1909, Root Gen. Corr., Box 65 (1909).

19. Butt, *Taft and Roosevelt*, I, 38.

20. Roosevelt to White, July 21, 1909, *TRL*, VII, 21.

21. Taft to Charles P. Taft, Sept. 10, 1910, TL.

22. Lodge to Roosevelt, April 29, 1909, *TR-Lodge*, II, 34.

23. *Ibid.*, 34–35.

24. Taft to Mrs. Taft, Oct. 3, 1909, TL; see also Taft to Knox, Oct. 9, 1909, TL.

25. Taft to Alfred R. Conkling, Feb. 25, 1909, TL.

26. Roosevelt to Taft, Dec. 15, 1908, *TRL*, VI, 1423.

27. Quoted in Graham H. Stuart, *The Department of State: A History of Its Organization, Procedure, and Personnel* (New York: Macmillan, 1949), 211.

28. Taft to Knox, Jan. 19, 1909, TL.

29. Francis Mairs Huntington-Wilson, *Memoirs of an Ex-Diplomat* (Boston: Bruce Humphries, 1945), 176, 190, 231; Katherine Crane, *Mr. Carr of State* (New York: St. Martin's Press, 1960), 100–1; Huntington Wilson, "The American Foreign Service," *Outlook*, LXXXII (March 3, 1906), 499–504; and *TRL*, VI, 1420.

30. Quoted in Stuart, *Department of State*, 211.

31. Huntington-Wilson, *Memoirs*, 199, 235.

32. Butt, *Taft and Roosevelt*, II, 563, 743.

33. *Ibid.*, 180; see also Order by the Secretary of State No. 24, June 14, 1910, in U.S. Department of State, Numerical Case 11120/87, National Archives, Washington, D.C. (Hereafter all references to State Department correspondence from the Numerical Case file will be cited as Num. Case.)

34. Henry Lane Wilson, *Diplomatic Episodes in Mexico, Belgium, and Chile* (New York: Doubleday, Page, 1927), 297.

35. Huntington-Wilson, *Memoirs*, 180.

36. *Ibid.*, 182. See also draft letter, Wilson to Knox, *ca.* Jan. 7, 1912, in Knox Corr., XVI, 2720–21, in which Wilson describes his duties to Knox, who was interested in securing a raise for Wilson.

37. Butt, *Taft and Roosevelt*, I, 371–72.

38. Huntington-Wilson, *Memoirs*, 231.

39. M. Nelson McGeary, *Gifford Pinchot* (Princeton: Princeton University Press, 1960), 116–21.

40. For a full treatment of the dispute, see Mowry, *Theodore Roosevelt*, 73–87.

41. Taft to Roosevelt, Dec. 24, 1908, Taft-TR.

42. Taft to Kent, June 29, 1909, TL.

43. McGeary, *Pinchot*, 127–29.

44. Stimson to Root, Nov. 12, 1909, Root Gen. Corr., Box 65 (1909).

45. George E. Mowry, *Theodore Roosevelt and the Progressive Movement* (New York: Hill and Wang, 1960), 77.

46. Taft to Longworth, Aug. 30, 1909, to Horace Taft, June 6, Sept. 6, and to Mrs. Taft, Oct. 3, TL.

47. Taft to Wickersham, Oct. 7, 1909, TL; McGeary, *Pinchot*, 146–47.

48. Taft to Horace Taft, Oct. 18, 1909, TL; Butt, *Taft and Roosevelt*, I, 245.

49. Taft to Kent, Sept. 19, 1909, TL.

50. Butt, *Taft and Roosevelt*, I, 235–36.

51. *Ibid.*, 235; see also Mowry, *Theodore Roosevelt*, 76–86; Mc-Geary, *Pinchot*, 157–60.

52. Lodge to Roosevelt, Jan. 15, 1910, *TR-Lodge*, II, 358.

53. Taft to P. A. Baker, May 21, 1910, TL.

54. Quoted in Butt, *Taft and Roosevelt*, II, 602.

55. Taft to Ballinger, March 7, 1911, TL.

56. Taft to Knox, March 11, 1911, TL; see also Butt, *Taft and Roosevelt*, II, 603–4.

57. Taft to Bannard, Nov. 10, 1912, TL.

58. Butt, *Taft and Roosevelt*, II, 695.

59. *Ibid.*

60. See Pringle, *Taft*, II, 728–30, for a more complete account of the Wiley case.

61. Butt, *Taft and Roosevelt*, I, 79.

62. Butt, *Taft and Roosevelt*, I, 110–11; see also Taft to W. S. Brown, Aug. 15, 1908, TL.

63. George K. Turner, "How Taft Views His Own Administration: An Interview with the President," *McClure's Magazine*, XXXV (June 1910), 216.

64. Richard Hofstadter, *The American Political Tradition* (New York: Vintage Books, 1959), 228.

65. Arthur F. Easterbrook to Sen. W. Murray Crane, Sept. 26, 1911, TPS 2, File 147.

66. See Pringle, *Roosevelt*, 309–13, and Mark Sullivan, *Our Times: The United States, 1900–1925* (New York: Charles Scribners's, 1926–1935), IV, 467–68, for a more detailed discussion.

67. See Wickersham to Taft, Oct. 26, 1911, TPS 2, File 2052; Sullivan, *Our Times*, IV, 406.

68. Taft to George B. Edwards, Dec. 3, 1911, TL.

69. Taft to Wickersham, Feb. 27, 1912, TL.

70. Taft to Horace Taft, Nov. 5, 1911, TL; Sullivan, *Our Times*, IV, 467–68.

71. Bannard to Taft, June 24, 1912, TPS 3, File 115.

72. Roosevelt to Hughes, Nov. 7, 1906, *TRL*, V, 490.

73. *TRL*, VII, 246; Butt, *Taft and Roosevelt*, II, 477–78.

74. Roosevelt to Garfield, April 28, 1911, *TRL*, VII, 246.

75. Butt, *Taft and Roosevelt*, II, 319, 619.

76. *Ibid.*, 618–19.

77. *Ibid.*, I, 355.

78. MacVeagh to Root, May 3, 1911, Root Gen. Corr., Box 87 (1911).

79. Butt, *Taft and Roosevelt*, II, 789.

80. *Ibid.*, I, 201.

81. Bannard to Taft, Nov. 7, 1912, TPS 3, File 115; Taft to Bannard, Nov. 10, 1912, TL.

82. Roosevelt had been D'Artagnan, Taft Porthos, and Root Athos in the Roosevelt cabinet, Helen Taft, *Recollections*, 302.

83. For a comprehensive history of the budgetary and appropriation process in Congress, see Lucius Wilmerding, Jr., *The Spending Power* (New Haven: Yale University Press, 1949), esp. 137–79.

84. "Economy and Efficiency in Government," Nov. 20, 1914, Taft Adrs., XXXIII, 300–01; see also "One of Taft's Reforms," *Washington Post*, March 28, 1910, in Scrapbook 24, 204, Knox Papers.

85. Taft to MacVeagh, Sept. 19, 1912, TL.

86. Quoted by Cornelius P. Cotter, "Legislative Oversight," in *Congress: The First Branch of Government*, ed. Alfred deGrazia (Washington: American Enterprise Institute for Public Policy Research, 1966), pp. 48–49. For more on Taft's attitude toward the commission, see Richardson, *Messages*, XXVII, 7930–31; "President Taft and the Cost of Government," *Outlook*, CII (Oct. 5, 1912), 235.

87. Quoted in Taft to MacVeagh, Sept. 19, 1912, TL.

88. Quoted in H. B. Gardner, "Proposal for a National Budget," *American Economic Review*, II (Dec. 1912), 970.

89. Taft to MacVeagh, Sept. 19, 1912, TL.

90. 272 U.S. 52 (1926).

91. Article on Government Economy, Feb. 6, 1915, Taft Adrs., XXXIII, 89.

92. For the organizational improvements made by the administration, see Howe, *Meyer*, 445–50; Franklin MacVeagh, "Departmental Economy," *Independent*, LXIV (Dec. 22, 1910), 1366–69; Richardson, *Messages*, XVII, 7885–88, 7909–10, 8063, XVIII, 8148–49, 8176–80, 8210, and especially the Special Message on Economy and Efficiency, Jan. 17, 1912, 8078–99.

93. Richardson, *Messages*, XVIII, 8078.

94. "Mr. Taft's Four Years," *Independent*, LXXIV (March 6, 1913), 489; see also Richardson, *Messages*, XVIII, 8194; and Franklin MacVeagh, "President Taft and the Roosevelt Policies," *Outlook*, CI (May 18, 1912), 115.

95. Taft to Horace Taft, Dec. 12, 1910, TL.

96. MacVeagh, *Outlook*, CI (May 18, 1912), 115.

97. Article on Government Economy, Taft Adrs., XXXIII, 94.

Chapter 4

1. Taft to Rep. John W. Dwight, as quoted in Butt, *Taft and Roosevelt*, I, 360.

2. Theodore Roosevelt, *Theodore Roosevelt: An Autobiography* (New York: Charles Scribner's, 1920), 382–83; see also Edward S. Corwin, *The President: Office and Powers, 1787–1957* (4th ed.; New York: New York University Press, 1957), 265–68.

3. Address to the Ellicot Club, Buffalo, N.Y., Feb. 22, 1908, Taft Adrs., IX, 50–51.

4. Address to Virginia Bar Association, Hot Springs, Va., Aug. 6, 1908, Taft Adrs., XI, 153.

5. Roosevelt to Root, June 2,1904, *TRL*, IV, 812–13.

6. L. White Busbey, *Uncle Joe Cannon* (New York: Holt, 1927), 211–14.

7. Butt, *Taft and Roosevelt*, I, 334; see also John Morton Blum, *The Republican Roosevelt* (New York: Atheneum, 1964), 73–87.

8. Speech of Acceptance, July 28, 1908, TPS 2, File 563.

9. Roosevelt to Longworth, July 11, 1910, *TRL*, VII, 100–101.

10. William J. Keefe and Morris S. Ogul, *The American Legislative Process: Congress and the States* (New York: Prentice-Hall, 1964), 159, 213–14.

11. Taft to Roosevelt, Oct. 9, 1908, TL; and Roosevelt to Taft, Oct. 12, 1908, *TRL*, VI, 1280.

12. Roosevelt to Taft, Nov. 10, 1908, *TRL*, VI, 1340–41.

13. Taft to Root, Nov. 25, 1908, Root Spec. Corr.; and Taft to Hon. Joseph H. Gaines, Dec. 1, 1910, TL.

14. Taft to Frank L. Dingley, Nov. 23, 1908, TL.

15. Taft to Mabel Boardman, April 15, 1912, TL; see also Kenneth Hechler, *Insurgency: Personalities and Politics of the Taft Era* (New York: Russell & Russell, 1964), 44.

16. Taft to Horace Taft, June 27, 1909, TL.

17. Taft to Hon. Halver Steeverson, Nov. 30, 1908, TL.

18. Taft to George S. Harding, Dec. 6, 1908, TL.

19. Taft to Bristow, Dec. 5, 1908, TL.

20. Taft to Harding, Dec. 6, 1908, TL.

21. Taft to Worthington, Dec. 5, 1908, TL.

22. *Ibid.*

23. Taft to Hon. Ernest M. Pollard, Dec. 22, 1908, TL.

24. Quoted in Butt, *Taft and Roosevelt*, I, 10; see also Mowry, *Era of Roosevelt*, 240.

25. Champ Clark, *My Quarter Century of American Politics* (New York: Harper, 1920), II, 4.

26. Taft to Roosevelt, March 21, 1909, TL.

27. Roosevelt, as quoted in Gwinn, *Cannon*, 142.

28. Turner, *McClure's Magazine*, XXXV (June 1910), 211.

29. Thomas R. Ross, *Jonathan Prentiss Dolliver* (Des Moines: State Historical Society of Iowa, 1958), 240.

30. Taft to Horace Taft, June 27, 1909, TL.

31. Clark, *My Quarter Century*, II, 5.

32. Taft to Gilbert, Aug. 11, 1908, TL.

33. Taft to Mabel Boardman, April 15, 1912, TL.

34. Taft to Payne, March 10, 1909, TL.

35. Taft to Payne, April 16, 1909, TL.

36. Taft to Hill, May 1, 1909, TL.

37. Taft to Perkins, May 3, 1909, TL; see also Taft to Henry Cabot Lodge, April 26, 1909, TL, and Taft to Lodge, April 30, 1909, TL.

38. Taft to Rep. E. J. Hill, June 16, 1909, TL.

39. Taft to Hon. John Dalzell, June 25, 1909, TL.

40. Taft to Mrs. Taft, July 11, 1909, TL; see also Taft to Underwood, July 3, 1909, and to Nelson W. Aldrich, July 24, TL.

41. Taft to Horace Taft, June 27, 1909, TL.

42. Butt, *Taft and Roosevelt*, I, 170.

43. Quoted in Leupp, *Outlook*, XCIX (December 2, 1911), 815.

44. 157 U.S. 429.

45. Quoted in Leupp, XCIX (Dec. 2, 1911), 815; see also Taft to Horace Taft, June 27, 1909, TL.

46. Taft to John A. Sleicher, June 25, 1909, TL; see also Taft to Prof. J. D. Brannan, June 25, 1909, TL.

47. Taft to Horace Taft, June 25, 1909, TL.

48. Richardson, *Messages*, XVII, 7771–72.

49. Taft to Horace Taft, June 27, 1909, TL; see also Gwinn, *Cannon*, 179.

50. Roosevelt to Lodge, Sept. 10, 1909, *TRL*, VII, 28.

51. Taft to Horace Taft, June 27, 1909, TL.

52. Taft to Mrs. Taft, July 11, 1909, TL.

53. Taft to Rollo Ogden, Jan. 15, 1911, TL.

54. Brannan to Taft, June 29, 1909, TPS 3, File 4.

55. Taft to Horace Taft, June 27, 1909, TL.

56. *New York Tribune*, June 17, 1909, 2.

57. Gwinn, *Cannon*, 181.

58. Taft to Baldwin, July 15, 1909, TL.

59. *Ibid.*

60. Taft to Horace Taft, Aug. 11, 1909, TL.

61. Taft to Mrs. Taft, July 8, 11, 1909, TL.

62. Butt, *Taft and Roosevelt*, I, 63, 379, 178.

63. Taft to Beveridge, July 13, 1909, TL.

64. Taft to Mrs. Taft, July 12, 1909, TL.

65. *New York Tribune*, July 17, 1909, 1.

66. Taft to Henry Taft, July 17, 1909, TL.

67. Taft to Mrs. Taft, July 18, 1909, TL.

68. Taft to Mrs. Charles P. Taft, July 18, 1909, TL.

69. Taft to Mrs. Taft, July 25, 1909, TL.

70. Taft to Vorys, July 26, 1909, TL.

71. Taft to Mrs. Taft, July 27, 1909, TL.

72. Taft to Aldrich, July 29, 1909, TL.

73. Taft to Charles P. Taft, Aug. 1, 1909, TL.

74. *New York Tribune*, Aug. 6, 1909, 1.

75. For an analysis of the tariff and Taft's views, see Pringle, *Taft*, I, 445–51; Leupp, *Outlook*, XCIX (Dec. 2, 1911), 812–13; Richardson, *Messages*, XVII, 7886, 7891–92; Taft to W. H. Miller, July 12, 1909, TL.

76. Lodge to Roosevelt, July 31, 1909, *TR-Lodge*, II, 343.

77. Butt, *Taft and Roosevelt*, I, 178–79.

78. Roosevelt to Lodge, April 6, 1910, *TR-Lodge*, II, 365–66.

79. See Roosevelt to Taft, March 19, 1903, *TRL*, III, 450–51; see also Gwinn, *Cannon*, 78–79, for Roosevelt's relations with Cannon.

80. Leupp, *Outlook*, XCIX (Dec. 2, 1911), 813.

81. See Taft to Charles H. Grosvernor, March 9, 1909, to William Dudley Foulke, July 16, and to Elbert F. Baldwin, July 29, TL; and Claude C. Bowers, *Beveridge and the Progressive Era* (New York: Literary Guild, 1932), 345.

82. Memorandum on the New Tariff Law, Sept. 16, 1909, in Knox Corr., VIII, 1245–46.

83. Clark, *My Quarter Century*, II, 6; see also Richardson, *Messages*, XVII, 7785–86.

84. Taft to Knox, Oct. 24, 1909, TL; Butt, *Taft and Roosevelt*, I, 200–1, 303–4.

85. Quoted in Butt, *Taft and Roosevelt*, I, 360.

86. Taft to Foulke, Nov. 18, 1909, TL.

87. Taft to Swift, Feb. 19, 1910, TL.

88. Taft to Mrs. Taft, Oct. 28, 1909, TL.

89. Quoted in Butt, *Taft and Roosevelt*, I, 222.

90. Richardson, *Messages*, XVII, 7814–46.
91. Hechler, *Insurgency*, 31.
92. Taft to Mrs. Taft, March 19, 1910, TL; see also Gwinn, *Cannon*, 207; Butt, *Taft and Roosevelt*, I, 307.
93. Gwinn, *Cannon*, 214, 221, 247.
94. Busbey, *Cannon*, 249.
95. Taft to Horace Taft, March 5, 1910, TL.
96. Butt, *Taft and Roosevelt*, I, 303–4; see also Taft to Tawney, Feb. 28, March 24, 1910, TL; and *New York Tribune*, June 22, 1911, 1.
97. Quoted in Butt, *Taft and Roosevelt*, I, 297.
98. Taft to Horace Taft, March 5, 1910, TL.
99. Richardson, *Messages*, XXVII, 7867–68; *New York Tribune*, June 1, 1910, 1.
100. Depew to Root, June 23, 1910, Root Gen. Corr., Box 70 (1910).
101. Hill, *New York Tribune*, June 21, 1910, 3.
102. *New York Tribune*, June 11, 15, 1910, 3, 1; for a detailed account of the progressive role in improving the railroad bill see Mowry, *Theodore Roosevelt*, 94–103.
103. Hill, *New York Tribune*, June 22, 1910, 3. (Hill apparently had special access to news about the administration. Taft had written earlier to his brother, "The Tribune has now a Washington editor-correspondent who is really excellent, and while he favors me unduly, he will give you the facts as it looks to us at any rate." Taft to Horace Taft, March 5, 1910, TL. In another letter to Charles P. Taft, the President admitted, "You have doubtless followed the tariff bill and my relation to it during the last two weeks in the newspapers. Rather the best account is given in the New York Tribune by its correspondent Hill, who has had better opportunities for information than almost any one." Taft to Charles P. Taft, Aug. 1, 1909, TL.)
104. Taft to Bannard, June 11, 1910, TL.
105. *New York Tribune*, June 24, 1910, 1.
106. Taft to W. S. Carter, June 23, 1910, TL.
107. Hill, *New York Tribune*, June 24, 1910, 4.
108. *New York Tribune*, June 26, 1910, 5. (See also June 22, 1910, 1, for a review of the record of the regular session of the 61st Congress.)
109. *Ibid.*, 6.
110. *Ibid.*, 5.
111. Taft to Charles P. Taft, Sept. 10, 1910, TL.
112. *New York Tribune*, Jan. 27, 1911, 1–2.
113. Taft to Roosevelt, Jan. 10, 1911, and to Bannard, Jan. 30, TL; Roosevelt to Taft, Jan. 12, 1911, TPS 3, File 26.

114. Taft to Hon. Sereno E. Payne, Jan. 26, 1911, and to Sen. W. O. Bradley, Feb. 27, TL.

115. See Taft to Payne, Jan. 26, 30, 1911, and to Dalzell, Feb. 13, TL.

116. See Taft to Aldrich, Jan. 29, 1911, TL; and *New York Tribune*, Feb. 21, 1911, 1.

117. *Congressional Record*, 61st Cong., 3d Sess., 1911, XLVI, Part 4, 3309.

118. Taft to Burton, March 1, 1911, TL.

119. Hill, *New York Tribune*, March 5, 1911, 3.

120. Clark, *My Quarter Century*, II, 7.

121. Taft as quoted in Hill, *New York Tribune*, March 5, 1911, 2–3.

122. Taft to Aldrich, March 11, 1911, TL. (Reference is to Joseph W. Bailey of Texas.)

123. *Congressional Record*, 62d Cong., 1st Sess., 1911, XLVII, Part I, 663.

124. Taft to Aldrich, March 30, 1911, TL.

125. Taft to Gov. Hoke Smith, May 25, 1911, TL.

126. Taft to Horace Taft, May 25, 1911, TL.

127. Taft to Sec. J. M. Dickinson, June 5, 1911, TL; see also Hill, *New York Tribune*, June 10, 1911, 4.

128. Quoted in Butt, *Taft and Roosevelt*, II, 644.

129. Taft to Clarence H. Kelsey, July 7, 1911, TL.

130. *New York Tribune*, April 20, 1911, 4.

131. Statement given to the Press, July 23, 1911, TL.

132. Taft to Horace Taft, Sept. 26, 1911, TL.

133. *New York Tribune*, March 5, 1911, 1.

134. Taft to Lodge, Dec. 30, 1910, TL.

135. Taft to Calderhead, Dec. 31, 1910, TL.

136. Hill, *New York Tribune*, March 5, 1911, 3, 5. (See Pringle, *Taft*, II, 599–600, for a more elaborate account of Taft's appointments to the tariff board.)

137. *Ibid.*; March 3, 1911, 4; Aug. 25, 1912, 2; *Congressional Record*, 62d Cong., 2d Sess., XLVIII, Part 3, 2318.

138. See Taft to Roosevelt, Jan. 6, 1911, to John V. Farwell, Jan. 7, TL.

139. Pringle, *Taft*, II, 618; for a more extensive account of the Lorimer affair, see 614–19.

140. Taft to Charles F. Adams, July 19, 1911, TL.

141. Taft to Charles P. Taft, Aug. 3, 1911, TL.

142. Taft to Aldrich, July 21, 1911, TL.

143. Taft to Horace Taft, Nov. 25, 1911, TL.

144. Taft to Charles Taft, Aug. 3, 1911, TL.
145. Taft to Bannard, Sept. 10, 1911, TL.
146. Taft to Hill, Aug. 9, 1912, TL.
147. Taft to Root, Aug. 18, 1912, TL.
148. Richardson, *Messages,* XXVIII, 8191–92.
149. For an explanation of "Dollar Diplomacy," see Ch. 7, pp. 261–62.
150. Taft to Mrs. Buckner A. Wallingford, Aug. 25, 1912, TL.

Chapter 5

1. Taft to Wallingford, July 14, 1912, TL.
2. Roosevelt to Arthur Hamilton Lee, Sept. 26, 1910, *TRL,* VII, 131; see also Pringle, *Roosevelt,* 351.
3. Taft to Root, Aug. 15, 1908, TL.
4. Taft to Hon. Howard C. Hollister, Sept. 16, 1908, TL.
5. "Personal Aspects of the Presidency," Feb. 28, 1914, Taft Adrs., XXXII, 204.
6. Roosevelt to Root, Aug. 18, 1906, *TRL,* V, 367.
7. William H. Taft, *Four Aspects of Civic Duty* (New York: Scribner's, 1906), 22–24.
8. *Ibid.,* 26–27.
9. *Ibid.,* 22–23.
10. Taft to White, March 12, 1909, TL.
11. Taft to Brown, April 1, 1909, TL.
12. Quoted in Butt, *Taft and Roosevelt,* I, 272.
13. *Ibid.,* 314.
14. Robert M. La Follette, *La Follette's Autobiography* (Madison: University of Wisconsin Press, 1960), 166, 321, 193.
15. Taft to Roosevelt, May 26, 1910, Taft-TR.
16. Quoted in Butt, *Taft and Roosevelt,* I, 41.
17. La Follette, *Autobiography,* 193.
18. Taft to Bannard, Dec. 30, 1909, TL.
19. Taft to Norris, Jan. 7, 11, 1910, TL.
20. Taft to Baldwin, Jan. 13, 1910, TL.
21. *New York Times,* Jan. 14, 1910, 1; *New York Tribune,* Jan. 15, 1910, 2.
22. Taft to Hitchcock, April 6, July 3, 1910, TL.
23. See Harlan Hahn, "President Taft and the Discipline of Patronage," *Journal of Politics,* XXVIII (May 1966), 378–82, for a discussion of the tactics.
24. As quoted by Lawrence F. Abbott, "The Roosevelt Campaign: A Review," *Outlook,* CIX (June 15, 1912), 337.

25. Butt, *Taft and Roosevelt*, II, 525; for a more general discussion of patronage as a weapon of party discipline, see Hahn, *Journal of Politics*, XXVIII (May 1966), 368–90.

26. Taft to Hitchcock, May 11, 1910, TL.

27. Taft to Hon. R. M. Montgomery, Feb. 25, 1910, TL.

28. Taft to Roosevelt, Dec. 22, 1908, Taft-TR, Box 215.

29. Quoted in Butt, *Taft and Roosevelt*, I, 15.

30. William Howard Taft, *Our Chief Magistrate and His Powers* (New York: Columbia University Press, 1916), 62–63.

31. Taft to Lyon, Feb. 9, 1910, TL.

32. Taft to Burton, May 9, 1911, TL.

33. *New York Tribune*, March 2, 1913, 6.

34. For Taft's challenge to senatorial courtesy on other patronage appointments, see Hahn, *Journal of Politics*, XXVIII (May 1966), 385–88.

35. Butt, *Taft and Roosevelt*, I, 260.

36. *Ibid.*, II, 463.

37. Taft to Charles P. Taft, April 19, 1910, TL.

38. Quoted in Butt, *Taft and Roosevelt*, I, 300–1, 356.

39. Taft to Hon. Horace H. Lurton, Sept. 3, 1910, and to Hon. W. A. Peters, Sept. 6, TL.

40. See Taft to Warren Thomas, Dec. 31, 1909, to Walter S. Page, Feb. 11, 1910, to Hy D. Davis, Feb. 28, to Burton, July 3, and to Charles P. Taft, Sept. 10, TL.

41. Butt, *Taft and Roosevelt*, II, 484; see Taft to Griscom, June 23, Aug. 20, 1910, and Griscom to Taft, Aug. 19, TL.

42. Taft to Charles P. Taft, Sept. 10, 1910. (Reference is to Lloyd Griscom, Republican county chairman from New York; and to William Loeb, former personal secretary to Roosevelt.)

43. Taft to Mrs. Taft, Sept. 24, 1910, TL.

44. Butt, *Taft and Roosevelt*, II, 519–20; Mowry, *Theodore Roosevelt*, 149–50.

45. See Taft to Root, Sept. 24, 1910, and to Charles Nagel, Oct. 11, TL.

46. Taft to Curtis, Aug. 23, 1910, TL.

47. Taft to William B. McKinley, Aug. 20, 1910, TL.

48. Roosevelt to Lodge, May 5, April 11, 1910, *TR-Lodge*, II, 380, 372.

49. *Ibid.*, 372.

50. Roosevelt to Gifford Pinchot, Aug. 17, 1910, *TRL*, VII, 113; see also Roosevelt to Sydney Brooks, Oct. 17, 1910, VII, 142.

51. Quoted in Butt, *Taft and Roosevelt*, II, 435.

52. Taft to Sec. James M. Dickinson, July 7, 1910, TL.

53. Quoted in Butt, *Taft and Roosevelt*, II, 484, 516.
54. Roosevelt to Lee, July 19, 1910, *TRL*, VII, 103.
55. Taft to Horace Taft, Sept. 16, 1910, TL.
56. Butt, *Taft and Roosevelt*, II, 524.
57. Taft to Horace Taft, Sept. 16, 1910, TL.
58. Taft to Horace Taft, Sept. 16, 1910, TL; see also Pringle, *Taft*, II, 571–72; and the Osawatomie and Colorado speeches in Theodore Roosevelt, *The New Nationalism* (Englewood Cliffs, N.J.: Prentice-Hall, 1961), 21–49.
59. Quoted in Jessup, *Root*, II, 163–64.
60. Taft to Root, Oct. 15, 1910, TL.
61. Taft to Charles P. Taft, Sept. 10, 1910, TL.
62. Roosevelt to Lee, Nov. 11, 1910, *TRL*, VII, 163.
63. Roosevelt to Stimson, Nov. 16, 1910, *TRL*, VII, 165; see also Roosevelt to Joseph B. Bishop, Nov. 21, VII, 168 for similar sentiments.
64. Roosevelt to White, Dec. 12, 1910, *TRL*, VII, 182.
65. Quoted in Jessup, *Root*, II, 185.
66. See Roosevelt to William Kent, Nov. 28, 1910, to Theodore Roosevelt, Jr., Aug. 22, 1911, and to Lodge, Dec. 23, 1911, *TRL*, VII, 176, 336, 465; Address at Newark, N.J., April 26, 1912, Taft Adrs., XXVIII, 240.
67. Quoted in Butt, *Taft and Roosevelt*, II, 645, 768, 804.
68. *Ibid.*, 804.
69. Taft to Horace Taft, Feb. 15, 1911, TL.
70. La Follette, *Autobiography*, 218; Butt, *Taft and Roosevelt*, II, 794.
71. See Mowry, *Theodore Roosevelt*, 172–74, for the origins of the National Progressive Republican League; *TRL*, VII, 194–95; Pringle, *Taft*, II, 765.
72. Root to Roosevelt, Feb. 12, 1912, as quoted in Jessup, *Root*, II, 173–75.
73. Taft to Horace Taft, Feb. 15, 1912, TL.
74. *TRL*, VII, 507.
75. Quoted in Butt, *Taft and Roosevelt*, II, 846–47.
76. Quoted in Jessup, *Root*, II, 180.
77. Taft to Bradley, Feb. 5, 1912, TL.
78. Taft to Horace Taft, Nov. 5, 1911, TL.
79. Taft to McKinley, March 12, 1912, TL.
80. Taft to Horace Taft, March 7, 1912, TL.
81. Taft to F. W. Cram, March 25, 1912, TL.
82. Taft to Col. J. C. Hemphill, April 12, 1912, TL.
83. Taft to Felix Agnus, Feb. 29, 1912, TL.

84. Taft to Charles F. Brooker, March 5, 1912, TL.

85. Taft to Horace Taft, March 1, 1912, TL.

86. Taft to Worthington, May 29, 1912, TL.

87. Taft to Samuel J. Elder, May 29, 1912, TL.

88. Butt, *Taft and Roosevelt,* II, 786–87.

89. Confidential Memorandum, Jan. 13, 1912, prepared by Charles D. Hilles, TPS 3, File 244.

90. Pringle, *Taft,* II, 764.

91. Taft to Rep. A. P. Gardner, April 17, 1912, TL.

92. Taft to Horace Taft, Jan. 13, 1912, TL.

93. Root to Robert Bacon, March 9, 1912, Root Gen. Corr., Box 91 (1912).

94. Address at Nahic, Mass., April 25, 1912, Taft Adrs., XXVIII, 214.

95. Pringle, *Taft,* II, 776–81.

96. Taft to Charles D. Wilby, May 3, 1912, TL.

97. Taft to Diekema, May 16, 1912, TL.

98. Taft to William Barnes, June 2, 1912, TL.

99. See Taft to Hilles, June 11, 12, 1912, and to Prof. J. D. Brannan, June 15, TL, for a further indication of Taft's role in the drafting of the Republican platform.

100. *New York Times,* June 20, 1912, 10.

101. Taft to Barnes, May 29, 1912, TL.

102. Taft to Hilles, June 14, 12, 1912, to Bannard, June 8, and to Hilles, June 18, TL.

103. Taft to Hilles, June 18, 1912, TL.

104. See *New York Times,* June 19, 20, 22, 23, 1912, 1, 3, 12, 1.

105. Taft to Mabel Boardman, June 26, 1912, TL.

106. Taft to Hemenway, June 26, 1912, TL.

107. Bannard to Taft, June 24, 1912, TPS 3, File 115.

108. John Emmet Hughes, *Ordeal of Power* (New York: Dell, 1964), 260.

109. Taft to Hilles, Aug. 7, 1912, TL; for a detailed account of Roosevelt's bolt and subsequent nomination as the Progressive candidate, see Mowry, *Theodore Roosevelt,* 248–73.

110. Taft to Myron T. Herrick, June 20, 1912, TL.

111. Taft to William Barnes, Jr., June 29, 1912, TL.

112. Taft to Wallingford, July 14, 1912, TL.

113. Taft to Edward Colston, July 14, 1912, TL.

114. *Ibid.*

115. Taft to Joseph P. Gaffney, Aug. 16, 1912, TL.

116. Speech of William Howard Taft Accepting the Nomination

for the Presidency by the Republican National Convention, Washington, D.C., Aug. 1, 1912, TPS 2, File 3399.

117. Butt, *Taft and Roosevelt*, II, 790, 630, 849.
118. George von L. Meyer to Taft, Oct. 19, 1912, TPS 3, File 327.
119. Hilles to Taft, Oct. 18, 1912, TPS 3, File 227.
120. See Walter L. Fisher to George L. Diekema, Sept. 19, 1912, and to Walter H. Wilson, Sept. 30, in Secretary's Private Files, 10,-692, in the Walter L. Fisher Papers, Manuscript Division, Library of Congress, Washington, D.C.; hereafter referred to as SPF.
121. "Taft's Disloyal Cabinet," *Kansas City Star*, Nov. 11, 1912, SPF.
122. Root to Robert Bacon, March 9, 1912, Root Gen. Corr., Box 91 (1912).
123. Root to Taft, May 15, 1912, Root Spec. Corr.; Root to Taft, Oct. 15, Sept. 4, 1912, TPS 2, File 152.
124. Root to Bacon, Sept. 11, 1912, Root Gen. Corr., Box 91 (1912).
125. See Daugherty to Taft, Sept. 26, 1912, Root Spec. Corr.
126. Taft to Horace Taft, Sept. 16, 1912, TL.
127. Taft to Charles Nagel, Oct. 16, 1912, TL.
128. Taft to Hilles, Aug. 7, 1912, TL.
129. See Taft to Catherine Meredith, Sept. 17, 1912, TL.
130. Taft to Hilles, Aug. 7, 1912, TL.
131. Taft to Horace Taft, Nov. 1, 1912, TL.
132. Taft to Bannard, Nov. 10, 1912, TL.
133. Press Statement, Nov. 5, 1912, TL.

Chapter 6

1. Quoted in Helen Taft, *Recollections*, 393.
2. Roosevelt to Trevelyan, June 19, 1909, *TRL*, VI, 1087.
3. Quoted in Butt, *Taft and Roosevelt*, II, 724.
4. *Ibid.*, I, 27.
5. Taft to Roosevelt, March 21, 1909, TL.
6. Taft to White, March 20, 1909, TL.
7. Taft to Roosevelt, March 21, 1909, TL.
8. Taft to White, March 20, 1909, TL.
9. Butt, *Taft and Roosevelt*, I, 13, 30, 26, 31.
10. Busbey, *Cannon*, 282, 284.
11. Taft to W. H. Miller, July 12, 1909, TL.
12. Taft to Foulke, July 16, 1909, TL.
13. Taft to Swift, Feb. 19, 1910, TL.
14. Taft to Bannard, Nov. 10, 1912, TL.

15. Taft to Nancy Roelker, Sept. 11, 1909, TL.

16. Richardson, *Messages*, XVII, 7783.

17. La Follette, *Autobiography*, 204.

18. Taft to Robert Taft, Oct. 28, 1909, TL.

19. Taft to Foulke, Nov. 18, 1909, TL.

20. Taft to Knox, Oct. 24, 1909, TL.

21. Taft to Robert Taft, Oct. 28, 1909, TL.

22. Taft to John V. Farwell, Feb. 19, 1910, TL.

23. Taft to Horace Taft, March 30, 1910, TL.

24. Turner, *McClure's Magazine*, XXXV (June 1910), 212.

25. See "President Taft's Interpretation of His Policies," *Outlook*, XCV (June 11, 1910), 272.

26. Leupp, *Outlook*, XCIX, 812.

27. Theodore Roosevelt, "The Tariff: A Moral Issue," *Outlook*, XCVI (Sept. 17, 1910), 102.

28. Butt, *Taft and Roosevelt*, I, 295–96; *TRL*, VII, 115.

29. Taft to Swift, Feb. 19, 1910, TL.

30. Richardson, *Messages*, XVII, 7814.

31. Taft to Lockley, Feb. 8, 1910, TL.

32. Taft to Bannard, March 2, 1910, and to R. L. O'Brien, Jan. 31, TL.

33. Sleicher to Root, Feb. 17, 1911, Root Gen. Corr., Box 87.

34. Taft to Sen. Frank P. Flint, Feb. 15, 1911, TL.

35. Taft to Penrose, March 2, 1911, TL.

36. *Congressional Record*, 62d Cong., 2d Sess., XLVIII, Part III, 2318.

37. Taft to Bannard, Nov. 11, 1912, TL.

38. See Hofstadter, *Age of Reform* (New York: Vintage, 1955), 186–98, for a more general treatment of the nature of the press of the period.

39. Busbey, *Cannon*, 275–78.

40. Taft to Guild A. Copeland, Feb. 9, 1910, TL.

41. Taft to Mallon, Jan. 13, 1910, TL.

42. Taft to Reid, April 7, 1910, TL.

43. Taft to H. H. Kohlsaat, March 14, 1910, TL.

44. John A. Stewart to Taft, Dec. 2, 1910, TPS 2, File 586.

45. Quoted in Butt, *Taft and Roosevelt*, I, 207–8.

46. Taft to Young, Nov. 15, 1909, TL.

47. Quoted in Butt, *Taft and Roosevelt*, I, 357.

48. Taft to O'Brien, Jan. 31, 1910, TL.

49. *Ibid.*, 234.

50. Taft to Kohlsaat, March 14, 1910, TL.

51. Quoted in Butt, *Taft and Roosevelt*, I, 236, 298–99.

52. "Personal Aspects of the Presidency," Feb. 28, 1914, Taft Adrs., XXXII, 206.
53. Taft to Mrs. Taft, Oct. 28, 1909, and to George von L. Meyer, Oct. 18, TL.
54. Taft to White, March 20, 1909, TL.
55. Quoted in Butt, *Taft and Roosevelt*, I, 207–8.
56. Taft to Dustin, Dec. 27, 1909, TL.
57. Taft to J. H. Cosgrave, Feb. 23, 1910, TL.
58. Taft to J. W. Pierce, April 14, 1910, TL.
59. Turner, *McClure's Magazine*, XXXV (June 1910), 221.
60. Taft to O'Brien, June 28, 1910, TL.
61. Quoted in Butt, *Taft and Roosevelt*, I, 311.
62. Taft to Cosgrave, Feb. 23, 1910, TL.
63. James E. Pollard, *The Presidents and the Press* (New York: Macmillan, 1947), 612; Butt, *Taft and Roosevelt*, II, 477–78.
64. Taft to Pugh, April 27, 1910, TL.
65. Quoted in Butt, *Taft and Roosevelt*, I, 311.
66. Taft to Loomis, July 13, 1910, TL.
67. Taft to McKinley, Aug. 20, 1910, TL.
68. See Taft to Herman Ridder, Feb. 25, 1910, TL; John Norris to Knox, Jan. 16, 1911, Knox Corr., XIII, 2092; see also memorandum of Charles M. Pepper, "Canadian Wood Pulp Development," Dec. 2, 1910, in Knox Corr., XII, 1898–99.
69. Knox to Sereno E. Payne, Feb. 4, 1911, Knox Corr., XIII, 2154.
70. See Charles M. Pepper to Knox, Feb. 7, 1911, Knox Corr., XIII, 2156; and *New York Times*, July 21, 1911, 1.
71. Pringle, *Taft*, II, 586.
72. *Congressional Record*, 61st Cong., 3d Sess., XLVI, Part III, 1469.
73. *Ibid.*, 2520.
74. Address before the Southern Commercial Congress, March 10, 1911, Taft Adrs., XX, 240.
75. Richardson, *Messages*, XVII, 7975.
76. Quoted in Sullivan, *Our Times*, IV, 399–400.
77. Fielding to Knox, Sept. 29, 1911, Knox Corr., XV, 2493–94.
78. Pringle, *Taft*, II, 584.
79. Taft to Henry Taft, Aug. 29, 1911, TL.
80. Taft to Col. J. C. Hemphill, Nov. 16, 1911, TL.
81. Taft to Bannard, Sept. 10, 1911, TL.
82. Butt, *Taft and Roosevelt*, I, 200; II, 756–57.
83. Taft to Horace Taft, Nov. 5, 1911, TL.
84. "The President's Journey," *Outlook*, XCIX (Nov. 11, 1911), 605–6.
85. Taft to Horace Taft, Nov. 5, 1911, TL.

86. Quoted in Butt, *Taft and Roosevelt*, II, 800; see also Taft to Horace Taft, Nov. 5, 1911, TL.

87. Quoted in White to Fisher, Dec. 10, 1911, SPF.

88. "Personal Aspects of the Presidency," Taft Adrs., XXXII, 202.

89. Butt, *Taft and Roosevelt*, II, 749.

90. "Personal Aspects of the Presidency," Taft Adrs., XXXII, 202.

91. Helen Taft, *Recollections*, 393.

92. Taft to Carpenter, Oct. 24, 1909, TL.

93. Butt, *Taft and Roosevelt*, II, 724.

94. Taft to Long, Feb. 20, 1910, TL.

95. Butt, *Taft and Roosevelt*, II, 724.

96. Quoted in Butt, *Taft and Roosevelt*, II, 749.

97. Taft, *Four Aspects of Civic Duty*, 44.

98. Quoted in Pringle, *Taft*, I, 378.

99. Richardson, *Messages*, XVII, 7770.

100. Taft to Kent, June 29, 1909, and to Horace Taft, Oct. 18, 1909, and March 1, 1912, TL.

101. Taft to Root, Oct. 15, 1910, as quoted in Jessup, *Root*, II, 363–64.

102. Richardson, *Messages*, XVIII, 8017, 8023–24.

103. Address at Banquet of Swedish-American Republican League, March 9, 1912, Taft Adrs., XXVII, 240.

104. Speech of Acceptance, Aug. 1, 1912, TPS 2, File 3399.

105. Taft to Bannard, Jan. 22, 1912, TL; see also Speech of Acceptance, Aug. 1, 1912.

106. See Taft to Hart Lyman (managing editor of the *New York Tribune*), March 27, 1911, TL. Similar letters were also sent to prominent editors such as Edward P. Mitchell of the *New York Sun*, Charles Clark of the *Hartford Courant*, Talcott Williams of the *Philadelphia Press*, and Lyman Abbott of the *Outlook*.

107. Taft to Charles Taft, March 1, 1912, TL.

108. Butt, *Taft and Roosevelt*, II, 775.

109. See Edward H. Butler to Hilles, Sept. 10, 1912, in U.S. Department of State, Decimal File 811.911/2, National Archives, Washington, D.C. (Hereafter all references to State Department Correspondence, unless otherwise indicated, will be to the decimal file.)

110. Taft to Bannard, Nov. 10, 1912, and to W. W. Keen, Sept. 17, TL.

111. Address at the Banquet of the Lotos Club, New York City, Nov. 16, 1912, Taft Adrs., XXX, 233–34.

112. "Personal Aspects of the Presidency," Taft Adrs., XXXII, 206–7.

113. Roosevelt to Taft, Sept. 12, 1907, Taft-TR.

Chapter 7

1. Taft to Gen. Leonard Wood, March 12, 1911, TL; see also Richardson, *Messages*, XVIII, 8039–40.

2. See Taft Adrs. in 1908 at Hartford, Feb. 15, VIII, 233–34; Ohio Society of Philadelphia, Jan. 14, VIII, 158; Tippecanoe Club of Cleveland, Jan. 29, VIII, 179; Lowell Board of Trade, Lowell, Mass., Feb. 8, IX, 42–43; Commercial Club of Chicago, April 4, X, 243–52; McKinley Club, Omaha, April 6, X, 10–11; Republican Club, Bridgeport, Conn., April 27, X, 179, for endorsements of the McKinley-Roosevelt policies.

3. Busbey, *Cannon*, 210; see also Jessup, *Root*, II, 53.

4. Address to Commercial Club, April 4, 1908, Taft Adrs., IX, 243. (For other speeches emphasizing trade expansion, see Taft Adrs. at Augusta Chamber of Commerce, Jan. 20, 1909, XIII, 139; Tacoma, Wash., Oct. 1, 1909, XV, 269; Tippecanoe Club of Cleveland, Jan. 29, 1908, VIII, 179–80.)

5. See Taft Adrs. at Ohio Society of Philadelphia, Jan. 14, 1908, VIII, 157; Tacoma, Wash., Oct. 1, 1909, XV, 269.

6. Address to Commercial Club, April 4, 1908, Taft Adrs., IX, 246. See also Taft's Shanghai Speech of Oct. 1907, in Davis, *Taft*, 283–90; and Taft to Alfred R. Conkling, Feb. 25, 1908, TL.

7. Huntington-Wilson, *Memoirs*, 181–82, 190.

8. Richardson, *Messages*, XVIII, 7801.

9. Address to Alaska-Yukon-Pacific Exposition, Seattle, Sept. 30, 1909, Taft Adrs., XV, 255.

10. Richardson, *Messages*, XVII, 7815. Taft himself labeled the measure a "subsidy" in his address at Tacoma, Oct. 1, 1909, Taft Adrs., XV, 271.

11. Richardson, *Messages*, XVIII, 8068, 8138–41.

12. Pringle, *Taft*, II, 650–51. In the Hay-Pauncefote Treaty the United States had agreed to operate the Panama Canal for "all nations" on terms of "entire equality." The administration interpreted "all nations" to mean "all except the United States," while Britain maintained the term implied no exceptions. See Richardson, *Messages*, XVIII, 8139. See also Knox to Laughlin, Jan. 17, 1913, AC 3686, Box 32, Knox Papers, for the American position on the tolls question.

13. Taft to Theodore Marburg, Aug. 21, 1912, and to A. B. Farquhar, July 15, TL.

14. Taft to Hon. John W. Griggs, Aug. 13, 1912, TL.

15. Richardson, *Messages*, XVIII, 8139.

16. Thomas A. Bailey, *A Diplomatic History of the American People* (New York: Appleton Century Crofts, 1964), 549–51.

17. Taft as quoted in Memorandum of E. T. Williams, "His Excellency Liang Tun-Yen's Call Upon the President," Dec. 17, 1910, 893.51/1406.

18. Charles Vevier, *The United States and China, 1906–13* (New Brunswick: Rutgers University Press, 1955), 58–59. See also A. Whitney Griswold, *The Far Eastern Policy of the United States* (New York: Harcourt, Brace, 1939), 133–75.

19. Griswold, *Far Eastern Policy*, 148–49.

20. Quoted in Davis, *Taft*, 284–86.

21. Straight to G. Casenave, Dec. 4, 1907, Straight Misc., Box 3, File 116D. See Huntington-Wilson, *Memoirs*, 167, for the opinion that Straight had significantly influenced Taft's thinking about China and Manchuria.

22. Address to Commercial Club, April 4, 1908, Taft Adrs., IX, 253.

23. Richardson, *Messages*, XVII, 7752.

24. See Taft to Sen. Eugene Hale, Dec. 22, 1908, to Lodge, Dec. 22, and to Henry S. Brown, April 1, 1909, TL; and Roosevelt to Taft, Dec. 22, Taft-TR, for Taft's interest in securing legislation on the subject.

25. Taft to Rollo Ogden, April 21, 1909, TL.

26. Taft to Mrs. Taft, July 14, 1909, TL.

27. For an extended account of the Crane incident, see Huntington-Wilson, *Memoirs*, 204–07; Knox to Taft, Oct. 3, 1909, Knox Corr., VIII, 1390–91; Taft to Knox, Oct. 3, 9, 11, 24, TL; and Knox to Taft, Oct. 12, TPS 2, File 102.

28. Address to the Commercial Club, April 4, 1908, Taft Adrs., IX, 253.

29. See " 'Holland' Reveals Real Role of the U.S. in Chinese Loan Negotiations," *Washington Post*, Feb. 12, 1913; Knox Corr., XX, 3346. (Holland was E. J. Edwards, a close friend and golfing partner of the President); Vevier, *U.S. and China*, 106–7.

30. Wilson to Fletcher, June 19, 1909, Num. Case 5315/227.

31. *Ibid.* See also Vevier, *U.S. and China*, 107. As a result of the Boxer uprising in 1900, China had granted the United States an indemnity of $25 million dollars to pay for damages to American property, but Roosevelt had decided to remit part of the indemnity to improve relations with China. By 1924, $18 million dollars had been turned back or not collected. Bailey, *Diplomatic History*, 482.

32. For the American basis, see Memorandum from W. Phillips to Knox, June 10, 1909, Knox Corr., VII, 1121–24, in which the United

States claimed the right to participate in the Hukuang Loan on the basis of a Chinese pledge of Sept. 1904 to give American and British capital preference in railway development from Hankow westward.

33. Taft to Prince Chun, July 15, 1909, TPS 2, File 102.

34. For reasons behind the Hukuang Loan, see Lewis Einstein, "The New American Policy in China," ca. Oct. 9, 1911, Knox Corr., XV, 2543–44; also Memorandum on "The Chinese Loan," Sept. 30, 1909, VIII, 1280–81; and " 'Holland' Reveals Real Role of the U.S. in Chinese Loan Negotiations," XX, 3346.

35. Statement to the Press, Jan. 6, 1910, Knox Corr., XXV, 1994–95.

36. Memorandum, Phillips to Knox, May 10, 1909, Knox Corr., VII, 1117–21, 1276; see also "The Chinese Loan," Knox Corr., VIII, 1274.

37. Knox to Sen. Eugene Hale, July 28, 1909, Knox Corr., VIII, 1239–40.

38. "America's 'Shirt Sleeve' Diplomacy Wins Chinese Loan Fight," *New York Herald*, Sept. 19, 1909, in Scrapbooks, AC 9631, Box 11, Knox Papers.

39. Quoted in Butt, *Taft and Roosevelt*, I, 145.

40. "The Chinese Loan," Knox Corr., VIII, 1282.

41. Straight to Fletcher, Feb. 20, 1910, Private Letters, 1260, Box 4, File 116C, Straight Papers.

42. Griswold, *Far Eastern Policy*, 135–41.

43. Huntington Wilson and Straight had become good friends while both served in the State Department. Wilson had been head of the Far Eastern Division and Straight had been consul-general at Mukden, China. Straight's candid letters to Wilson indicate that Straight had a sympathetic listener regarding his hopes for a stronger U.S. role in Manchuria. Fortunately, from Straight's standpoint, Wilson became assistant secretary and Knox's righthand man, an invaluable position from which to lobby for a change in American policy toward China, Japan, and Russia. See in particular Straight to Huntington Wilson, Dec. 30, 1907, Straight Misc., Box 3, File 116D, for an indication of their relationship.

44. Williams, "Recollections of Willard Dickerman Straight and His Work," Correspondence, Box 5, File 105, Straight Papers; see also Memorandum on the Chinchow-Aigun Railway Project, Feb. 10, 1910, X, 1639, and Undated memorandum on China, XII, 1998, Knox Corr., for background to the Chin-Ai Railroad scheme.

45. Statement to the Press, Jan. 6, 1910, Knox Corr., XII, 1996–97; see also Undated memorandum on China, XII, 1998; and Memorandum from the Division of Far Eastern Affairs to Knox, March 31, 1910, X, 1674, Knox Corr. for background.

46. Quoted "From the Novoye Vremya of June 24–July 7, 1910," AC 9172, Box 5, Knox Papers.

47. Memorandum of Miller, Sept. 19, 1910, Knox Corr., XI, 1759.

48. Memorandum of Talks between Knox and Liang Tun-yen, Dec. 5, 1910, TPS 2, File 102.

49. "Excerpt from letter of February 2nd, 1911," in "Copies of Major's Letters used for 'Asia'" Box 4, File 119B, Straight Papers.

50. Memorandum, The Chin-Ai Project, Aug. 16, 1910, 893.77/1058.

51. See Taft to Knox, Sept. 1, 1910, TL.

52. See Memorandum for the Secretary, Sept. 24, 1910, 893.51/125; J. P. Morgan to Knox, Sept. 27, 1910, 893.51/128; see also Knox to American Legation, Peking, Sept. 29, 1910, 893.51/122.

53. Taft to Knox, Nov. 7, 1910, TL; Knox to American Legation, Peking, Oct. 6, 1910, 893.51/138.

54. Knox to American Legation, Peking, Nov. 25, 1910, 893.51/209.

55. Williams, "His Excellency Liang Tun-yen's Call upon the President, December 17, 1910," 893.51/1406.

56. See Knox to American Legation, Peking, Dec. 10, 1910, 893.51/236; Memorandum, Division of Far Eastern Affairs to the Secretary, Dec. 28, 1910, Knox Corr., XII, 1931–35; and E. T. Williams, Memorandum of the Far Eastern Division, Jan. 14, 1911, 893.51/1408. Note that although Woodrow Wilson repudiated the consortium in 1913, he was forced in November 1917 to readopt the Taft policy of supporting American participation in such a consortium as the price for maintaining American influence in China. See Bailey, *Diplomatic History*, 637.

57. R. S. Miller to Knox, Jan. 29, 1912, 893.00/1028.

58. Wilson to Taft, Feb. 26, 1912, 393.00/1105.

59. The resolution read: "Whereas the Chinese nation has successfully asserted the fact that sovereignty is vested in the people, and has recognized the principle that government derives its authority from the consent of the governed, thereby terminating a condition of internal strife; and

"Whereas the American people are inherently and by tradition sympathetic with all efforts to adopt the ideas and institutions of representative government: Therefore, be it

"*Resolved, etc.*, That the United States of America congratulate the people of China on their assumption of the powers, duties, and responsibilities of self-government, and express the confident hope that in the adoption and maintenance of a republican form of government the rights, liberties, and happiness of the Chinese people will be secured and the progress of the country insured." *Congressional Record*, 62d Cong., 2d Sess., XLVIII, Part III, 2645, 4906.

60. Wilson to American Legation, Peking, March 2, 1912, 893.00/-1121-1400.

61. Quoted in Williams, "His Excellency Liang Tun-yen's Call upon the President," 893.51/1406.

62. Huntington-Wilson, *Memoirs*, 218.

63. Williams, "His Excellency Liang Tun-yen's Call upon the President," 893.51/1406.

64. Straight to Fletcher, March 26, 1911, and to H. P. Davidson, Feb. 15 (canceled), Correspondence, 1260, Letterbook, Box 3, Straight Papers; see also Knox to Taft, Sept. 12, 1911, TPS 2, File 102.

65. Jessup, *Root*, II, 250.

66. Taft to John Barrett, Dec. 7, 1908, TL.

67. See Munro, *Intervention and Dollar Diplomacy*, 151–59.

68. See Knox to Taft, Sept. 28, 1909, TPS 2, File 229.

69. Munro, *Intervention and Dollar Diplomacy*, 106, 533; see also "Arbitration Treaties," Address at Sacramento, Calif., Oct. 13, 1911, Taft Adrs., XXIV, 2–4.

70. For reasons behind the convention see Wilson to A. A. Adee, Jan. 13, 1911, 815.51/207; Arbitration Treaties, Taft Adrs., XXIV, 7–8; Knox to Shelby M. Cullom, Feb. 13, 1911, and Rough Notes on Honduran Loan, Feb. 1911, TPS 2, File 451; and Rough Notes (undated), Knox Corr., IX, 1513.

71. Knox to Cullom, Feb. 13, 1911, TPS 2, File 451.

72. "Honduran Loan," Presidential Message of Jan. 26, 1911, in Subject File, Box 193, Root Papers.

73. Knox to Taft, Jan. 23, 1911, TPS 2, File 451.

74. Dearing to Wilson, March 14, 1912, 817.51/393.

75. See Wilson to Taft, March 15, 1912, TPS 2, File 496; Taft to Wilson, March 15, 1912, TL. For a copy of the letter sent to senators, see Taft to Sen. Joseph Bailey, March 14, 1912, TL.

76. Wilson to Taft, Sept. 19, 1912, TPS 2, File 2180.

77. Address to Americus Club, May 2, 1910, Taft Adrs. XVIII, 240.

78. "Arbitration Treaties," Oct. 13, 1911, Taft Adrs., XXIV, 6.

79. See Wilson's address at Baltimore, May 4, 1911, in Knox Corr., XIV, 2313–15; and Knox's press interview in 1912, "Interview with the Honorable Philander C. Knox, Secretary of State," AC 9631, Box 13, Knox Papers.

80. Richardson, *Messages*, XVIII, 8150.

81. See Knox to Taft, Dec. 30, 1910, TPS 2, File 451. See also enclosed memorandum by Wilson, "Proposed Adjustment of the Debt of Honduras by the United States," TPS 2, File 451; and Taft to James Speyer, Dec. 27, 1910, TL.

82. Quoted in "Central American Treaties," *Newark Evening News,* Aug. 17, 1911, in Scrapbook 24, AC 9631, Box 11, 140, Knox Papers.

83. Huntington-Wilson, *Memoirs,* 215. Knox shared the same view and did not miss an opportunity to praise the bankers for their co-operation with the department.

84. See A. A. Adee to American Legation, Buenos Aires, Aug. 30, 1909, and Wilson to Charles W. Sherrill, Sept. 30, 1909, Num. Case 835.34, for an indication of Taft's personal interest in the Argentine contracts.

85. Wilson to Sherrill, Sept. 30, 1909, Num. Case 835.35.

86. See Seward W. Livermore, "Battleship Diplomacy in South America: 1905–1925," *Journal of Modern History,* XVI (March 1944), 34–36; Richardson, *Messages,* XVII, 7881; Knox to Sen. Eugene Hale, Jan. 29, 1910, General Correspondence, Box 72 (1910), Knox Papers; and "Dollar Diplomacy," undated memorandum *ca.* 1910, 160/12.

87. *Congressional Record,* 62d Cong., 3d Sess., XLVI, Part IV, 3519.

88. Draft A of Secretary Knox's Reply to the President of the Senate Resolution of Feb. 27, 1911, 835.34/270.

89. *Congressional Record,* 62d Cong., 3d Sess., XLVI, Part IV, 3519; see also Knox to President of the Senate, March 30, 1911, 835.34/270; and Richardson, *Messages,* XVIII, 7979.

90. See "Dollar Diplomacy," 160/12; Munro, *Intervention and Dollar Diplomacy,* 238–55; Huntington-Wilson, *Memoirs,* 213; Fletcher to Knox, June 13, 1911, 825.23/145; Stimson to Taft, Feb. 28, 29, 1912, TPS 2, File 512; Howard to Knox, Sept. 16, 1912, 823.34/13; and Taft to Dalzell, March 11, 1910, TL.

91. Taft to Mrs. Taft, Oct. 15, 17, 1909, TL.

92. See Taft to Knox, Nov. 10, 1910, 812.00/358; and Knox to Taft, Nov. 11, 1910, 812.00/358.

93. Taft to Knox, March 11, 1911, TL; Knox to Taft, March 15, 1911, Knox Corr., XV, 2230; and Butt, *Taft and Roosevelt,* II, 602.

94. Taft to Wood, March 12, 1911, TL; see also Richardson, *Messages,* XVIII, 8039–40.

95. Taft to Knox, March 11, 1911, TL.

96. Taft to Slayden, Sept. 12, 1912, TPS 2, File 95c.

97. Taft to Farquhar, Sept. 11, 1912, TL.

98. Wilson, *Diplomatic Episodes,* 210.

99. Taft to Meyer, March 14, 1911, TL.

100. See Taft to Knox, March 27, 1911, 812.00/1159; and Knox to Taft, March 29, 1911, 812.00/1159; Memorandum from Rudolph

Forster (Assistant Secretary to the President) to the Department of State, April 17, 1911, 812.00/1441.

101. See Rudolph Forster to Wilson, March 19, 1911, 812.00/1095; Taft to Knox, March 20, 1911, TL; and Norton to Knox, March 27, 1911, 812.00/1275.

102. Taft to Roosevelt, March 22, 1911, TL.

103. Richardson, *Messages* XVIII, 8041–42.

104. Taft to Sloan, April 18, 1911, TL.

105. Quoted in Butt, *Taft and Roosevelt*, II, 645.

106. Howard to Taft, July 30, 1912, TPS 2, File 95c.

107. Daugherty to Carmi Thompson, Sept. 8, 1912, TPS 2, File 95c.

108. Roosevelt to Taft, March 14, April 1, 1911, *TRL,* VII, 243, 245.

109. Roosevelt to Garfield, April 28, 1911, *TRL,* VII, 246. It is interesting to note Roosevelt's position on Cuban intervention in 1906 when he wrote Lodge: "Just imagine my following the Buchanan-like course of summoning Congress for a six weeks' debate . . . as to whether I ought to land marines to protect American life and property—the fighting would have gone on without a break, the whole island would be a welter of blood." Roosevelt to Lodge, Sept. 27, 1906, *TRL,* V, 428. Taft, of course, had actually been used by Roosevelt to straighten out political affairs in Cuba and had eventually requested the President to use troops in Cuba.

110. Memorandum from the Office of the Solicitor, Feb. 26, 1912, TPS 2, File 95b.

111. Memorandum of J. Reuben Clark, Jr., "The Mexican Situation," Oct. 1, 1912, Knox Corr., XIX, 3207.

112. Memorandum of J. Reuben Clark, Jr., "Suggestive Points on the Mexican Situation," Feb. 1913, Knox Corr., XIX, 1504.

113. Taft to Gus J. Karger, July 22, 1913, TL.

114. See Mowry, *Era of Roosevelt,* 191–92, for a discussion of the background of the arbitration treaties. See also John P. Campbell, "Taft, Roosevelt, and the Arbitration Treaties of 1911," *Journal of American History,* LIII (Sept. 1966), 279–80; Jessup, *Root,* II, 80–81.

115. Taft to Marburg, Jan. 31, 1910, TL.

116. Quoted in Address at Connecticut State Fair, Hartford, Sept. 7, 1911, Taft Adrs., XXI, 276.

117. Butt, *Taft and Roosevelt,* II, 634.

118. Address at Connecticut State Fair, Taft Adrs., XXI, 276–77.

119. Campbell, *Journal of American History,* LIII (Sept. 1966), 280–81.

120. Address to Methodist Conference, Ocean Grove, N.J., Aug. 15, 1911, Taft Adrs., XXI, 215; see also Andrew Carnegie to Taft,

Dec. 15, 1912, Knox Corr., XX, 3274; Francis B. Loomis to Dr. Nicholas Murray Butler, Oct. 31, 1911, Root Gen. Corr., Box 78, in which Hilles allegedly admitted that he did not know why Knox had not consulted with the Senate.

121. See Campbell, *Journal of American History*, LIII (Sept. 1966), 280; Address at Connecticut State Fair, Taft Adrs., XXI, 279. For the text of the treaties, see Senate Docs., 62d Cong., 1st Sess., Nos. 91 and 92 (Serial 6108).

122. Address before the Pennsylvania Society, New York City, Jan. 21, 1911, TL.

123. See Campbell, *Journal of American History*, LIII (Sept. 1966), 281–82; Taft to Knox, Aug. 12, 1911, TL; and Knox to Taft, Aug. 12, Knox Corr., XV, 4449–50; *TRL*, VII, 289, 326–27.

124. Quoted in Butt, *Taft and Roosevelt*, II, 635.

125. Taft to William J. Bryan, Jan. 16, 1912, TL.

126. Address at Marquette, Mich., Sept. 20, 1911, Taft Adrs., XXII, 99; *TRL*, VII, 289.

127. Address at Connecticut State Fair, Taft Adrs., XXI, 282–83.

128. Address at San Francisco, Oct. 13, 1911, Taft Adrs. XXIV, 32.

129. Address to Chamber of Commerce, Los Angeles, Oct. 16, 1911, Taft Adrs., XXIV, 78.

130. Taft to Bryan, Jan. 16, 1912, TL.

131. Taft to Carnegie, March 28, 1912, TL; see also Campbell, *Journal of American History*, LIII (Sept. 1966), 286–87; Knox to Hilles, Jan. 18, 1912, TPS 2, File 107; and Root to Bacon, March 9, 1912, Root Gen. Corr., Box 91.

132. *New York Times*, Sept. 30, 1911, 2, 3.

133. See Taft to Knox, Sept. 30, 1911, TL; Adee to Taft, Oct. 1, 764.67/38; Knox to Taft, Oct. 2, Adee to Knox, Oct. 3, and Adee to American Embassy, Constantinople, Oct. 4, 765.67/21, 76, 51.

134. Taft to Knox, Dec. 20, 1911, and Knox to Taft, Dec. 27, 867.00/357.

135. See Taft to Wilson, Sept. 22, Oct. 1, 1912, TL; Wilson to Taft, Sept. 23, 765.67/384.

136. Taft to Wilson, Oct. 1, 1912, TL; see also Wilson to Taft, Oct. 8, 1912, 765.67/424.

137. Rockhill to Knox, Oct. 9, 1912, 765.67/432.

138. Taft to Edwin Ginn, Oct. 22, 1912, TL.

139. See Knox to Taft, Jan. 25, 1913, TPS 2, File 4195; Richardson, *Messages*, XVIII, 8161–62.

140. Straight to Excellency (unnamed), Jan. 29, 1911, Correspondence, 1260, Box 3, Letterbook, Straight Papers.

Chapter 8

1. Taft, *Our Chief Magistrate*, 157.

2. Roosevelt, *Autobiography*, 357, 363–65.

3. Taft, *Our Chief Magistrate*, 139–40.

4. Address to Tippecanoe Club of Cleveland, Jan. 29, 1908, Taft Adrs., VIII, 170.

5. Taft, *Our Chief Magistrate*, 112–13.

6. Address to Laymen's Missionary Movement, New York, April 20, 1908, Taft Adrs., X, 155.

7. Address to the Virginia Bar Association, Hot Springs, Aug. 6, 1908, Taft Adrs., XI, 153.

8. Address to the Ellicot Club, Buffalo, Feb. 22, 1908, Taft Adrs., IX, 50–51.

9. Taft, *Our Chief Magistrate*, 147.

10. Quoted in Louis Koenig, *The Chief Executive* (New York: Harcourt, Brace & World, 1968), 26.

11. White to Fisher, Nov. 10, 1911, Private Files, Box 10, Fisher Papers.

12. Quoted in William Manners, *TR and Will: A Friendship That Split the Republican Party* (New York: Harcourt, Brace & World, 1969), 5.

13. Taft, *Our Chief Magistrate*, 144.

14. *Ibid.*

15. Address at Hill School, Pottstown, Pa., Nov. 15, 1913, Taft Adrs., XXXI, 21.

16. Taft, *Our Chief Magistrate*, 145.

17. *Ibid.*, 146–47.

18. Roosevelt, *Autobiography*, 479.

19. Taft, *Our Chief Magistrate*, 147–48.

20. 272 U.S. 52 (1926).

21. Taft, *Our Chief Magistrate*, 76.

22. 272 U.S. 118.

23. *Ibid.*, 122.

24. *Ibid.*, 135.

25. *Ibid.*

26. *Ibid.*, 172.

27. Quoted in Mason, *Taft*, 254.

28. "The President and His Administration," *Outlook*, C (Feb. 10, 1912), 301.

Selected Bibliography

Manuscript Collections

The Papers of Walter L. Fisher, Manuscript Division, Library of Congress.
The Papers of Philander Chase Knox, Manuscript Division, Library of Congress.
The Papers of Elihu Root, Manuscript Division, Library of Congress.
The Papers of Willard D. Straight, Olin Library, Cornell University.
The Papers of William Howard Taft, Manuscript Division, Library of Congress.

Records in the National Archives

Record Group 59: General Records of the Department of State Numerical File, 1906–1910.
Decimal File, 1910–1926.

Government Documents and Printed Records

Papers Relating to the Foreign Relations of the United States, 1908–1913. Washington, D.C.
Porter, Kirk H., and Donald B. Johnson, eds., *National Party Platforms, 1840–1956.* Urbana, Ill.: University of Illinois Press, 1956.
Richardson, James D., ed., *A Compilation of the Messages and Papers of the Presidents.* 20 vols. New York: Bureau of National Literature, 1897–1914.
U.S., *Congressional Directory.*
U.S., *Congressional Record.*

Autobiographies, Letters, and Memoirs

Butt, Archibald, *The Letters of Archie Butt.* Garden City, N.Y.: Doubleday, Page, 1924.

——, *Taft and Roosevelt: The Intimate Letters of Archie Butt.* 2 vols. Garden City: Doubleday, Doran, 1930.

Clark, Champ, *My Quarter Century of American Politics.* 2 vols. New York: Harper, 1920.

Hoover, Irwin Hood, *Forty-Two Years in the White House.* Boston: Houghton Mifflin, 1934.

Huntington-Wilson, Francis Mairs, *Memoirs of an Ex-Diplomat.* Boston: Bruce Humphries, 1945.

La Follette, Robert, *La Follette's Autobiography.* Madison: University of Wisconsin Press, 1960.

Kohlsaat, H. H., *From McKinley to Harding.* New York: Scribner's, 1923.

Longworth, Alice Roosevelt, *Crowded Hours.* New York: Scribner, 1933.

Pinchot, Gifford, *Breaking New Ground.* New York: Harcourt, Brace, 1946.

Roosevelt, Theodore, *The Letters of Theodore Roosevelt,* Elting E. Morison, and John M. Blum, eds. 8 vols. Cambridge: Harvard University Press, 1951–1954.

——, *The New Nationalism.* Englewood Cliffs: Prentice-Hall, 1961.

——, *Theodore Roosevelt: An Autobiography.* New York: Charles Scribner's, 1920.

Stimson, Henry L., and McGeorge Bundy, *On Active Service in Peace and War.* New York: Harper, 1948.

Straus, Oscar S., *Under Four Administrations.* Boston: Houghton Mifflin, 1922.

Taft, Helen Herron. *Recollections of Full Years.* New York: Dodd, Mead, 1914.

Taft, Horace Dutton, *Memories and Opinions.* New York: Macmillan, 1942.

Taft, William Howard, *Four Aspects of Civic Duty.* New York: Scribner's, 1906.

——, *Our Chief Magistrate and His Powers.* New York: Columbia University Press, 1916.

White, William Allen, *The Autobiography of William Allen White.* New York: Macmillan, 1946.

——, *Selected Letters of William Allen White, 1899–1943,* Walter Johnson ed. New York: Holt, 1947.

Wilson, Henry Lane, *Diplomatic Episodes in Mexico, Belgium and Chile.* New York: Doubleday, Page, 1927.

Secondary Sources

Bailey, Thomas A., *A Diplomatic History of the American People.* New York: Appleton-Century-Crofts, 1964.

——, *Presidential Greatness.* New York: Appleton-Century-Crofts, 1967.

Barber, James David, *The Presidential Character: Predicting Performance in the White House.* New York: Prentice-Hall, 1972.

Beale, Howard K., *Theodore Roosevelt and the Rise of America to World Power.* New York: Collier Books, 1962.

Blum, John M., *The Republican Roosevelt.* New York: Atheneum, 1964.

Bowers, Claude G., *Beveridge and the Progressive Era.* New York: Literary Guild, 1932.

Burns, James MacGregor, *Presidential Government: The Crucible of Leadership.* New York: Avon Books, 1965.

Busbey, L. White, *Uncle Joe Cannon.* New York: Holt, 1927.

Coletta, Paolo E., *William Jennings Bryan: Political Evangelist, 1860–1908.* Lincoln: University of Nebraska Press, 1964.

Crane, Katherine, *Mr. Carr of State.* New York: St. Martin's Press, 1960.

Davis, Oscar King, *William Howard Taft: The Man of the Hour.* Philadelphia: Ziegler, 1908.

deGrazia, Alfred ed., *Congress: The First Branch of Government.* Washington: American Enterprise Institute for Public Policy Research, 1966.

Duffy, Herbert S., *William Howard Taft.* New York: Minton, Balch, 1930.

Fenno, Richard, *The President's Cabinet.* New York: Vintage, 1959.

Glad, Paul W., *The Trumpet Soundeth: William Jennings Bryan and His Democracy, 1896–1912.* Lincoln: University of Nebraska Press, 1964.

Griswold, A. Whitney, *The Far Eastern Policy of the United States.* New York: Harcourt, Brace, 1938.

Gwinn, William Rea, *Uncle Joe Cannon: Archfoe of Insurgency.* Bookman Associates, 1957.

Hargrove, Erwin C., *Presidential Leadership: Personality and Political Style.* New York: Macmillan, 1966.

Hechler, Kenneth W., *Insurgency: Personalities and Politics of the Taft Era.* New York: Russell and Russell, 1964.

Hofstadter, Richard, *The Age of Reform.* New York: Vintage, 1955.
——, *The American Political Tradition.* New York: Vintage, 1959.
Howe, M. A. deWolfe, *George von Lengerke Meyer.* New York: Dodd, Mead, 1920.
Hughes, Emmet John, *The Ordeal of Power.* New York: Dell, 1962.
Jessup, Philip C., *Elihu Root.* 2 vols. New York: Dodd, Mead, 1938.
Kallenbach, Joseph E., *The American Chief Executive: The Presidency and the Governorship.* New York: Harper & Row, 1966.
Keefe, William J., and Morris S. Ogul, *The American Legislative Process: Congress and the States.* New York: Prentice-Hall, 1964.
McGeary, Martin Nelson, *Gifford Pinchot.* Princeton: Princeton University Press, 1960.
Manners, William, *TR and Will: A Friendship That Split the Republican Party.* New York: Harcourt, Brace, & World, 1969.
Mason, Alpheus Thomas, *William Howard Taft: Chief Justice.* New York: Simon and Schuster, 1965.
Moos, Malcom, *The Republicans.* New York: Random House, 1956.
Mowry, George E., *The Era of Theodore Roosevelt: 1900–1912.* New York: Harper, 1958.
——, *Theodore Roosevelt and the Progressive Movement.* New York: Hill and Wang, 1960.
Munro, Dana G., *Intervention and Dollar Diplomacy in the Caribbean, 1900–1921.* Princeton: Princeton University Press, 1964.
Neustadt, Richard, *Presidential Power.* New York: John Wiley, 1960.
Nevins, Allan, *Henry White: Thirty Years of American Diplomacy.* New York: Harper, 1930.
Nye, Russel B., *Midwestern Progressive Politics.* New York: Harper & Row, 1965.
Petersen, Svend, *A Statistical History of American Presidential Elections.* New York: Frederick Ungar, 1963.
Pollard, James E., *The Presidents and the Press.* New York: Macmillan, 1947.
Pringle, Henry F., *The Life and Times of William Howard Taft.* 2 vols. New York: Farrar & Rinehart, 1939.
——, *Theodore Roosevelt.* New York: Harcourt, Brace & World, 1956.
Ross, Ishbel, *An American Family: The Tafts—1678 to 1964.* Cleveland: World, 1964.
Ross, Thomas R., *Jonathan Prentiss Dolliver.* Des Moines: State Historical Society of Iowa, 1958.
Rossiter, Clinton, *The American Presidency.* New York: Harvest Books, 1960.

Sorensen, Theodore C., *Decision-Making in the White House*. New York: Columbia University Press, 1963.

Stuart, Graham, H., *The Department of State: A History of Its Organization, Procedure, and Personnel*. New York: Macmillan, 1949.

Sullivan, Mark, *Our Times: The United States, 1900–1925*. 6 vols. New York: Scribner's, 1926–1935.

Vevier, Charles, *The United States and China, 1906–1913*. New Brunswick: Rutgers University Press, 1955.

Weber, Max, *From Max Weber*. H. H. Gerth and C. Wright Mills, eds. New York: Oxford University Press, 1958.

Wilmerding, Lucius, Jr., *The Spending Power*. New Haven: Yale University Press, 1949.

Articles

Abbott, Lawrence F., "The Roosevelt Campaign: A Review," *Outlook*, CI (June 15, 1912), 331–40.

Baldwin, Elbert F., "President Taft's Cabinet," *Outlook*, XCI (March 27, 1909), 691–702.

Campbell, John P., "Taft, Roosevelt, and the Arbitration Treaties of 1911," *Journal of American History*, LIII (September 1966), 279–97.

Fisk, George M., "The Payne-Aldrich Tariff," *Political Science Quarterly*, XXV (March 1910), 35–68.

Gardner, H. B., "Proposal for a National Budget," *American Economic Review* (December 1912), 970–72.

Hahn, Harlan, "President Taft and the Discipline of Patronage," *Journal of Politics*, XXVIII (May 1966), 368–90.

Leupp, Francis E., "President Taft's Own View," *Outlook*, XCIX (Dec. 2, 1911), 811–18.

Livermore, Seward W., "Battleship Diplomacy in South America: 1905–1925," *Journal of Modern History*, XVI (March 1944), 31–49.

MacVeagh, Franklin, "Departmental Economy," *Independent*, LXIV (Dec. 22, 1910), 1366–69.

——, "President Taft and the Roosevelt Policies," *Outlook*, CI (May 18, 1912), 110–16.

"Mr. Taft's Four Years," *Independent*, LXXIV (March 6, 1913), 488–89.

Phillips, David Graham, "The Treason of the Senate," *Cosmopolitan Magazine*, XLI (August 1906), 368–77.

"A Political Balance Sheet," *Outlook*, XCIV (April 2, 1910), 742–46.

"The President's Journey," *Outlook*, XCIX (Nov. 11, 1911), 605.

"President Taft and the Cost of Government," *Outlook*, CII (Oct. 5, 1912), 235.

"President Taft's Interpretation of His Policies," *Outlook*, XCV (June 11, 1910), 272.

Roosevelt, Theodore, "The Tariff: A Moral Issue," *Outlook*, XCVI (Sept. 17, 1910), 102.

Turner, George K., "How Taft Views His Own Administration: An Interview with the President," *McClure's Magazine*, XXXV (June 1910), 211–21.

Index

Taft, William Howard (*cont.*)
and magazine subsidies, 126, 134,
145–47, 209–11, 233; and naval policy, 129, 134, 145, 236–38, 277; and
newspaper publishers, 204–6, 209–
11; newspaper reading habits,
226–29; organizational reforms, 85–
92; party leadership, 155, 162–67,
178–80; and patronage, 163–70,
186–87; personal qualities, 1, 6–8,
12–14, 21, 25–27, 30–32, 34, 36, 42–
43, 48–49, 64, 73, 85, 93, 104, 109–
10, 123–24, 133, 142, 149–50, 155–56,
159–61, 163, 172, 180–83, 188–89,
201–4, 209, 214–16, 228–29, 234–35,
237, 273; and "policy of harmony,"
98–99, 103–8; and political contributions, 43–45, 134; political experience, 4–27; political style, 37,
41–49, 58–59, 65, 67–68, 71–72, 75–
76, 81, 83–87, 92–93, 104, 110, 115,
119–25, 129–30, 133–34, 139, 142,
149, 155–56, 160–61, 167–68, 170,
172–74, 176–77, 183–84, 188–89, 194,
201–4, 206, 209, 214–20, 222–32,
226–34, 275, 288, 295–96, 298, 305–
6; postelection statement of 1912,
200; press relations, 213–22, 224–29,
233–35, 238–39, 241, 267, 271; and
progressives, 75, 183, 185–86, 189,
191, 193–96, 198, 200, 214, 216, 231–
33; and public image, 83–84, 120–
22, 124–25, 128, 131, 133–35, 137,
142, 147, 150, 159–60, 162, 181–85,
201–35, 262, 267, 271, 280; and purge
of 1910, 170–72; and reciprocity,
140–42; and renomination, 173,
181–85, 187–92, 195; and responsible party government, 157–59, 163–
68, 170–72, 193–94, 293–94; and
Roosevelt, differences, 19–21, 176–
78, 237; and Roosevelt, similarity
of views, 50–53, 236–37, 292–94;
Roosevelt's effect on presidency
of, 2–3, 94, 154, 182, 201–2, 220,
215–16; and Roosevelt's "New
Nationalism," 178, 182–83, 231,
232–33; and Senate, 275–76, 278–
79, 281, 283; and "senatorial courtesy," 168–69; and Shanghai
speech, 23, 242–43; and special
messages, 91, 110, 230, 233–34; and
special session of Congress, 104,

139–40, 148–53; and State Department, 68–72, 238–39, 241, 257–58,
259, 265–66, 283–87; and treaty-
making powers, 260–61, 293; and
veto, 101–2, 111–13, 115–16, 118,
134, 148–50; view of judiciary,
108–10, 168, 178, 182, 189, 191,
195–96, 200, 229–33, 305–6; view of
presidency, 54, 89–90, 95, 100–1,
150–51, 216, 229–33, 267–69, 275,
287–88, 289, 291–305; and wars,
280; western tour of 1909, 206–7,
218–19; western tour of 1911, 224–
25, 280–81; and world court, 276–
77
Taft-Katsura Memorandum, 22–23
Tariff commission, 54, 123, 129, 145–
46, 149–50
Tariffs, Taft and, 96–97, 118, 141–44,
148–51, 207–8, 228; *see also* Canadian reciprocity *and* Payne-Aldrich tariff
Tawney, James A., 98–99, 122–23
Tennessee Coal and Iron Company,
79, 80
Trevelyan, George, 29
Turco-Italian War of 1911–12, 283–
86
Turkey, 269, 283–86

Underwood, Oscar W., 106–7, 139
U.S. Department of Agriculture, 74
U.S. Department of Interior, 74
U.S. Department of Navy, 90–91;
dispatches warships without presidential approval, 270
U.S. Department of State, 262, 264–
65; and Argentine battleship contracts, 263–64; and bankers, 262–
63; Bureau of Trade Relations, 239;
and Canadian reciprocity, 136; and
Chin-Ai Railway Project, 250–53;
and Chinese currency loan, 253–
55; and Crane incident, 245; Division of Far Eastern Affairs, 69,
250, 252, 257; Division of Information, 329; Division of Latin
American Affairs, 261; and Honduras Loan, 259–60; and Hukuang
Loan, 246–50; and Knox, 67–72;
and Mexican revolution of 1911,
266–74; and Open Door policy,
257; reorganization of, 68–69, 90,

WILLIAM HOWARD TAFT

Designed by R. E. Rosenbaum.
Composed by York Composition Co., Inc.
in 11 point linotype Janson, 3 points leaded,
with display lines in Centaur.
Printed letterpress from type by York Composition Co., Inc.
on Warren's Olde Style India, 60 pound basis,
with the Cornell University Press watermark.
Illustrations printed by Art Craft of Ithaca.
Bound by Vail-Ballou Press
in Columbia book cloth
and stamped in All Purpose foil.

Library of Congress Cataloging in Publication Data
(prepared by the CIP Project for library cataloging purposes only)

Anderson, Donald F
    William Howard Taft: a conservative's conception
of the Presidency.

    Bibliography: p.
    1. Taft, William Howard, Pres. U.S., 1857–1930.
2. United States—Politics and government—1909–1913.
3. Executive power—United States. I. Title.
E761.A83   353.03′13′0924   73-8408
ISBN 0-8014-0786-9

Anderson, Donald F
　　William Howard Taft: a conservative's conception of the
Presidency [by] Donald F. Anderson. Ithaca [N. Y.] Cor-
nell University Press [1973]

　　ix, 355 p.　illus.　22 cm.

　　Bibliography　p. 341[-346].

　　1. Taft, William Howard, Pres. U. S., 1857–1930.　2. United
States—Politics and government—1909–1913.　3. Executive power—
United States.　I. Title.

E761.A83　　　　　　　　　　　353.03′13′0924　　　　　　73–8408
ISBN 0-8014-0786-9　　　　　　　　　　　　　　　　　　　　MARC
Library of Congress　　　　　　　　73 [4]